INFORMATICS IN ELEMENTARY EDUCATION

IFIP Working Conference on
Informatics in Elementary Education
(up to 13 years of age)
Malente, near Kiel, F.R.G., 25-29 July 1983

organised by
Working Group 3.1 of
IFIP Technical Committee 3, Education
International Federation for Information Processing

Programme Committee
F. B. Lovis (U.K.), P. Bollerslev (Denmark), U. Bosler (F.R.G.),
E. D. Tagg (U.K., *Editor*), J. D. Tinsley (U.K., *Editor*),
T. J. van Weert (The Netherlands)

Organising Committee
U. Bosler, K.-H. Hansen, F. Holst,
G. Jacobsen, I. Moors, H.-J. Waldow (all F.R.G.)

NORTH-HOLLAND
AMSTERDAM • NEW YORK • OXFORD

INFORMATICS IN ELEMENTARY EDUCATION

Proceedings of the IFIP WG 3.1 Working Conference on
Informatics in Elementary Education
Malente, near Kiel, F.R.G., 25-29 July 1983

edited by

J. D. TINSLEY
Education Officer
Birmingham Education Department, U.K.

and

E. D. TAGG
Formerly Senior Lecturer in Mathematics
University of Lancaster, U.K.

1984

NORTH-HOLLAND
AMSTERDAM • NEW YORK • OXFORD

© IFIP, 1984

All rights reserved. No part of this publication may be reproduced, stored in a retrieval system, or transmitted, in any form or by any means, electronic, mechanical, photocopying, recording or otherwise, without the prior permission of the copyright owner.

ISBN: 0 444 86811 9

Published by:
ELSEVIER SCIENCE PUBLISHERS B.V.
P.O. Box 1991
1000 BZ Amsterdam
The Netherlands

Sole distributors for the U.S.A. and Canada:
ELSEVIER SCIENCE PUBLISHING COMPANY, INC.
52 Vanderbilt Avenue
New York, N.Y. 10017
U.S.A.

Library of Congress Cataloging in Publication Data

IFIP WG 3.1 Working Conference on Informatics in
   Elementary Education (1983 : Malente, Germany)
   Informatics in elementary education.

   1. Education, Elementary--Data processing--
Congresses.   2. Computer-assisted instruction--Congresses.
3. Elementary schools--Data processing--Congresses.
4. Middle schools--Data processing--Congresses.
I. Tinsley, John David.   II. Tagg, E. D., 1913-
III. International Federation for Information Processing.
Working Group 3.1.   IV. Title.
LB1028.43.I34   1983   372'.0285'4   83-19461
ISBN 0-444-86811-9 (Elsevier)

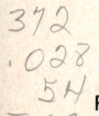

PRINTED IN THE NETHERLANDS

PREFACE

Technical Committee 3 (TC 3) of the International Federation for Information Processing (IFIP) oversees the activities of four Working Groups, one of which, WG 3.1, is concerned with the field of secondary education.

A Working Conference on "Microcomputers in Secondary Education" was organised by WG 3.1 at the Centre International d'Etudes Pédagogiques de Sèvres (France) in April 1980. After this event it very soon became clear that it was time to plan a Working Conference on Informatics in Elementary Education (up to 13 years of age). Since TC 3 has, as yet, no Working Group which embraces the field of elementary education, WG 3.1 was asked to extend its activities and to organise this Working Conference.

The Conference duly took place at the Gustav-Heinemann-Bildungsstätte (Haus Seehof), Malente, FRG, from 25 to 29 July 1983 and was attended by 48 invited delegates from 16 different countries. A total of 17 papers were presented and a number of subsequent discussion sessions was carefully recorded. These papers and discussion reports form the main point of the contents of these proceedings.

It should be recorded that once it became clear that this Working Conference would attract participation from so many countries, TC 3 took the decision to set up a further Working Group, WG 3.5, to plan and to organise future activities in the field of informatics and the elementary school.

The onerous task of organising the logistics of this Conference was undertaken by a committee from the staff of the IPN - Institute for Science Education, Kiel, under the chairmanship of Dr. Ulrich Bosler. The site proved ideal, the weather superb and the arrangements for our accommodation quite excellent. We are most grateful to Dr. Bosler and his team for all the hard work which made our stay so pleasant and, in particular, to the secretaries from IPN, Mrs. Freya Holst and Mrs. Ingrid Moors, who worked so hard and willingly to enable us to meet the deadlines for the publication of these Proceedings.

And, finally, as Chairman of WG 3.1, may I express my personal thanks to the two Editors of this book, who worked as hard as any one and who never allowed either the complexity of their tasks or the superb weather to deprive them of their cool.

All concerned with this Working Conference are conscious that it dealt with a field of rapid and exciting change and of unlimited opportunity. We hope that our efforts will help and encourage others to jump in and get their feet wet.

Frank Lovis

Chairman WG 3.1

EDITORIAL

The welcome addresses of Dr. Plett and Dr. Bosler contained material of interest and significance for the conference and permission was therefore sought - and granted - to include these in the Proceedings with the other invited papers and discussions. The papers and discussions are arranged in the order in which they were presented. The discussions took place at the end of each session and were summarized by the rapporteurs.

We are very grateful to the following for the special contributions they made to the completion of these proceedings.

1) Jean Foster for retyping many of the early revisions of the paper and overseeing the final preparation of the proceedings.

2) Dr. Ulrich Bosler and the two ladies he brought from IPN, especially Ingrid Moors who typed a great number of revisions of papers during the conference, including some complete revisions.

3) To Brian Samways and Birmingham Educational Computing Centre (BECC) for providing text processing facilities to enable the discussion reports to be revised quickly.

4) To all the rapporteurs for the speed and accuracy in the production of their reports and, in some cases, for recording them on the text processor.

5) To Gloria Jones for volunteering to type in discussion reports.

6) To the North-Holland Publishing Company for their efficiency in handling the manuscript.

David Tinsley
Donovan Tagg   Editors

TABLE OF CONTENTS AND PROGRAMME

Monday 25th July

OPENING SESSION — 1

  Welcome by
  P.C. Plett
  F. Lovis
  U. Bosler — 3 / 7

OPENING ADDRESS:

  INFORMATICS IN ELEMENTARY EDUCATION: HOPES AND FEARS
  B. Levrat — 9

Tuesday 26th July

Session 1 — 17

  MOTION IN MINDSPACE
  T. Bonello-Kubath, F. Kubath — 19

  MICRO-PRIMER: A FOUNDATION COURSE FOR TEACHERS IN PRIMARY SCHOOLS
  R. Jones — 27

  DISCUSSION
  Chairman: J.D. Tinsley   Rapporteurs: D. Martin, B. Levrat — 35

Session 2 — 37

  WHY I USE A COMPUTER DURING MY PHYSICS LESSONS
  K.G. Ahlström — 39

  COMPUTERS AS A TOOL FOR CHILDREN AT ELEMENTARY LEVEL AND ITS
  IMPACT ON SCHOOL MATHEMATICS
  H. Löthe — 45

  DISCUSSION
  Chairman: P. Bollerslev   Rapporteurs: R. Jones, H. Bauersfeld — 49

Session 3 — 51

  WISCONSIN SUMMER COMPUTER FEST
  M.V. DeVault — 53

  STATUS REPORT: INSERVICE COMPUTER LITERACY TRAINING
  C.D. Martin, R.S. Heller — 61

  DISCUSSION
  Chairman: P. Bollerslev   Rapporteurs: B. Samways, C.J. Watkins — 67

Wednesday 27th July

Session 4 — 71

- A TEACHER PERSPECTIVE OF COMPUTER LITERACY FOR CHILDREN
  M.M. DeVault — 73
- COMPUTING IN BIRMINGHAM PRIMARY SCHOOLS
  C.J. Watkins — 79
- DISCUSSION
  Chairman: F.B. Lovis
  Rapporteurs: F. Kubath, P. Gorny — 89

Session 5 — 91

- INTRODUCING COMPUTERS TO PUPILS IN A NON-TECHNOLOGICAL SOCIETY
  E. Schmidt, N. Tovgaard — 93
- COMPUTERS AND EDUCATION: EXPERIENCES IN A JAPANESE JUNIOR HIGH SCHOOL
  S. Yoshimura, R. Kuroda — 99
- DATALÆRE IN ELEMENTARY SCHOOLS: EXPERIMENTS IN GRADE 5
  N. Tovgaard, E. Schmidt — 105
- DISCUSSION
  Chairman: E.D. Tagg
  Rapporteurs: T. Bonello-Kubath, C. Berdonneau — 111

Thursday 28th July

Session 6 — 113

- PROBLEM SOLVING USING THE MICROCOMPUTER
  W.G. Cathcart — 115
- INTRODUCING COMPUTERS IN LONDON PRIMARY SCHOOLS
  B. Weaver — 125
- DISCUSSION
  Chairman: T. van Weert
  Rapporteurs: M.V. DeVault, E. Schmidt — 133

Session 7 — 135

- PROGRAMMING TRAINING FOR CHILDREN OF 11 - 14 YEARS OLD
  M. Nakanishi, A. Aiba — 137
- INTRODUCTION TO INFORMATICS: A SYLLABUS FOR MIDDLE SCHOOL
  J. Fonjallaz — 145
- DISCUSSION
  Chairman: U. Bosler
  Rapporteurs: M.M. DeVault, G. Plancke-Schuyten — 153

Session 8 — 155

SPRITES WITH FIRST GRADERS
C. Berdonneau — 157

MICROS IN THE PRIMARY CLASSROOM: ITMA TRAINING MATERIALS
J. Stewart, R. Fraser, J. Petty, H. Burkhardt — 161

SOFTWARE FOR THE ELEMENTARY SCHOOL
G. Fisher — 169

Session 9 — 177

DISCUSSION GROUPS
Chairman: T. van Weert
Rapporteur: W.G. Cathcart, R.G. Lauterbach — 179

Friday 29th July

Session 10 — 187

COMPUTERS IN ELEMENTARY EDUCATION:
A SOLVABLE PROBLEM WITH PROBLEMATICAL SOLUTIONS
R.G. Lauterbach — 189

THE DISPARITY OF COMPUTER EXPERIENCE:
A CASE FOR ORIENTING THE SYLLABUS FOR ELEMENTARY EDUCATION?
H. Bauersfeld — 199

DISCUSSION
Chairman: U. Bosler
Rapporteurs: R. Petty, P. Bollerslev — 207

Session 11 — 211

CLOSING ADDRESS: CONFERENCE REVIEW
B. Levrat — 213

DISCUSSION
Chairman: F.B. Lovis
Rapporteurs: E.D. Tagg, J.D. Tinsley — 215

List of Participants — 217

# OPENING SESSION

OPENING ADDRESS

Ministerialrat Dr. Peter C. Plett
Heinemannstr. 2, D 5300 Bonn 2

Ladies and Gentlemen, I would like to welcome you cordially here in Malente on behalf of the Federal Republic of Germany. Your working conference will deal with part of a theme which is at present occupying western industrialized nations, and in particular Western Europe.

In order to hold their own in economic matters, in particular vis-à-vis the United States of America and Japan, the Western European countries decided within the European Community, in early June to conduct comparative analyses in the field of the new information technologies in education in addition to the existing exchange of experience in order to increase the transferability of teaching programmes and software between member countries and in order to identify those equipment systems which can best be used for educational purposes.

With this aim in mind, both national and international expert meetings will be held within the next two years. Your work therefore has the full support of a topical subject in nearly all industrialized countries.

This conference deals with an important and interesting sector, namely the age group up to 13 years of age. While you will handle technical questions, I would like to use this opening address to put to you some administrative aspects so that you will know during your deliberations what we in the Federal Republic of Germany need to know about the theme, in terms of information required for policy-making.

I will begin by giving you a brief outline of the situation of informatics in elementary education in the Federal Republic of Germany to the extent that I am familiar with it. I will then mention pilot experiments and in a few sentences talk to you about the computer programming competition.

And finally I shall discuss the questions and hypotheses mentioned during my address which confront the Federal and Länder governments when they have to take decisions in this field.

THE SITUATION OF INFORMATICS IN ELEMENTARY EDUCATION

I would like to point out that elementary education as defined by you, i.e. up to the age of thirteen, does not correspond to fixed stages in German education. We have the kindergarten level of the 4 - 5 year olds, which in Germany is part of the elementary level. It is followed by the level of the 6 - 9 year olds, the so-called 4-year primary school. The 10 - 15 year olds attend different forms and types of school and together belong to secondary level I.

As far as I know, there is no such subject as informatics at the kindergarten and primary school level. In secondary level I, instruction focuses on informatics in grades 9 and 10 of this type of school. In Land Berlin informatics may be chosen as a compulsory optional subject and in Bavaria in intermediate schools as an optional subject. In a few other countries the contents of informatics may optionally be included in other subjects, mostly mathematics.

Since information instruction in secondary level I is confined to grades 9 and 10, that is to say to the 15 - 16 year olds, it can be summed up for your working conference that there is at present no informatics instruction in elementary education up to 13 years of age.

Of course, this is an official statement, which does not exclude the fact that even younger pupils at some school or other in Germany play with the computer in their leisure hours, perhaps with the aid of older pupils or a teacher. The pilot experiments in this field all take place in grades 9 and 10, i.e. for 15 and 16 year olds, and therefore need not be mentioned here. The same can be said about the federal computer programming competition. Here, too, there is a secondary I level, which, however, includes only 14 - 16 year olds.

In this year's computer competition, a pupil of secondary level I successfully worked on a very interesting solution to an old problem. When some of you arrived in Hamburg today and looked for the way to Seehof at Malente or whenever you arrived in a strange city and looked for the quickest way to a destination, you probably would have liked to have a computer-aided automatic information machine which you could have asked for the quickest connection to Seehof or to any other 1983 main street. Such an automatic information machine would have printed out within seconds when to take which means of transport and where, which connection to take, how, where and when, and at what time you would arrive at your destination. A pupil of secondary level I in the Federal Republic of Germany has tackled this problem and written an easily intelligible programme in BASIC. For this he recieved the special prize awarded by the Federal Minister of Education and Science to a participant from secondary level I for a particularly outstanding achievement.

As you can see from the competition and in particular from the awarding of the prize, the Federal Government thinks that the participipation of younger pupils is desirable.

Let me now say something about the questions and hypotheses.

1) The school will not be able to halt the advance of the microcomputer in all fields of life. The microcomputer will pervade children's toys, leisure time and working life.

2) The school may ignore this advance if it holds the view that the microcomputer does not belong in the curriculum. However, one day it may have to accept the fact that any undesirable developments force a belated response by the school; this is what has happened with so-called traffic education.

3) If the microcompunter is used in informatics, this is done for data acquisition and data processing; that is to say, computer utilization is a cultural skill.

4) The school cannot afford not to teach its pupils a cultural skill which they will need in the future. It it did so it would run the risk of creating computer illiteracy.
5) Given the present number of lessons, we must find out which subjects will have to be reduced in favour of informatics or in which subjects informatics could be integrated.
6) At what age or in what grade should informatics first be taught?
7) Which benefits and drawbacks for the child are entailed by the early start of informatics instruction?
8) What would the curriculum look like for different age groups?
9) Should there be special hardware for young children?
10) Should there be special software for young children?
11) Which programming languages should be taught and is it necessary at all to use programming languages?
12) What experience has been gained in other countries?
13) With regard to which questions are pilot experiments and/or research projects required?

The Federal Government would be pleased if you were able to provide answers to some of my hypotheses and questions from your international deliberations.

From the Conference papers I have gathered that this international Conference in Germany admits only a single conference language: English. If this is possible here in Germany this week (and I am not sure at all whether a German language conference would be feasible in England or France), something has been achieved in the field of colloquial languages which is still to be achieved in the case of computer languages. There are BASIC, Pascal, Fortran, Cobol, Elan and many other computer languages. Perhaps it would be a precedent if the International Federation for Information Processing could agree on some international standards, for example on a single computer programming language. This would be a unique example; for the fact that only a single language is admitted as conference language here is a rare exception internationally.

I hope that this Working Conference will be a success and that you, the participants, will have a pleasant stay in this lovely North German landscape.

WELCOME ADDRESS

Ulrich Bosler
Chairman, Local Organizing Committee

Ladies and Gentlemen, on behalf of the IPN - Institute for Science Education in Kiel I may say welcome to Malente! But what is IPN? The Federal Republic of Germany has a decentralized educational system. The responsibility for education rests with the "Länder" which are individual states like Bavaria or Northrhine-Westphalia. The IPN is the main institute of the Federal Government which works nationwide. On our main board you will find representatives of the federal ministry of education as well as of all the "Länder". The main subjects of the institute are biology, chemistry, physics, and the theory of education. One area is computer science.

The title of this working conference is "Informatics in Elementary Education". For me it is a question rather than a statement. It is not a conference for people who have produced results after a long period of work. It is a working conference in an uncharted landscape. Our main questions are:

- Have we yet reached the stage where we can evaluate the introduction of computing systems into elementary classes?
- Are we able to demonstrate examples of good practice which will encourage teachers to adapt their teaching methods to adopt new strategies?
- Are we seeking a fundamental or just peripheral change in traditional learning systems at the elementary school stage?
- Are there useful analogies which can be drawn from the introduction of modern scientific topics into the elementary curriculum?

I think we should have enough scepticism about our own work and the work of some of our colleagues. In my judgement we must be sensitive to the different educational traditions of the countries represented here in our working conference.

We should ask ourselves whether it is necessary to use a computer for the new learning approaches we have identified. Why should we use a computer to draw a square on a video screen? What is wrong with the blackboard, paper and pencil or even the sand at the seaside? Children can make circles by holding hands in the garden! The computer only requires us to use our brains. Surely we can use our bodies and our emotions as well as our brains for our learning.

I hope that this working conference will provide an open atmosphere here in Malente so that we can answer some of the questions.

INFORMATICS IN ELEMENTARY EDUCATION :
HOPES AND FEARS

Bernard C. Levrat
University of Geneva
24, rue Général Dufour
1211 GENEVE 4
Switzerland

1. INTRODUCTION

On the eve of George Orwell's 1984, TC 3 and its working group WG 3.1 take a timely initiative in inquiring about what will happen in elementary schools in the next few years with the introduction of computers. In January, the well known weekly magazine "TIME", instead of a person, nominated the computer "Machine" of the Year indicating that it deemed the advent of the personal computer the most important event of 1982. Certainly, the fast selling hardware (2.8 million units for $4.9 billion in 1982) strikes the imagination of every ambitious young person, especially with the virtually limitless market for software. There is no doubt that micro-computers in every guise will profoundly affect many people's lives.

Americans are optimistic as ever in the face of new technological developments. The same issue of TIME quotes a survey by Yankelovitch, Skelly and White indicating that 68 % of them believe that "the computer revolution will improve the quality of their children's education". They fail, however, to indicate how this is to be accomplished. If one reads books like MINDSTORMS by Seymour Papert or listens to Jean-Jacques Servan-Schreiber, founder of the "Institut Mondial de Programmation", one can hope to see very positive effects of computers in schools, both in the most advanced countries and in the Third World. Pessimists will fear that the whole school business may be governed by the ruthless laws of the market alone : aggressive advertising and promotional actions could do more to shape the use of computers in school than reasoned policies.

To be sure, parents and educators alike want the best possible means of preparing youngsters for life although there might be considerable differences between the objectives or the time scale involved. Some may resent the cultural imposition of teaching material produced outside, others will question the effectiveness of the new methods proposed. To tell the truth, virtually all experimentation has been on too limited a scale to satisfy these fundamental concerns. Most use of computers in elementary schools has relied on the efforts of dedicated individuals. We shall have the privilege to hear some of them present their work in the coming sessions and in demonstrations. By putting all these together, by asking pertinent questions and making informed remarks in the discussions, we may hope to help in deciding the best ways for elementary school children to use computers.

2. DIDACTICS

Most use of computers in education is at the secondary and university level. In extrapolating our experiences to younger classes, we may remind ourselves that often a single person is in charge of a class for all the subjects. Actions which have been possible through mathematics or science teachers are not feasible. Rather than turning the problem to teachers who are already technically oriented, one has first to convince and then to retrain a very dedicated personnel attached to the transmission of traditional values and skills.

It is not required, however, that the teacher become an expert on computers. If properly programmed machines were available in the classroom or in a somewhat enlarged school library, one could imagine the children sharing their time between the traditional classroom and the perhaps more stimulating computer environment. This scheme would most likely meet with the hostility of the teachers, if they resent it as direct competition and a possible substitute for a sizeable number of them. This need not be: one could achieve a reduction in the class size, which any teacher would welcome. Another alternative is cooperation with the teachers, accepting computers as new tools, able to provide additional services not previously available.

In fact, there is no real choice. Elementary school is viewed as the great equalizer in today's society. Many children will have access at home to the family personal computer. They will derive a great advantage from this headstart if schools do not offer an equal opportunity to prepare for the world of tomorrow. They could also experience frustration if they fail to find at school tools which are readily available at home.

There is also a growing concern about differences according to sex. In its March 1983 issue, "Psychology Today" asks the following question "Second-Class Citizens ?" and then states

"... from video arcades to keyboard camps, girls find the world of computers a mostly male domain.... the so-called computing culture places obstacles before them. These obstacles, while not unsurmountable, present genuine problems. Unless they are removed, the girls of today may find themselves second-class citizens in the computer-intensive world of tomorrow."

Hopefully, this will be remedied in elementary schools, provided that the mostly female teacher population accepts working with computers. It is also possible that the present uses and programming of computers will have to be adapted to suit their tastes.

In the following pages, I shall discuss some possible uses of computers in schools. Much of the early experience with computer literacy involved highly trained staff and substantially better student/staff ratio than we can expect in elementary schools. We shall have to judge the relevance of the models in the light of what is compatible with the egalitarian role which elementary schools must play.

3. CREATING A NEW INTELLECTUAL ENVIRONMENT

Young people are motivated and stimulated by direct contact with computing systems. A surprisingly large number of them feel comfortable with programmable machines and derive genuine pleasure in figuring out the intricacies of any particular system. They bring to it an enthusiasm, perseverance and even insight that few adults can match.

The programming languages developed so far to communicate with computers have been designed by people with their own biases towards certain areas of science or the needs of the business community. They are better suited to perform astronomical calculations in split seconds or to maintain many sorts of records than to provide a comfortable basis for developing a partnership in solving all kinds of problems.

In spite of this severe language handicap, children will spend hours with computers if they can bring them to play their own games. They are all too ready to invest much of their time acquiring the skills to achieve the highest scores in "asteroids, "adventure" or "space invaders". Given the opportunity to write their own programs, they will immerse themselves in the task of making their machine look smarter and prettier than any other.

Could so much time and effort be wasted or even damaging ? Any of us who has programmed, has experienced the intense satisfaction of successfully completing a challenging program, and the even more rewarding feeling of "fixing a bug" which eluded us for days. This is always done at a price : less social life and loss of interest for other matters while struggling with our problem. Spending too much time with a computer could spell disaster for a youngster if it trapped him in a closed world of his own. It is my feeling however, that, after some enthusiastic initial experiences, most kids will be able to take or leave their computer habit without damage to their social life but with much improved problem solving skills.

One of the most influential advocates of this view is Seymour Papert who says in his book MINDSTORMS[1] :

> "... the computer presence might have more fundamental effects on intellectual development than did other technologies, including television and even printing. ... Even the best of educational television is limited to offering quantitative improvements in the kinds of learning that existed without it. "Sesame Street" might offer better and more engaging explanations than a child can get from some parents or nursery school teachers, but the child is still in the position of listening to explanations. By contrast, when a child learns to program, the process of learning is transformed. It becomes more active and self-directed. In particular, the knowledge is acquired for a recognizable personal purpose. The child does something with it. The new knowledge is a source of power and is experienced as such from the moment it begins to form in the child's mind."

4. ENRICHMENT OF THE LEARNING ENVIRONMENT

Elementary school teachers are experts in guiding children through learning sequences to suit their individual needs. With the help of an interactive computer, a teacher can ask every pupil in the class to play the lessons best suited to his needs at a particular moment. Because of the time it takes to develop and test such materials, one has to realise that teams of teachers and computer professionals will be required to invest many man-years of effort until one has a reasonably complete set of useful courseware at one's disposal.

The first example which comes to mind is drill and practice. Devices with voice output like Texas Instruments' "Speak and Spell" give a new incentive to learn how to spell correctly without the pressure of spelling contests. There exist countless programs for all kinds of machines to exercise arithmetic, enrich the vocabulary, tell correct sentences from incorrect ones, with the computer keeping scores, pointing out mistakes and, in the best cases, offering relevant helping sequences.

If a true dialogue can be established between the child and the computer which will present new knowledge and encourage its understanding by means of carefully planned questions, one enters the realm of tutorial programs. The best known collection of them exists on some large CDC computers with many terminals and the PLATO system. Similar techniques can be used on personal computers with elementary schools in mind and excellent examples have been demonstrated. It must be pointed out, however, that the preparation is time consuming and non-trivial with the consequence that no small adjustments can be made and teachers who want to use the product have to accept it as delivered.

It is also possible to use the computer to generate rich, creative, manipulatable environments for the learner. Quoting from Bork and Franklin[2]:

"One form of controllable world has the computer duplicating or enhancing a typical laboratory environment... (One factor missing is the possibility of injury if the experiment is not done correctly.)...
The laboratory environment can be extended greatly. Realms of experiences can be provided that are difficult or impossible to realize in the world as it exists. In as much as experience is the basis for intuition, these controllable worlds can give the user a feel for phenomena and the consequences of theories that was previously available only to the deeply talented or after much study."

Although these thoughts were inspired by work done mostly with college students, they could have far reaching consequences in a strategy leading gifted elementary school children to proceed at their own pace, building their insight and intuition far beyond what the best teachers could be expected to achieve.

5. EXTENSION OF LEARNING RESOURCES

We are entering a new era where telecommunications and computers combine together to offer large numbers of exciting new possibilities. Big computers can store and organise billions of pieces of information. They can be accessed through communication networks and relevant data will flow to small, inexpensive local or personal computers, where it can be displayed in a variety of forms to satisfy the end user.

Currently, such advanced technologies work for banks, airline reservation systems and all sorts of electronic mail. They distribute specialized information to trained users. One can begin to see their relevance to education by looking at what is happening with book libraries. In many countries, work is in progress to build computerized catalogues of all the books available. When one wants to access a given book, pressing a few keys on a terminal connected to the system will locate the closest library where it is available. But the power of computing systems to store and retrieve allows also a search for books and articles on a given subject, the central computers searching their files to provide complete answers to a given query phrased on the terminal.

While scientists are using telecommunication satellites to consult data bases on the most recent advances in their field, school children could browse through an encyclopedia stored on their local computer or access some bigger machines to get help in solving a given problem. Quite often, information retrieval is not sufficient, a good deal of work has yet to go into the so-called knowledge based systems until they make sense out of the simplest questions a child can ask. Just what response should Saint-Exupéry's Petit Prince get when he types :" S'il te plaît, dessine-moi un mouton." ?

Coming back to earth, one can understand the predicament of governments which are to set up general facilities to make possible some of the above. The number of distinct, mutually exclusive options recommended by experts is already very large and brave souls who are willing to push forward know already that advances in technology could make their solutions obsolete long before they are implemented. Yet, the promises of instantaneously accessible sources of knowledge are so exciting that several countries are investing a great deal towards an immediate solution: France is transforming its telephone system into a terminal system, Japan works on a knowledge-based fifth computer generation and a number of American companies compete to offer all kinds of new value-added services. I am sure that many things are going on in all the countries represented here. It holds so much promise for a new outlook on the teaching process that we must make sure that the needs of schools, particularly at the elementary level, are not forgotten.

6. INFORMATICS AND THE CURRICULUM

With computers in the classroom, it is reasonable to assume that school educators will consider a study of the computer as a natural part of their curriculum. Such a need is not felt about the telephone or the television set, which also play important roles in the lives of growing young persons. Why should we have a different attitude about computers ? I believe it is because they are becoming part of everyone's cultural and professional environment; one cannot use them effectively without knowing something about them.

One often hears that computers are only as smart as the people who program them. Here is not the place to argue about that, although complete systems come through the work of many people and the total result is greater than simply the sum of the parts. In any event, programming is what makes computers so different from other media. Ideas and imagination are stored and distributed to be finally delivered through some particular hardware, where the intricacies of the electronic devices need not concern us.

Teaching about computers is non-trivial and teachers will need advice on what concepts are appropriate at each stage of learning. Experienced teachers from various countries and cultural backgrounds will have different ideas and it could be one of the valuable contributions of this working conference to compare various work done so far and come up with some practical recommendations.

7. NEW TECHNOLOGIES

Computing and storage devices have been in constant progress since electronic computers were invented around 1945. It is not a steady growth of little improvements as in other industries but great leaps forward that change the complete scene and have unsettling effects on the long range planning necessary in education.

On the positive side, let us remark that studies on the introduction of computers in elementary schools, which would have been mostly theoretical 10 years ago, have taken a great urgency because small, affordable computers are becoming generally available. The good ideas on what to teach and how to teach it have not become obsolete. It is fascinating to see that any community which really wants to experiment with them can do so without millions from government educational programs but with its own resources.

There may be some hesitation because the micro-computers of tomorrow will be more powerful than those of today. They will be somewhat cheaper too, although the basic price of displays, keyboards and printers is not expected to drop as rapidly as the cost of electronic components. Waiting may also bring in wonderful gadgets like voice output or computer controlled video-disks, even some sorts of robots that can be more fun to program than physically static computers.

Progress in software and applications is usually much slower than in hardware technology. There is so little software for elementary school education that we must get started now and devote most of our attention to pedagogical issues. The process of evaluating the potential of new technologies can be left to research labs in universities. In order to be ready when they come, we should be aware of their existence without letting them become a distraction.

8. GETTING STARTED

This Keynote address will find its conclusion in four days' time after listening to all the contributions and discussions. I beg people more experienced in teaching than in computing to accept my apologies for all the computerese jargon that my colleagues in computing and I are all too prone to use. Their questions and their competent advice is part of what is needed to make the Working Conference useful. The various sessions will concentrate on different aspects of informatics in elementary education. They were carefully balanced by the Programme Committee, whose preparatory work was excellently done.

It remains to be seen if we can agree on a set of recommendations about what must be started, what must be absolutely avoided and what requires more study and experimenting. There is a lot of work to do before Friday, and some fine entertainment to be enjoyed, thanks to the organizing Committee, but I know I can count on your stamina since you are the kind of people who come to work when everyone else is on vacation.

BIBLIOGRAPHY

1) Seymour Papert.
    MINDSTORMS. Children, Computers and Powerful Ideas.
    Basic Books, Inc., N.Y. 1980.

2) Alfred Bork and Stephen Franklin.
    The role of personal computer systems in education.
    In Alfred Bork : Learning with Computers. Digital Press, 1981.

SESSION 1

MOTION IN MINDSPACE

Toni Bonello-Kubath
and
Frank Kubath

Metropolitan Separate School Board
Toronto, Ontario
Canada

The integration of the computer into the classroom environment is currently challenging educators to understand more clearly how children learn, rather than what they should learn. Educational values, objectives and approaches are being reexamined. Pilot experiences to date suggest that the new technology will significantly alter our thinking, as well as our life styles. Traditional teaching is no longer appropriate in the face of an information explosion.

Computers seem to offer a closer realization of pedagogical ideals: self-directed learning, greater focus on process both divergent and convergent, open-ended investigations, teacher as facilitator, immediate access to a variety of resources, co-operative exchange of new understandings/discoveries/inventions, more time to personalize teacher-student interaction. Computers free and enable children to pursue their wonderings effectively. Learning is ongoing and dynamic. Ideas can play and move in a multi-dimensional mind-space. Computers invite youngsters to grasp the 'wholes', to search as Einstein did for the simple principles that govern our world.

"Education is that which liberates human potential and thus the person...that which shows people how to achieve 'liberating control' over both their environment, and themselves." (1)

"...we are at a point in history where we have an unprecedented technology upon which to build educational systems that distinguish between the transmission of past heritage and the eliciting of new understanding." (2)

As educators finally enter the Information Age and accelerating technological developments signal significant changes yet to come, the responsibility to reevaluate instructional objectives and methodologies presses. The prospect of living in an increasingly intelligent and interactive environment suggests that the human intellect, receiving greater and more sophisticated bodies of information, will be consistently challenged to integrate this information in order to make meaningful decisions in daily life. The ability to use content to generate new information will supplant present emphasis on the retention of specific content.

"In altering the info-sphere so profoundly, we are destined to transform our own mind...the way we think about our problems, the way we synthesize information, the way we anticipate the consequences of our own actions...We may even alter our own brain chemistry...A smarter environment might make smarter people." (3)

Toffler argues that the computer's facility to store and interrelate large numbers of causal forces enables us to deal with problems of greater complexity. The computer can identify subtle hitherto unnoticed patterns from vast amounts of data and allow people to form new and imaginative solutions.

"...computers can be expected to deepen the entire culture's view of causality, heightening our understanding of the interrelatedness of things, and helping us to synthesize meaningful 'wholes' out of the disconnected data whirling around us." (4)

Gutenburg's invention of the printing press changed man's attitude toward knowledge -- it became something both decipherable and accessible. The medium of the printed word itself also had an impact -- it began to shape thinking styles. Computers, too, will change how we perceive knowledge, as well as the way we think. The goals of new curricula must foster effective and varied use of information technology, as well as enable students to function beyond its capabilities.

The style of thinking used by Albert Einstein was considered revolutionary in his time, but may indeed be the model for everyone's thinking as the computer is fully implemented in the web of our lives.

"Einstein's intellectual contribution is eminently synthetic, as was his exceptional openness of thought. He linked phenomena together and formulated connections, but these phenomena were already known and he only used existing mathematical tools...his originality did not spring from new data extracted from experimentation or from a mathematical invention...Rather, his genius led him to a new association of known facts and formulas ...He was an architect of scientific thought; none of the elements were invented by him, but the construction was his, and it was marked by his spirit of simplification." (5)

Through an examination of actual student-computer experiences across the elementary panel, we hope to support the above position by pointing to the computer-related learning possibilities that are rapidly unfolding. Coping with the present is not enough. Our aim is to organize and project these possibilities into a vision for tomorrow.

Canadian primary students (4 to 8 years) are exposed to a large amount of information transmitted by electronic media. Television 'programs' required passive reception on the part of the child. Now, with computers, they can begin to think more actively in a 'dialogue' mode. Dialoguing, sending messages to direct incoming information, entailed a technical difficulty which inhibited the fluency of the interaction between the student and the program. Information-entering devices simpler than a typewriter - (QWERTY) - style keyboard, were needed. One of the simplest ways of indicating choice is pointing to the selection. Therefore 'pointing methods' of input such as 'light pens' or 'touch screens' were attractive. The simplicity of light pen design and construction made it a good device for young student use. With it children were able to indicate their choices and control the program with a minimum of concern about the method of 'speaking' to the computer. The beginning of an interactive environment adapted and adapting to the person using it had begun.

The eye movements of students playing 'Space Invader' type games appeared to be structured into vertical and horizontal formats. Noting a seeming improvement in the rate reading skills developed after playing these games, led to the hypothesis that the standard print format for reading and writing could also be taught to students under their control. Seeing print in a vertical plane (on a blackboard) and then copying it to a horizontal plane (on a desk) was usually learned through the patient practice of printing on lined paper. Understanding the organization of vertical and horizontal positioning of the coordinate system used for print, developing the ability to rotate this frame of reference, and proportionately reducing or expanding the size of letters within it, are very complex tasks for young students, especially in combination.

Pursuing the idea of interacting and adapting environments led to the use of a 'joystick' as a tool for teaching printing/writing skills. This was a simple device for entering direction information into the computer. The child, working on a horizontal plane, could press the vertical stick slightly forward (away from his body) and see a block of light move proportionately upward on the video screen. Likewise, a pull moved the light block proportionately downwards, left pressure moved it left, etc. This seemingly unremarkable process enabled the child, through psychomotor experience in hand-eye coordination, to establish a consistent, testable understanding of relationships within vertical and horizontal coordinate planes.

These 'mathematical' skills all occur on the 'concrete' level, without formal mathematical notation. Nevertheless, this experience can constitute a basis for later development of formal mathematics. This controllable interaction at the child's 'concrete stage' of thinking is an exciting prelude to the move to 'formal operations' that the use of LOGO and its robot can provide.

The introduction of LOGO into the classroom environment added a further intellectual tool. LOGO, developed by Seymour Papert, is a language appropriate for youngsters -- one which they can make sense of, yet powerful enough to meet sophisticated programming objectives. In the LOGO environment, children are encouraged and guided in their experiments with Turtle geometry. Students become increasingly adept at transferring an understanding of how they move in space to programming the parallel motion of the Turtle (another instance of syntonic learning.) Manoeuvering an actual Turtle robot, of which the screen graphic is a representation, proved to be a valuable concrete experience, even for senior elementary students. They could ascribe greater meaning to the screen Turtle. For primary pupils, one might also suggest that the robot prompted empathy, which in turn facilitated growth out of the egocentric perspective.

Developmentally children moved through significant programming stages with LOGO. Initial immediate-mode drawings were produced via a series of single instructions. The use of REPEAT soon enabled them to organize their instructions more efficiently. Later they could teach the Turtle how to draw a particular design, which it remembered and executed in its entirety upon request. Before long they were able to help the Turtle incorporate these smaller designs into larger, more complex patterns. Papert would argue that this developmental line compares to one's gradual construction of a knowledge network -- from data accumulation to classification to conceptualization to relationships to theories and systems. Papert also suggested that in the computer-rich setting, he found evidence of early development of formal thinking -- a challenge to the Piagetian theory of cognitive development. Might LOGO involvement also compare to the process of language development? Whereas late primary students (8-9 years) tend to write stories where events are noted in chronological order, early junior students (9-10 years) begin to categorically arrange and analyze their experiences. 'Playing' with LOGO may facilitate this transition. Proficiency in reading depends heavily on a child's ability to classify and bring that level of abstract thinking to the processing of the printed page. Might LOGO or LOGO-like contexts also assist in the remediation of reading problems?

Devising programs, according to Papert, entails serious theory building giving

> "...children unprecedented power to invent and carry out exciting projects. ...learning is not 'active' simply in the sense of interactive. Learners in a physics microworld are able to invent their own personal sets of assumptions about the microworld and its laws and are able to make them come true. They can shape the reality in which they will work for the day, they can modify it and build alternatives." (6)

In so doing children begin to formulate 'powerful ideas' -- intellectual structures or models which enable the child to organize incoming or forthcoming knowledge. Information is in formation. The question of whether a theory is 'right' or 'wrong' has no bearing on a child's experience in the microworld of Turtle geometry. Papert explains that many of the theories we construct in the course of early learning are eventually cast aside in favour of others which are more encompassing and/or more consistent with what is believed to be true. Children can learn as much about theory building from the 'false' theories that are ultimately abandoned as they can from the 'true' ones. "For they surely gain more in their intellectual growth by the act of inventing a theory than they can possibly lose by believing, for a while, whatever theory they invent."(7)

Linking Papert's ideas to recent brain research raises new questions for exploration. While joined by the corpus callosum, the left and right hemispheres of the brain perform different but mutually beneficial functions. The left hemisphere controls, for instance, language, the understanding of mathematics and logic, while the right hemisphere handles perception, fantasy, music and art appreciation.

Whereas the left brain focuses on the parts, the right brain tries to see the whole. Currently, there is valid concern that education as we know it limits itself to left-hemisphere skills in order to yield a finished product that can be 'accountable'. A balanced use of the two hemispheres is desirable. LOGO appears to nurture this -- at any time one is able to see the whole in relation to its parts. Ideas can be readily sculptured and tested.

The same arguments could be made for programming in BASIC. Experience with 10-13-year-old gifted youngsters proved that with proper guidance, students could soon devise programs which yielded: 1) graphic art -- flat images, cursor-controlled animation and later more complex animation using subroutines; 2) musical melodies -- sometimes combined with graphics; 3) programs which solved for unknown mathematical values; 4) programs which simulated real-life situations and required decision-making on the part of the operator; 5) interactive tutorial programs which taught other students subject-related material; and 6) modified versions of established games as well as original games. The possibilities were virtually unlimited to the creative student, working together with a teacher, who did not have to be a master programmer, just open and enthusiastic about student ideas, willing to permit experimentation, and prepared to provide needed resources.

It is interesting to note that children tackled programming with genuine enthusiasm only when they came upon a worthwhile idea. What was occasionally mistaken by the teacher as apathy or inability to master programming skills proved to be a creative lull. Once they came upon a compelling idea, they proceeded to integrate all previously taught programming tools. Furthermore, once into a program, it was never really finished. As new skills were learned or new ideas came to mind, the 'big picture' (algorithm) of the program was revised and changes were made accordingly. Children were in control of their learning; it was ongoing and ever broadening in scope. (Though identified as gifted, these students, in groups of 15-20 at a time, worked with 1-3 computers in a special one-day-per-week situation. Regular students working with a greater number of computers each day of the week might very well yield the same kind of results.)

Higher level processes are certainly involved in the writing of computer programs. One can almost sense the pulse of a divergent-convergent cycle rhythmically operating throughout the endeavour. Fred Bell suggests:

> "Writing a computer program requires analysis and synthesis of the subject under consideration as well as the program itself. A student cannot write a program to tutor others, play a game, simulate a situation, or solve an exercise without analyzing the topic being studied and synthesizing it into a coherent teaching/learning program. The synthesis required in writing the program properly and the analysis in debugging it provides additional practice at synthesizing and analyzing. Since many non-tutorial computer programs are higher-level applications of topics, the student programmer must evaluate the appropriateness of alternative approaches to the topic and the program. When a student writes computer programs to extend and clarify topics in school, the six steps in problem

-solving (posing the problem, precisely defining the problem, gathering information, developing a solution strategy, finding the solution and checking the solution) must be carried out. On the other hand, most so-called 'problems' in textbooks are really exercises for practicing skills, which require only one of the six steps of problem solving; namely, finding the answer." (8)

The use of music and word processors in the classroom further contributed to the generation of open-ended environments. In preparation for the use of word processing, primary students had the opportunity to work with a simple 'music processor'. On the computer screen they were able to manipulate tone symbols represented in traditional music format. With the immediate aural feedback, the students were able to compare and revise objectified ideas matched against their internal constructs. Determining the next note generally required playing the entire piece through, or at least the immediate few bars, to refresh the memory of the music pattern as well as maintain and pursue the integrity of the composition. The structural skills derived from composing and editing music appeared to be transferrable to language processing. Even very young students, using simple word processors, had improved writing fluency. Concern about handwriting legibility was reduced, and the labours of editing for spelling and grammar were minimized since the printing was standardized by the computer. Children could better focus on the creative expression of their ideas, often working together discussing plotlines more fully before implementing them in their stories. The word processor invited students to see the 'whole' first in their minds and then visually on the screen, something they didn't do as readily when writing directly into a notebook.

Marrying music and word processors within a single framework should encourage transference between the two systems. Notational similarities can be generalized. Synergistic thought, in exploring the interaction between words and notes, becomes an even more exciting possibility. Enabled to edit music and language ideas in relation to one another, the dimensions of a child's thought processes increase. No longer confined to a linear vehicle, thinking will possibly involve parallel, yet interactive channelling, with pooling from different directions within a multi-dimensional mindspace.

Some current progressive thoughtware has already paved the way in this direction. In a visual representation, students are provided with the opportunity to manipulate and alter three-dimensional images. Other programs, such as GERTRUDE'S SECRETS (The Learning Co., California -- Ann Piestrup), set up an environment wherein the child can wander, investigate, hypothesize, test, evaluate and ultimately assimilate a part of that environment. Accompanied by a map displaying the architectural layout of Gertrude's home, students can design their own route through the various rooms containing different kinds of puzzles, stopping and working in any room of their choice, checking out instructions if they so choose, leaving the more difficult version(s) of a puzzle type temporarily to attempt another category. The child controls his/her learning rate and direction. No two children really learn in exactly the same way. The opportunity for each child to move toward certain understandings on the basis of a unique pattern of connections, and possibly in the process discover new understandings, is exciting. Knowledge is indeed something children can shape for themselves; they can become their own epistemologists.

Proposed thoughtware could progress in stages toward intricate concept networks as follows: 1) recognition of interrelationships among facts, presented in different representational modes, resulting in the formulation of mental constructs; 2) links among these fact clusters or concepts will in turn be established, forming generalizations; 3) finally explanations or theories generated by the student will tie these generalizations together meaningfully to act as a unifying force.

The future learning environment may be flexibly rather than rigidly structured, open-ended versus directed, divergent versus convergent lateral versus linear/sequential, focusing on how to think rather than what to think, requiring the student to be a resourceful participant rather than a passive observer/recipient, independent and inner-directed rather than dependent and other-directed. It will be a place where a child learns how to ask effective questions. (It is a question which tells where thinking is going, while an answer only tells where thinking rests momentarily.) Content can be any -- for it is the processing of information which will constitute essential learning.

With tools such as LOGO, learning can be ongoing. Ideas are always in motion in mental space that is dynamic. Reading, processing text for meaning via the sampling of graphics, syntax and semantics, will have a significant new interactive quality with the computer. Writers can convey their ideas in multi-dimensional format. Readers have more simultaneous information to process, along with the opportunity to move toward more encompassing, more powerful understandings.

Self-actualized people, people who have scaled Maslow's hierarchy, also tend to be higher-level thinkers. Maybe the computer will generate this condition as a more typical societal characteristic. Our entire value system will have to be reconsidered and revised. Our definition of the gifted and giftedness may also have to be altered.

The computer can almost be seen as a microcosmic representation of the logic binding the societal macrocosm. The computer might be hailed as 'logic at its best'. Ironically, it is also a creative catalyst, a vehicle into a new and divergent thinking age. It frees us from the necessity of being the bearers of societal organization to consider other possibilities, to ponder as Einstein did, the simple rules that govern life and the universe.

FOOTNOTES

1. Thomas Dwyer, "Heuristic Strategies for Using Computers to Enrich Education"; Taylor, R. (ed.) THE COMPUTER IN THE SCHOOL: TUTOR, TOOL, TUTEE (New York: Teachers College Press, 1980), page 88.

2. Ibid., page 92.

3. Alvin Toffler, THE THIRD WAVE (New York: Bantam Books, 1980), pages 172 and 175.

4. Ibid., pages 174-175.

5. Louis Armand, "The Grandeur of Einstein"; DeBroglie, Armand and Simon, EINSTEIN (New York: Peebles Press, 1979), pages 216-217.

6. Seymour Papert, MINDSTORMS: CHILDREN, COMPUTERS AND POWERFUL IDEAS (New York: Basic Books, Inc., 1980), page 126.

7. Seymour Papert, "Teaching Thinking", COMPUTERS IN EDUCATION -- WCCE 1970, Part 1 (Amsterdam: North-Holland Publishing Co., 1970), page 62.

8. Fred Bell, "Classroom Computers: Beyond the 3R's", CREATIVE COMPUTING September 1979, page 69.

BIBLIOGRAPHY

1. Armand, Louis "The Grandeur of Einstein"; DeBroglie, Armand and Simon, EINSTEIN (New York: Peebles Press, 1979).

2. Bell, Fred "Classroom Computers: Beyond the 3R's", CREATIVE COMPUTING September, 1979.

3. Dwyer, Thomas "Heuristic Strategies for Using Computers to Enrich Education"; Taylor, R. (ed.) THE COMPUTER IN THE SCHOOL: TUTOR, TOOL, TUTEE (New York: Teachers College Press, 1980).

4. Papert, Seymour MINDSTORMS: CHILDREN, COMPUTERS AND POWERFUL IDEAS (New York: Basic Books, Inc., 1980).

5. Papert, Seymour "Teaching Thinking", COMPUTERS IN EDUCATION -- WCCE 1970, Part 1 (Amsterdam: North-Holland Publishing Co., 1970).

6. Toffler, Alvin THE THIRD WAVE (New York: Bantam Books, 1980).

MICRO-PRIMER
A FOUNDATION COURSE FOR TEACHERS
IN PRIMARY SCHOOLS

Ron Jones

Educational Inspector for Microelectronics
Lincolnshire, England

> To introduce microcomputers into 27,000 Primary
> Schools and to train 54,000 Primary Teachers in
> their use presented the British Government with an
> enormous task. The solution lay in the creation of
> MICRO PRIMER, a distance-learning package supported
> by a short tutor-led course, produced by the
> Micro-electronics Education Programme (MEP) team.
> In this paper, the project co-ordinator describes
> the background to the project and the various
> components and the hidden curriculum contained
> therein.

The Department of Industry's "Micros in Primary Schools" Scheme was officially announced in July 1982 by the Prime Minister with the following words: "I am delighted to announce a scheme giving pound for pound support to primary schools buying a microcomputer package. I hope this scheme will mean that by the end of 1984, every primary school has its own microcomputer and will be giving young people the experience they need with the technology of their working and daily lives..."

The scheme came into operation on the 1st October 1983 and supports a primary school's choice of system from three British designed and built microcomputers. It is not the intention of this paper to examine the 'hardware' on offer, rather it aims to give the background which led to Government support for the use of the technology with young children within the primary school sector; to relate the extent of the current developments and finally to explore future trends. The role of the teacher is discussed within this structure ; this is related to an examination in some detail of the training materials which are an integral part of the Department of Industry Scheme, and the new skills which will be demanded of both teachers and children.

THE BACKGROUND

For the head of the British Government to make an announcement concerning the lower strata of the education service came as something of a surprise to many people, including those in primary schools especially as it came at a time of severe government cutbacks which have resulted in tight financial restraints. It does, of course, reflect the concern of many in positions of responsibility that Britain is now in the grip of a technological revolution, and in order that our future generations might come to terms with rapidly changing conditions, children of school age must be given the opportunity to gain the necessary experience with - in the Prime Minister's words - "... the technology of their future working and daily lives." But the announcement was important in other ways for it represented not only the involvement of two major government departments sharing the responsibility - the Department of Industry (DOI) and the Department of Education & Science (DES), but also their positive involvement at a remarkable speed.

A national survey carried out in early 1980 revealed that only 32 primary schools in England were using microcomputers, and these were scattered throughout the length and breadth of the country in tiny conglomerates. Yet within two and a half years since that survey, 27,000 primary schools are being offered the opportunity to avail themselves of a sohpisticated piece of high technology which only a few years ago would have been confined to multi-nationals and the big banks. How did this remarkable change come about ?

As far as the primary schools are concerned it can be traced, with the exception of a tiny minority, to May 1978. That is the date when BBC television's Horizon progamme 'Now the Chips are Down' was first screened, and when several progressive primary schools saw for the first time the implications for education of the technology based on the microprocessor - the chip. The programme allowed the nation a glimpse into the world of tomorrow - which in Japan and the United States of America was the world of today. This revealed that there were nations already coping with the revolution in information technology which had resulted in the creation of whole new industries based on the infinite applications of chip technology.

The momentum, started by BBC television, was given further impetus by the Council for Educational Technology (CET) in December 1978 when it published a statement entitled "Microelectronics: their implications for education and training" (1). In this important document the members of the symposium threw down the following four challenges which are relevant to all in education:

1. What can we do to help people to prepare themselves for a rapidly changing society ?

2. What can we do to help people fit themselves for employment in new and technologically advanced occupations ?

3. What can we do to help people fill their leisure hours, whether the the result of a reduced working week, or the enforced leisure of unemployment ?

4. What can we do to help people to maintain their self-esteem when there are no jobs for them ?

It is against this kind of challenge that the pressure for the introduction of microelectronics in primary schools was born, and why it is important that it is viewed in the wider social and technological context rather than as small children in classrooms armed with a learning tool. This also helps to account for the fact that it is believed to be important for our future as a nation that _all_ children and _all_ teachers should be involved in using the new technology, if we are to help create a technologically literate people.

It was against this background of challenge that a few schools began to explore various uses of the new technology, and why in March 1981 at a conference held at Homerton College, Cambridge, a number of these pioneering teachers came together for mutual support and to share ideas and experiences. It was at this conference that it was decided that, in the interest of expanding further the uses of the micro, a national body should be created. From this grass roots movement emerged Micros and Primary Education (MAPE) (2). This national organisation which now has 14 regions which correspond to those organised under the Microelectronics Education Programme (3) aims 'To promote and develop the awareness and effective use of microelectronics as an integral part of the philosophy and practice of primary education.'

MAPE has emerged against the background of meeting a national need, and has been very active in promoting 'awareness' not only amongst primary teachers, but also in many other areas of interest, indeed through the constant need for sponsorship big business has gradually become aware of the technological needs of the primary sector of education. MAPE, through its steering committee, provided a body of expert knowledge which was made available for use by the Microelectronics Programme, and indeed the organisation supplied the MICRO-PRIMER co-ordinator and the software development officer for the in-service training package which is an integral part of the DOI Scheme.

It is interesting to note that the word 'microcomputer' does not appear in the aims or title of MAPE. This was a deliberate omission, because it has been the intention of the organisation from the beginning to keep the technology as broadly based as possible, for the time will soon come when the microcomputer itself is but a small part - albeit an essential part, of a whole information technology system - and MAPE must adapt to such developments in the future. MAPE has also aimed in its pioneering development to prevent 'microelectronics' from becoming a subject within the primary school curriculum, for it believes that the new technology is so essential that it must be absorbed into the very fabric of primary education in the United Kingdom.

CURRENT DEVELOPMENTS

It is this fundamental belief in the importance of the use of the technology rather than in the technology itself which has allowed the move forward in such a short time from the simple use of the microcomputer as merely a drill and practice tool. Not only has it far more potential than that, but it would not reflect the future needs of society, and would certainly not merit the injection of considerable government aid if it was to be used in such a limited way.

Neither has it been linked only into mathematics and science. It has, despite its short existence as a learning tool, successfully bridged many areas of the curriculum. It is now seen as a powerful thinking tool which extends the children's range of experiences through its use in simulations. It is enabling quite young children to handle complex data and to see the computer as a powerful aid to learning. It is allowing them to gain first hand experience with the new technology which is the very key to prosperity in a nation whose economy is so closely linked with technology.

There are two major problems which need to be overcome in order to promote the developing use of micros within primary schools. The first and foremost is the attitude of the teaching profession; how to encourage 54,000 primary teachers to take their first faltering steps across the technological threshold; the second is for committed teachers to take on board the educational implications of the new technology in terms of curriculum changes based on new skills which are urgently needed.

The main problem over the next two years is gently and with sympathy, to lead 54,000 classroom teachers to take their first bite of the technological cherry, for they will have to form the core of the trained teachers who will then, hopefully, pass on their new found skills to their colleagues. The danger is that the children will absorb the technology with such alacrity that this will create a culture gap between themselves, their teachers and their parents.

To help in trying to avoid this danger, the Microelectronics Education Programme (MEP) team, turned its attention in April 1982 to the creation of an in-service education training package. The package, which was launched just eight months later, in November 1982, is known as MICRO-PRIMER, and is a foundation resource for teachers.

It is worth examining in some detail the ingredients of the MICRO PRIMER, which is a multi-media training package designed to be used for distance learning. The size of the training task which had to be completed in a two year period was just too large to be tackled by the normal tutor-led approach. A fresh approach was devised, where to qualify for the DOI Scheme, two teachers from each school would agree to undertake a period of training which consisted of approximately 30 hours of self-study supported at a later date by a 12 hour tutor-led course organised by the teachers' Local Education Authority. The 30 hour distance-learning element of MICRO PRIMER has two main parts; materials which are specific to the microcomputer chosen under the scheme and non-specific materials which cover the wider implications of the new technology.

Before describing the various components, it is worth dwelling on the aims of the package. It aims to introduce teachers to some of the uses of micros in schools emphasising 'some' because it is hoped that many teachers will accept the challenge of experimenting and exploring uses which have not yet been discovered - such is the state of the art, it is still fresh and at the innovative stage of development. Secondly, MICRO PRIMER aims to give teachers confidence in using the micro throughout the curriculum. In this it encourages teachers to take the whole system home and use the training materials in private until they have come to terms with it. It also introduces teachers to some of the concepts behind information technology, and finally to some of the social and educational implications of information technology, and the urgent need to absorb new skills.

OVERVIEW

The components of the MICRO PRIMER package have been designed with a particular planned sequence in mind, but could be used in a variety of ways to suit the user. The Overview offers a suggested path known as ROUTEWAY. This details 22 'work units', each work-unit directing the reader to study specific sections of the package and urging the user to attempt various practical activities which are essential to the learning process. These activities increase in complexity as the beginner's confidence grows, yet offers the experienced user a good deal of food for thought.

STUDY TEXT

This is the core of distance-learning in the package. It is divided into seven self-contained work units which introduce various facets of microcomputing to the teacher: hardware; social implications; models of learning; applications in primary schools; classroom management; the teacher's role; and future prospects. It leads the teacher in gentle steps from a simple explanation of a microcomputer system to a discussion of the different relationships that arise in a classroom when a micro is present. It does this through the use of clear text, effective illustrations and cartoon pictograms to suggest follow-up activities. It should be emphasised that the STUDY TEXT is not a text book; rather it has been developed to be used in context with other parts of the foundation course and is designed to be used within the carefully planned sequence, the MICRO PRIMER'S ROUTEWAY. It is indicative of the use of new technology that the STUDY TEXT was written and edited in just eight weeks - a task which daunts many traditional publishing houses !

READER

The Reader contains 25 articles and case studies gleaned from many sources. The articles are grouped in three sections; social implications, computers in the classroom, and implications for primary education. They are designed to give the teacher a rapid up-date not only on the state of the technology, but also on its social and educational implications. The articles will in this context provide a very useful source of topics for discussion as the READER is carefully integrated at certain points in the STUDY TEXT for this purpose.

CLASSROOM CASE-STUDIES

In order to remind the teacher-student ploughing a lonely furrow that the whole scheme is designed to be used with the children in the classroom, Julian Coleman, of BBC radio, has written and produced four case-studies in sound. These sound illustrations allow the student to break away from text-based information and learn something of other teachers' use of the micros in the classroom. The case-studies, which are presented on two cassettes cover the use of micros in structured reinforcement; in data-handling; in simulations. Case Study 4 illustrates some management problems; each mini-broadcast lasts approximately twenty five minutes.

THE EASEL

This flip-over machine easel is designed to stand by the side of the micro system and complements the manufacturers guide.

- Side 1 - the system guide helps the student to connect together the various components to create the microcomputer system, and get it running.

- Side 2 - is an activity guide which encourages the students to practice various activities with the micro, exploring its potential.

The Easel used is specific to the particular machine ordered through the DOI Scheme.

SOFTWARE PACKS

The packs contain 30 programs for use by the teacher in the classroom. They have been tried and tested, and are for use with a wide range of children, from reception infants through to upper juniors (ages 5-11). They also cover a wide range of subject areas within the curriculum. In addition, the packs also contain programs which help with skills development, using and handling facts and other information and trying out possible problems through simulations. Each program is fully described in accompanying booklets so that the teacher can learn the thinking behind the design of the programs.

Built into the MICRO PRIMER are possible ways of solving the second major problem of helping teachers, once they have taken the initial steps to recognise the need to identify new skills, especially those skills associated with information technology. Philip Virgo in a recently published Bow Paper 'Learning for Change' (4) urges a shift in the curriculum. He argues: "We can no longer afford to spend one or two decades of detailed preparation for a single life-long career progression. Instead we should aim, like our ancestors, to impart those basic skills almost certain to be in continuous demand and to build a system capable of responding rapidly to changes and disseminating new skills to any age group when necessary."

He identifies three new skills which he would like to add to basic literacy and numeracy. The first is the concept of simulations; the second is problem structuring and solving; the third 'the basic skills of running a business.'

TUTORIAL RESOURCES MATERIAL

An essential part of MICRO PRIMER is a tutored course provided by the teachers' Local Education Authority (LEA). The tutored element of the total package was refined by LEA advisers during a series of three day MEP courses on which advisers were introduced to the distance-learning components of MICRO PRIMER.

The result of these refinments, based on the experience of LEA Primary Advisers, are the Tutor Guidelines provided by MEP in a Tutorial Resources Folder.

Because of the possible wide application of the material, the Guidelines and associated Tutorial resources have been developed with flexibility in mind and are offered as suggestions rather than a prescription for the course which LEA's are required to run under the DOI Scheme.

Accompanying the Guidelines which contain material for seven activity sessions is a set of 30 specially designed overhead projection transparancies. The Guidelines are designed to be used in connection with a DES video MICROS IN PRIMARIES - STARTING OUT. The video is supported with teachers' notes and a video observation grid.

The suggested course is produced on seven laminated session card, A to G, and for each of these sessions there is a statement of AIMS; a list of EQUIPMENT and MATERIAL; NOTES where appropriate, and a set of ACTIVITIES. Each session is based on a minimum time of two hours.

Session A is designed for use where an LEA distributes the microcomputer and MICRO PRIMER package at a pre-training meeting. Sessions B - G make up a tutored course which is designed to follow on from the distance-learning part of MICRO PRIMER, or some such introductor course. These sessions cover the following:- Sharing Experience; Exploring Software; New Skills - Information Handling; New Skills - Problem Solving; New Skills - Problem Structuring and Logical Thinking; The Teacher's Role.

FUTURE TRENDS

So much for the current developments; having recognised the need, the Government through its development agency MEP has provided the means of training large numbers of teachers who are about to take the leap forward into the future, thus enabling their students to begin to use the technology of their future lives. We have already taken the first faltering steps on the road to creating a technologically literate teaching force, and there is already the beginning of a pattern in their use of technology. At first structured reinforcement will prevail as the major use, but gradually with the growing confidence of the teaching force, much more ambitious uses of new technology will develop in such areas as information handling, which involves the development of such skills as data collection, the accessing of data, its storage and retrieval, its manipulation and use; and in the detailed questioning and interrogation of data.

The third part of this new learning strategy is still in its infancy: the development of such life skills as flexible thinking, of evaluating and decision making through the use of complex simulations, which involve children working in small groups. A great deal of exciting curriculum development work lies in the future. Teachers will begin to form program design teams to cope with this type of use. It will be these design teams, hopefully backed by their Local Authorities working through the MEP regional structure, which will serve to unlock the ideas which are within the imaginative and innovative classroom teacher.

Seymour Papert's ideas expressed in his book 'Mindstorms' (5) will begin to take effect within the primary sector with the development of the language LOGO, for it represents a stimulating vision of education for the future - collaboration between computers and children. His vision does not allow for computers 'programming' children, rather the reverse. He envisages the child programming the computer, mastering the powerful technology and coming into contact with some of the deepest ideas within science, mathematics and other areas of the curriculum. The future does not require that all teachers become programmers, far from it, but it will require that teachers, as program originators and developers, establish a means of accurately conveying their ideas to the program writers - the encoders.

It will be essential for future developments that a structure is established very quickly which will enable this collaboration to take place on a national basis. In this way, it will bring a steady flow of well produced, well documented software. This will require further Government initiative. The 'Hardware' is now available and will be required in greater quantities than one, or even two per school. An even greater requirement will be the continuance of the programming teams established by MEP for the creation of MICRO PRIMER.

Another promising area for development for the future will be in the area of control technology. Children need to be aware of the power of the microprocessor to control far more than the visual display unit. They need to 'play' with the processor's control of electronic circuits and electric motors. This needs to be linked to technology and design, even at the primary stage as a natural extention to the child's mastery of such technical toys as LEGO and Fischertechnik. Types of toys which are capable of being converted into a myriad designs - where the children do not merely follow a recipe design, but work at solving a design problem in their own way, thus encouraging the concepts of 'EXPLORATION AND INNOVATION.'

CONCLUSION

The micro has provided a means of unifying the education service, for it is a revolutionary tool at all levels, but we should not lose the opportunity it offers for mutual respect and co-operation. It demands from all of us in the education service the recognition that new skills are required of ourselves and of our children if we are to become technologically literate; it is through these skills that we will be able to cope with a rapidly changing world. Already the development teams are made up of people from different strata of education and such experience needs to be shared - on an international basis. the DOI Scheme which represents co-operation at the highest level has just come at the right moment in time. The key to training is that active involvement leads to commitment. Professor Gosling in his occasional paper "Microcircuits, Society and Education" (6) summarises the spirit of the future in which primary schools are actively involved when he says: " From sand is the silicon micro-circuit created, from sand the optical fibre. The most common and worthless material about us, available in inexhaustible quantities, suddenly is transformed to be the key to all our futures, in a world so different from the one we know that merely to turn our minds to it stuns our imaginations. The task of education in helping our kind to make the transition to a new life-style is one which will demand all our skills, insights, flexibility. Yet the role of education is central for it is in the mind of man that the revolution to come will be fought. In the kingdom of sand all things become possible, and only imagination rules."

REFERENCES:

(1) Microelectronics : their implications for Education and Training
    (CET, 3, Devonshire Street, London.)

(2) MAPE - Micros and Primary Education. An organisation for teachers in Primary Schools. Details from the Secretary, Mr. Barry Holmes, St. Helen's School, Bluntisham, Cambridgeshire, England.

(3) MEP (Microelectronics Education Programme. Director, Mr. R. Fothergill, Coach Lane Campus, Newcastle upon Tyne NE7 7XA, England.)

(4) Philip Virgo - Learning for Change. A Bow Group Paper
    (Bow Publications Ltd. 240 High Holborn, London WC1 7DT.

(5) Seymour Papert - Mindstorms. (Basic Books)

(6) W. Gosling - Microcircuits - Society and Education (CET as above)

(7) Ron Jones - Microcomputers their uses in Primary Schools (CET)

Session 1 - Discussion

Rapporteurs: C.D. MARTIN, B. LEVRAT

As chairman, TINSLEY thought the two papers illustrated very well the following two basic questions:
- What are the children able to do with informatics?
- How can we stop teachers preventing them from doing it?

He then invited questions from the audience.

VAN WEERT wanted some clarification about the use of word processors allowing "students to see the 'whole' first in their minds and then visually on the screen". KUBATH used the analogy of teaching language: both phonics/sound and the visual shape of the letters are used to distinguish different words. Similarly, in constructing essays, using the video screen, the child has the flexibility of reconstructing sentences and moving things on the screen to help develop ideas; by building his text in pictorial format, he goes from iconic understanding to a more abstract representation. BONELLO-KUBATH, working with teachers who used word processors with children, noted that these children tended to discuss and develop the complete story as a whole while working at the word processor.

PLANCKE-SCHUYTEN expressed the hope that programming will help the pupil 'learn to learn'. How will the problem-solving skills from a computer environment transfer to a non-computer environment? This is one of the big concerns of the work which is going on at the Pedagogical Laboratory in Ghent. The KUBATHs found that the same concern was valid when teaching thinking and research skills aside from the computer. They concluded that transferring techniques have to be taught to teachers. Synthesis must be part of the curriculum because it does not happen by magic. JONES stated that, in the U.K., they tried to avoid the transfer of skills problem altogether by including the computer in a natural way in all subject areas, eliminating the 'expert syndrome'.

LOVIS posed a possible problem inherent in the U.K. training program. When only two teachers in a school received the computer training mentioned by JONES, there is the danger that they would be offered better positions elsewhere. How can the school carry on the computer program with the loss of the two teachers? JONES replied that the falling birthrate had decreased teacher mobility. In addition, teachers are forming user groups to train and bring along new colleagues.

GORNY stressed the changes occurring in the socio-cultural background. Most of our communication relies on sequences of symbols. Computer systems give us the possibility to handle and change pictorial, that is spatial, information about complex relations and objects. Perhaps some of the predictions of MacLuhan will come true now, when more comfortable and cheaper graphics systems will be available. School systems will have to cope with the challenge of widening thinking skills to include pictorial and spatial information.

BONELLO-KUBATH expressed gratitude that the essence of their talk had been understood. The problem is to define literacy to include the ability to work with all kinds of symbols, music, text, and pictures. Information like files can be organised in a spatial way, relating to a house or a desk-top as it has been done at MIT. KUBATH commented that students are already familiar with video-screens due to arcade games. He didn't see that traditional literacy would be replaced, but rather enhanced by graphics.

JONES cited examples of two simulations in which the computer was used to enhance other literacy skills such as writing, research, and interpretive thinking by posing the problem and providing the record-keeping for the solution of the problem.

LOETHE asked the participants to comment on the appropriateness of the programming languages being used with elementary students. He assumed that the British project is using BASIC to keep the price of the computer down. JONES pointed out that technology and languages are not as important as the integration of computers in the classroom. The main issue is to get the teachers trained rather than to get bogged down in arguments about languages.

BONELLO-KUBATH started teaching BASIC with graphics and then moved to LOGO. She found that children who were successful with BASIC were not interested in LOGO, whereas children who were not successful with BASIC did move readily to LOGO. There may be some sequence in going from one language to another. The important issue is not necessarily which language, but how to approach programming with children using an open-ended method. KUBATH stated that he had the luxury of implementing a philosphy of using whatever medium he needed to present what he was trying to teach. He had a lot of hardware and software available, as well as several programming languages such as LOGO, BASIC, FORTH, Assembly language, etc. Later children used these languages at the expense of some confusion, but they did master the 'multilingual' environment.

M. DeVAULT asked if the U.K. program was open-ended and could be moved from teacher to teacher. JONES stated that the government would offer a computer to each school ready to provide two teachers willing to go through the material and then take the 12 hrs follow-up training which is essential. Regions are establishing their own courses to create large groups of trained teachers. The next step is to teach specification writing to teachers so they can communicate with programmers to create good software.

TINSLEY invited the authors to sum up their position. The KUBATHs had been concerned that their ideas were radical. They were encouraged that the audience was able to understand them from such a brief presentation. JONES's main concern was to emphasize the breadth of moving a large number of people into the future. Children must learn to move from structured information to information handling, problem structuring and solving, and control technology (robotics).

SESSION 2

WHY I USE A COMPUTER DURING MY PHYSICS LESSONS

K.G. Ahlström

Kungsbergskolan Comprehensive School

Linkoping
SWEDEN

It is difficult for teachers to explain how computers work in society because pupils have limited understanding of life outside school. Instead we must find applications in the classroom which can develop a wider perspective.

I often use a computer in my physics classes. It can be used as an intelligent calculator and make remarks such as "just fine !" or "sorry !" "you made a mistake ! try again !". After these experiences, my pupils and I can discuss how they reacted when they got these replies from the computer.

This paper gives examples of experiments to measure time and calculate velocity. The computer is used to present and sort out data so that questions can be asked "what sort of information do you need ? how fast did the computer work compared with you ?"

Many teachers have to teach about computers with very little knowledge about computers. If the computer is not regarded as a computer but as another measuring instrument the teacher's self confidence increases. In that situation, a physics teacher will dare to use the computer. It is necessary to use computers at school. Our pupils must face a reality where computers existing and are important.

Since 1982, the Swedish Board of Education has directed that every pupil in a comprehensive school must receive education about computers and about how they are used in Society. This will not lead to a new school subject, but will be introduced by co-operation between teachers of mathematics and civics who will be expected to co-operate and integrate topics within their existing subjects.

The following is an important quotation from the instructions given by the Board of Education: " The purpose of education (about computers) is to give the pupils such knowledge that they are interested and confident enough to take up an attitude towards, and have an influence on the use of computers in our society."

The following instructions are included in the Board of Education Report which was written in 1980.

- Data and informatics. How can we transmit, interpret, store and process information ? What is the information explosion ?

- Computer system and computer program. How is a computer system built up ? What parts does a computer system consist of ? What is the purpose of the program ?

- Personal index. What does the law say ? What is integrity ? What about public documents ?

- The historical development. What are the advantages and disadvantages ? What are the reasons for ADP ? How can computers be used at home, in a place of work, in administration and in commercial and industrial life ?

- Computers and the working environment. How do computers influence employment ? How vulnerable is a society which depends on computers ?

- Practical experience by data processing.

The curriculum will be changed rapidly. The teaching should be very practical. Pupils' own experience and questions are the starting points. Educational visits are of importance. The pupils must take prime responsibility for the planning of the educational visits. It is not necessary to have access to the use of a computer system. If a school has a computer system every pupil ought to work for some time at a terminal. The course should include about 20 lessons. There will be no time to teach every pupil how to write programs in BASIC.

The Teachers. Thus all pupils in Sweden should receive instruction about computers. As a result, many teachers will have to teach about computers without having had adequate training. I myself am a teacher in mathematics and physics in a Swedish comprehensive school. My only education on computers has been the result of my own efforts. Many teachers are and will be in the same situation with enthusiasm our most important motive. Under such circumstances we must find situations where teachers are encouraged to use a computer in their teaching. The extent of teacher education should change however now that the Board of Education is investing in further training.

Every school must have computers. I think it is difficult to teach about computers and how a computer can work in society without using at least one computer. The pupils must have a chance to be seated in front of a terminal. Not until then will their fear disappear. After that they will know that people control the working of computers. They also know that a person can use a computer without knowing how it works. Others may have constructed the computer and the program - but anyone can handle it - after some training. computers change life in society. It is difficult to explain to pupils how a computer can work in society. Society outside school is not well known to the pupils, but we can use computers in school to find out how the computer can change the conditions of our pupils' society - the class and the classroom. We can compare this situation with a reality where we have no access to a computer. After these impressions we can start to understand the role of computers in society outside school. Below I will relate how and why I use a computer and how my pupils react.

The computer in the physics laboratory. I use the computer in the physics laboratory. I have many reasons for that. One of the most important ones is the computer I use. It can measure times, frequency, temperature, voltage and current with an external interface and simple BASIC commands. In a similar way, other teachers will be able to find appropriate uses of computers within their own subjects, for example, mathematics, civics or mother tongue.

You must find suitable experiments which show how the computer works and its characteristics. Pupils learn by experience in the laboratory. From these experiences they must draw conclusions about what the computer means in society outside school. For the present I have about fifteen experiments and demonstrations. I use them in my classes at suitable opportunities.

Why I Use a Computer during my Physics Lessons

I use the computer when I can find reasons to use it. The computer must be a part of our everyday life. Sometimes I make demonstrations, sometimes my pupils use the computer in different experiments. The programs are stored on a cassette tape. The programs can be classified like this: the computer used as an intelligent calculator, the computer used as a measuring instrument or the computer used to collect and process data. Some programs are formulated in such a way that the computer guides the pupils. They get instructions from the computer. I have devised the programs. The pupils only write what the computer asks them to do.

The computer as an intelligent calculator. In class 7 we work with balanced levers, windlasses, blocks and tackle and inclined planes. The pupils use them to lift weights of cement. Intuitively they will find out the Golden rule of mechanics " when you gain in force you lose in distance." The last experiment is with the inclined plane. Before the experiment we discuss which job is heavier - to lift or to roll the wagon up the inclined plane, or are both equal ? Each pupil formulates his hypothesis. They observe as carefully as possible. The height and the length of the inclined plane are measured. The forces to lift or roll the wagon are measured with a dynamometer. Every result is given to the computer. The computer calculates the work to lift or roll the wagon. Why a computer ? Why not just paper and pencil or a calculator ? Well there is a line in the program which compares the two tasks. If one work is ten per cent greater than the other one - the computer gives the instructions - You must control your experiment and your measurements. Do it again - If it is smaller than ten per cent the computer tells the pupil - Good. Go on. It is striking to look at their faces. They are happy when they are successful and they will try again when the computer says so. Their protests are weaker compared with when I tell them. What is the power of the computer ? We discuss it afterwards. I tell the pupils that I have made the program. Consequently they do what I have told them. Thus a simple experiment has been a lesson in what the computer means in our reality and in our society.

In Class 8 we work with Ohm's law. Earlier we have done experiments with simple circuits, we have connected and read off volt and am meters. Ohm's law has been demonstrated, by means of the computer. The pupils are given resistors and are supposed to find out their resistance. The resistance and the tolerance (5 or 10%) are printed on the resistor in fully written out text. The pupils make their experiments. The instruments are read. The measurements are given to the computer. The computer calculates the resistance. Resistance and tolerance, given in fully written text, are also given to the computer. It compares and decides if your results are approved or whether you must do it again. The same reaction and the same discussion as before - What do you need to know ? You have to connect and read the instruments - and that is troublesome and difficult. The next thing I have to do is to buy meters, connectable to the computer. The computer would then take care of this troublesome detail. Then the discussion would be amplified to robots, factories without workers, production where computers work and persons supervise.

The computer used for measurements. A computer can measure short times. The computer I use has simple BASIC commands such as TIME (1). The pupils can test their reaction times. We use other methods, but they find it most amusing to work with the computer. Why a computer ? There are many reasons. The computer starts with a random number generator. It repeats the experiment ten times and calculates the average. But most important, it is programmed to show how far the pupils would move during the reaction time. They find out how far a car can go after something has happened before the driver presses the brake. The computer calculates the braking distance at every 5Km/h from

0 to 100 km/h and presents the results on the screen. I don't think pupils in the seventh class have the patience to calculate the values themselves. By means of a computer a teacher does not need to invent simple examples. The pupils can use their own measuring results. I urge the pupils to discuss the results with their parents. I hope they drive the family car. In the same way the computer can be of help when you measure the speed of sound. You can examine a person's power, you can measure how radioactive radiation pierces different materials and so on. The pupils try to work with and without computers.

The computer stores and processes data. What sort of data is relevant to the pupils ? If you have access to a computer, it can help the pupils to produce their own data. It must be more meaningful. If the pupils process the data side by side with the computer they can compare. How quickly and carefully does a person work compared to a computer ? In the seventh class I make the following experiment. At the beginning and the end of a staircase I place photocells and lamps. The photocells are connected to the computer. The computer can measure the time it takes a pupil to run upstairs. Every pupil is furnished with a piece of paper. They write down name, the length of the staircase and the time to run upstairs. After running, they have to calculate their velocities both in m/s and km/h. They have access to calculators (which means computer power.) The pupils gather in front of the staircase. Every pupil's name is given to the computer with an INPUT command. The pupil runs upstairs. The computer measures time and writes it on the screen. When all pupils have run, I wait until they have finished their calculations. Gathering in front of the computer, a push on RETURN and the table with names and results is presented on the screen. The pupils are given the task to sort the results from the fastest to the slowest one. When they are ready, a new gathering in front of the computer. A new push on RETURN and the sorted list is presented after a short while. Afterwards, we discuss the experiment. What sort of knowledge did you need ? How fast did the computer work compared to you ? I consider that the experiment will give the pupils a better image of how a computer collects and processes data than a report on how fast a great computer works in an office. The reason is that the experiment is made in the pupils' everyday life. Some pupils accept the reality of the computer without criticsm. They do not need to think. The demands on them are less. Other pupils think this reality is senseless. One pupil said "If the computer were better, then we could let it run upstairs too!" Unfortunately I do not have a printer. I would like the pupils to have their names and results on a paper written out by the computer. In the same way, the computer can measure how fast a pupil moves his hand. If the program above is modified and every pupil states his weight the computer can calculate and give a table of the required forces in numerical order.

The computer takes over. You can in simple experiments show how a computer can change a job to a matter of routine. The computer impoverishes our working life. The computer handles most of the work and a person supervises. In the ninth class we do laboratory work on energy. Coefficient of utilization is very important. In an experiment we settle the coefficient of utilization when water is warmed in a saucepan on an electric plate. You determine the energy change of water and the electric energy. The whole experiment is operated by the computer. The pupil types in two measurements, the weight of water and the effect of the hotplate. At the right moment the computer urges the pupils to put on or take off the saucepan, to switch on and off and to put the thermometer into and out of the water and to stir the water. The computer operates the rest. It measures the initial and final temperature and calculates the rise of temperature. The time taken in seconds is registered by the computer. The computer calculates the heat and electric energy and the coefficient of utilization in percent. At last the computer presents every measurement and all calculations. The computer then suggests a new experiment. Determine the coefficient of utilization but use no lid on the saucepan.

The same discussion afterwards. How did the computer change our attitude to the experiment ? Was it easier or more difficult ? Was it funny or boring ? Should we or should we not use computers?

Again the teacher. In Sweden many teachers must teach about computers with very little knowledge of computers. If they are able to regard the computer as just another measuring instrument, physics teachers will feel at home. Teachers are familiar with different kinds of measuring instruments. The new thing with the computer is the programming but the program is often saved on a cassette tape. If teachers' self confidence increases, they will start to use computers in their teaching. It is necessary to use computers at school. Our pupils must face a reality where computers exist everywhere and are an important part of our life. We must therefore introduce the computer as early as possible in the comprehensive school.

Editorial Footnote

In Swedish schools, classes 7 and 8 refer to pupils of ages 14 and 15 respectively.

COMPUTERS AS A TOOL FOR CHILDREN AT ELEMENTARY LEVEL AND ITS IMPACT ON SCHOOL MATHEMATICS

Herbert Löthe

PÄDAGOGISCHE HOCHSCHULE
ESSLINGEN
FRG

The theory and practice of teaching mathematics will change drastically in the future. Already today, it is a fact that most pupils learn the concepts of different kinds of numbers by exploring their environment and not by a teaching process. This situation is in principle true - though not obvious - of nearly all mathematical disciplines, when we think of them in the light of sophisticated computer systems.

When discussing the relevance of the elements of computer science and the impact of computer use on elementary education, we first of all feel concerned about school mathematics. I personally believe that theory and practice of teaching mathematics will change drastically under this impact. These changes are rather obvious in arithmetic. Hence I will start by discussing this topic.

ARITHMETIC

Today the pupil is led from the concept of number (e.g. as a cardinal) to the decimal system together with its related algorithms and further on step by step in a rather systematic way to the complete system of real numbers. The sequence of teaching is strongly influenced by the scientific way of expanding the system of numbers. In the future we can no longer decide to teach this whole course of instruction in this way. The main points are the following. Children seldom learn a particular thing at the time the teacher supposes. Fundamental abstractions like the natural, whole numbers and fractions are learned much earlier than planned by the curriculum designers. This learning happens when children explore and discover the world around them. Nowadays they are finding numbers everywhere in impressive representations as digital displays of clocks and other devices. "Counting with a carry" is demonstrating the mechanism of the decimal system. Though a mathematician might not be very content with this limited concept of number it is very useful in mental calculations and other traditional computational skills. From this situation a new role for teachers emerges. They have to supplement and enrich this special concept of numbers by others, this particular number system by others, this concept of operation (e.g. addition as counting) by others and so on.

As a second device for exploring, children use pocket calculators which they find at home, at department stores, but - at least in Germany - not at school. Nevertheless this mathematical machine is a fascinating thing for children. They are able to learn the concept of fraction (in decimal representation) only by exploring the calculator and they can use it in a reasonable way when they have grasped the relationship between arithmetical operations and measurements, especially in real life examples and word problems. The calculator demonstrates to an eight or nine year old pupil the result of 2:5 as 0.4 which makes sense for instance as 0.4m = 40 cm. The calculation "2 divided by 5" also makes sense, when embedded in a word problem like "a string of 2m is to be cut and distributed among 5 boys." Similar explorations are made by children with

with negative numbers, e.g. in problems concerning debts and accounts. However, some topics of the number system are not covered by the exploration of calculators and the interpretation in terms of real-life situations. For instance, children are not able to get sense out of calculations like $(-2) \times (-3) = 6$. But this completion of the mathematical system is hard to motivate at all. On the other hand, an incomplete calculus in the mathematical sense is no hindrance to excellent work with real-life problems.

CONCLUSIONS

Though the pocket calculator does not establish too rich a mathematical environment, I hope that my sketch of the impact of this device on elementary education in mathematics gives enough evidence for the following general statements concerning the development of didactics:

- The syllabus of school mathematics will change, because some parts will become obsolete as for instance the complete calculus of fractions (without the concept of decimal fractions). On the other hand appropriate elements of informatics will be integrated.

- The didactics of mathematics and the practice of teaching will have - at least on a long-term basis - a drastic change, though the incompetency of the present teacher generation will slow down this process. In the future teachers have to proceed in their teaching from the fact that elementary mathematics has become an experimental subject for the pupils.

- The learning of mathematics will be for the pupils more a process of exploring the mathematical environment than a participation in a systematic sythesis of the subject.

- The role of the teacher will change correspondingly; she or he will have to clear up the concepts, to present supplementary information, to guarantee that all pupils have the same chance for discovering and so on.

In the following I would like to present some examples for this kind of work in mathematics education.

TURTLE GEOMETRY

Seymour Papert ([7]) introduced in 1968 a mathematical environment which he likes to call "mathland". There are a lot of opportunities for children in this environment to explore, to think about, to experiment with and so on; but over all there is an opportunity for the children to acquire insight into their own thinking. Besides this aspect, I also would like to stress that this kind of geometry should be included in the syllabus. Turtle Geometry is a geometry of motion; the turtle constitutes a mental model of motion, of course as a simplification of real movements. Pupils have to ask themselves "How do I move ?" "What are the elements of my movements ?" "How can I give some commands which describe a movement ?" and so on.

In this way pupils build up a mental model of the computer as a performer of commands which describe the motion in discrete steps. This approach to geometry, which is only feasible with computers, is much more helpful in physics than for instance the euclidean way (see [3], [6]). Activities can start with geometrical and physical problems nearly at any level at school and these ideas can be extended during school time and afterwards to nearly arbitrary complexity (e.g. turtle in the space of General Relativity; see [2]).

MODULAR DESIGN

All children play a lot with sets of building blocks starting with wooden blocks and going on to Lego, Fischer-Technik and similar things. Present school mathematics contains only a few examples of using this mental technique, for instance in tiling the plane. But the main characteristics of modular thinking such as breaking down complex things into adequate and multi-functional parts, interfacing, organising a hierarchy of modules and so on - are stressed by computer science when we think of a more mathematical and less technical context. Tools for modular design are modular computer languages and systems (e.g. Logo).

For children of grade 2 or 3 it is a motivating activity to combine elementary figures (triangles, squares, circles etc.) to form more complex drawings like houses, trees, churches and towers and using these results as building blocks for a street or a landscape (see for instance [4], [9]).

As an observer of these activities one can isolate different characteristics and steps of the work and think about auxiliary materials. Important concepts are building blocks which can be blown up (input variables), building blocks with turtle states before and after drawing (orientation, interfacing), "circles" as polygons of 36 sides on the screen (approximation, accuracy as resolution of the screen), repeated use of the same elements (control structures, tail recursion) and others.

This kind of work is the favourite matter for an introduction in computer use with Logo (e.g. [1], [8]), because children (and even adults) can learn the mechanisms of editing and running programs and the elements of language for structuring and controlling in a nice and motivating environment.

The consciousness of the underlying informatical objectives and of the characteristics of the working style can lead to further work with other subject matter. The use of procedures as building blocks can - for instance in the context of number theory problems - motivate the concept of the output of a procedure because it is impossible to combine procedures which manipulate numbers or other data to larger entities without an output mechanism. Procedures with input and output (and without side effects) represent exactly the mathematical concept of function. This important concept is rather difficult to understand because traditional school mathematics does not put it in concrete enough terms. According to my experience, even an average student teacher cannot work with this concept in a productive way.

THE METHOD OF SYSTEMATIC TRIALS (ITERATION)

This method is one of the most powerful ideas of mathematics, which becomes as nested intervals even more important as a link between finite and infinite mathematics.

Very early in their work in turtle geometry, pupils have to deal with problems like the hypotenuse in a right angled triangle, the diagonals of a square or other incommensurable lines. The only helpful hint a teacher can give is: "Try it !" Pupils will make trials to get the length of a line in a more or less systematic way; by commanding the turtle FOWARD :S BACK :S with different values for S they can find out a value which approximates the right one to a given accuracy (in this case the resolution of the screen.) In a similar way children can get approximations for angles in figures they want to define as procedures for drawing.

In carrying on this working style in geometry one can define an environment for exploring the fundamental constructions of triangles in terms of turtle geometr (as we have done in our project, see [5]). In parallel with an euclidean development pupils can discover these constructions and learn approximate methods by themselves.

Besides geometry the same habit of solving problems is needed in tasks like "Which rate of interest will double an account by compound interest in seven years ?" By using a calculator pupils of grade 6 can solve this problem with the method of systematic trial and error. As we know, this method becomes very important and unavoidable at post-elementary level in defining and calculating roots and other irrational numbers.

I would like to stress that pupils can only acquire this exploration method when they are allowed to use computers (or to a minor extent pocket calculators). Only with these devices can the pupil experiment with drawings, numbers or other things in a way that allows short-term responses on trials.

Besides these examples of concepts - from mathematics or informatics - are others like the concept of variables which can be very different depending on the mental model of the computer which is used.

I have tried to show that there are fundamental ideas - as part of previous mathematics or newly brought into our field of vision by the presence of computers - which can be learned by pupils starting at elementary level and proceeding on in a spiral way through the whole of school mathematics. The examples also indicate that future school mathematics will incorporate more thoughful methods; even pupils at elementary level can employ these methods to a certain extent when computers are used as a tool for experiment in a rich mathematical environment.

REFERENCES

[1] Abelson, H., Logo for the Apple II (Byte/McGraw Hill, Peterborough 1982)

[2] Abelson, H. and diSessa, A., Turtle Geometry (The MIT Press, Cambridge, London, 1981)

[3] diSessa, A., Velocity Space and the Geometry of Planetary Orbits, Am.J.Physics 43 (1975)

[4] Hanninger, J., Ein Unterrichtsversuch zu geometrischen Erfahrungen in der Grundschule, Logo-Papier Nr.2, Logo-Projekt, Pädagogische Hochschule Esslingen (Dez. 1982)

[5] Hoppe, H.-U., Das Logo-Konzept für den Computereinsatz im Mathematikunterricht, Logo-Papier Nr. 4, Logo-Projekt, Pädagogische Hochschule Esslingen (Apr. 1982)

[6] Löthe, H. und Quehl, W., Natürliche Geometrie und Dynamik, Logo-Papier Nr. 7, Logo-Projekt, Pädagogische Hochschule Esslingen (Juni 1983)

[7] Papert, S., Mindstorms, Children, Computers and Powerful Ideas (Basic Books, New York 1980, German edition: Birkhäuser Verlag Basel, Boston, Stuttgart 1982)

[8] Solomon, C., Apple Logo, Introduction to Programming through Turtle Graphics (Logo Computer Systems - Apple Computer 1982)

[9] TI Curriculum Guide (Texas Instruments 1981)

Session 2 - Discussion

Rapporteurs: R. JONES, H. BAUERSFELD

LOETHE stated that as far as he was aware there was no evidence to prove the educational value of LOGO (reply to PLANCKE-SCHUYTEN) but that it currently provided the best available tool for children to develop a research style. He would like to explore the use of other languages such as PROLOG and SMALLTALK based on UK experiences.

LEVRAT, after posing the question of the necessity for teachers and children to learn a programming language, expressed concern that it would be difficult to persuade teachers to learn LOGO. LOETHE agreed about the difficulty but felt that its importance to the changes which were already happening within mathematics made it very important that teachers did learn this particular language. The use of TURTLE geometry on the one hand, and LISP on the other was vital for the purposeful use of data processing and for file building. The language provided a fundamental structuring method which teachers of mathematics would need to master.

HANSEN stated that he could not agree with the idea of excluding computer literacy from the elementary school curriculum because it could lead to the dangerous "black box" approach in education. LOETHE defended his position because he felt that the computer in the real world was outside the experience of young children and should therefore be left to the secondary stage of education when the children could be made more aware of the implications.

MARTIN asked for a definition of computer literacy, to which LOETHE stated that to him it was being aware of computer applications in the real world. He used the "car driving" analogy. Martin stressed the need for pupils to have a mental model of the computer. LOETHE again expressed his concern about allowing computer literacy to become a subject discipline at the elementary school level.

HANSEN and CATHCART expressed their views; the former basing his argument in favour of computer literacy on the need to introduce young children to technology; CATHCART stated that as computers were a "grass roots" phenomenon because of their use in homes, especially in Canada, parent and pupil pressures would eventually force schools to introduce computer literacy into the curriculum.

TAGG made two points: the first was that he abhorred the idea expressed by AHLSTROM of children obeying computers, he felt that children had the need to understand and to argue. His second point concerned the use of the computer in encouraging the development of an engineering style of thinking. AHLSTROM defended his position because within his style of use an essential ingredient was the teacher's discussion with his pupils which he based on a quote from DIS - Rapporten 1980:
> "The purpose of education is to give the pupils such knowledge that they want to dare and can take up an attitude towards, and have an influence on the use of computers in our society."

In replying to STEWART, AHLSTROM stated that there were no science teachers using computers with very young children in Sweden, but when he returned home he would approach his government for investment in this area, because he believed it to be an area of need.

SESSION 3

WISCONSIN SUMMER COMPUTER FEST
A Curriculum Demonstration and Teacher Education Experience

M. Vere DeVault

Department of Curriculum and Instruction
University of Wisconsin
Madison, Wisconsin
U.S.A.

The Wisconsin Summer Computer Fest is designed to serve as a curriculum demonstration center. Issues related to computer literacy are explored and solutions are demonstrated in work with 500 children in grades 1-12. Eighty graduate students participate in the planning and implementation of the program. Issues under continuing investigation include: the ways technology can sustain humane and aesthetic environments in the classroom, how students can assume control over their interactions with computer environments, and how to meet the need to provide computer literacy education for all youth.

The impetus for computer literacy education in the schools comes from society at large. Though there is much activity in computer education, after four or five years of rather feverish activity, the major questions still asked are "How will we use computers in the school curriculum?" and "How shall we prepare teachers for this new task they confront?". As schools proceed with plans for the implementation of computer programs, there is a great need for the establishment of study centers in which answers to these two major questions can be sought. The Wisconsin Summer Computer Fest is such a center.

The Wisconsin Summer Computer Fest, sponsored by the School of Education at the University of Wisconsin-Madison, was initiated in the summer of 1982. It has two purposes: first, as a curriculum demonstration center, it serves as a vehicle to develop and field test instructional materials in computer literacy education for the schools; second, as a teacher education center, it provides the opportunity to explore many curriculum issues as faculty and graduate students study the issues, develop a curriculum, and demonstrate its implementation for five hundred children, in grades 1 to 12.

Approximately 30 graduate students, twenty-two of them at the Ph.D. level, participated in a spring seminar when the curriculum for the WSCF was developed. These graduate students then served as instructors during the summer and were supported by fifty additional graduate students serving as assistants and enrolled in a graduate course associated with the WSCF. In all, more than 80 graduate students were substantially involved in the development and implementation of the program. The range of expertise of these graduate students varied greatly, although all had teaching experience. Among the 30 instructors, all were familiar with microcomputers and had some competence in programming in BASIC as prerequisites for their joining the spring seminar as potential instructors. Some had considerable expertise in several programming languages and had taught computer literacy courses in schools. There were no such requirements for assistants. Their computing experience varied greatly: some had no experience with computers, while others had taught computer science courses in secondary schools and in the Madison Area Technical College.

These two goals, curriculum demonstration and teacher education, were implemented in five labs: four for computers and one for computer-related activities. The four computer labs used Apple II, VIC-20, ATARI 800, and the IBM-PC, respectively, for grades 1-3, 4-6, 7-8, and 9-12. Each computer lab included ten or eleven computers with children working much of the time in pairs. As forty children were on hand for each grade level at any given time, twenty in each grade level group were in the computer lab while the other twenty were in the Computer Related Activities Lab (CoRAL, as it came to be called).

PLANNING ACTIVITIES OF THE SPRING SEMESTER

There was a clear indication at the beginning of the spring seminar that all aspects of the program were open for discussion and development of ideas coming from participants. It was apparent that this could be no ivory tower seminar as decisions had to be made early enough in the semester to permit extensive planning and preparation before summer. The seminar represented a mixture of the theoretical, contemplation of issues and philosophies, and the practical, the need to make decisions and to move toward implementation of the summer curriculum. The study of curriculum issues surrounding computer literacy education gave direction to four specific activities: the development of workbooks designed to teach BASIC at each of the age levels; the development of activities in the CoRAL; the design and preparation of the labs; and the planning of activities to be undertaken with the children on a day-to-day basis.

The workbooks were write-in texts with the level and amount of reading appropriate to the grade level for which they were planned. The four workbooks: Apple for the primary grades (48 pages); VIC-20 for the intermediate grades (64 pages); ATARI for the junior high group *80 pages); and IBM for the senior high group (96 pages).[1] The general nature of the workbooks was planned by the seminar participants working as a whole and the manuscripts were prepared by seminar participants working at their respective levels.

The CoRAL represented one of the most creative and difficult parts of the planning task. Considerable study was undertaken before making final decisions concerning the purchase of any particular materials or the inclusion of specific activities. Ultimately, the CoRAL included: programmable vehicles (Big TRAK, DATSUN); computer memory for music (CASIO); Children's Discovery System (miniature computer toy with a variety of cartridges); instructional computerized systems (SPEAK AND SPELL, SPEAK AND MATH); art activities; drama; literature; electronics (small computerized kits); field trips; and video games.

In planning the day-to-day computer activities in the computer labs, seminar participants carefully selected software and made decisions about its use as a supplement to the workbook activities. The primary children also spent a substantial amount of time with LOGO. The high school group experienced the widest range of student expertise: some high schoolers had no computer experience, whereas others approached the whiz-kid level. In addition to the use of the workbook for most of these high schoolers, special projects were undertaken by many, and all were given introductory experiences with word processing and VisiCalc.

These activities (development of workbooks, planning the CoRAL, preparing the design for the labs, and planning for the day-to-day operation of the WSCF) were, of course, crucially important to the success of the program. The study and discussions that centered around key issues, however, seem to have made the most lasting contribution to evolving practices in the schools' implementation of computer literacy education. It is to these issues that we now turn.

CURRICULUM ISSUES

The manner in which basic issues are resolved will determine the nature of computer literacy education in the schools of the next decade, and our study of these issues is a continuing one. Our understanding of each issue and our appreciation for its implications will be expanded and altered, no doubt, in the light of continuing experience with the Wisconsin Summer Computer Fest. School faculties who observe and share in our efforts over the next few years will also have an impact on our thinking. It is our expectation that taking a position on each of these issues will make a contribution to the direction in which schools move in the development of computer literacy education.

   Issue #1. Computer technology and its impact on classroom environments.

   WSCF position: Computer technology should be used in ways that assure the continued support of the humanistic environment schools have always valued highly.

The twentieth century has witnessed a continuous struggle between the technology or behaviorism of E.L. Thorndike and the humanistic or socially oriented philosophy of John Dewey. By the mid-twenties, the dichotomy between the two emphases was well established (Fox & DeVault, 1978). The push of the Thorndikian supporters for the attainment of minimum essentials and the equally strident supporters of Dewey for a socially oriented activity-centered curriculum has echoed down through the decades to the present time. Innovations of the sixties were typically initiated under the auspices of supporters of one or the other of these two positions. Educational technology in the form of behavioral objectives, management systems, measurement strategies, and learning packets resulted in programs such as Individually Prescribed Instruction (IPI) in which children worked alone, followed a sequence of several hundred learning booklets, were tested following the completion of each booklet, and were provided with teacher or aide assistance only as needed.

During that same decade, attempts to individualize instruction were drawing on the philosophies of John Dewey and his followers as the open classroom movement got underway. Such classrooms depended upon a rich learning environment, informal relations between teachers and children, a wide variety of reading materials and activities, and the teachers' awareness of the needs of individual learners. Supporters of open classrooms deplored predetermined objectives, prescribed instructional procedures and the use of objective tests.

IPI and the open classroom are representative of many efforts made in the sixties and early seventies to create new approaches to schooling. An interesting phenomenon took place as these programs were created in research centers or in the minds of parents and teachers eagerly seeking an alternative to the public schools. In the hands of classroom teachers over a few months or years, the character of each of these extremes moderated, taking on many of the characteristics associated with its counterpart. IPI, and similarly developed programs, in the hands of hundreds of classroom teachers was revised on teacher recommendation to include more group work, to include teacher presentations of some of the material, and to encourage individual students to undertake project activities associated with their study of mathematics. The open classrooms, responding to the demands of parents and the increasing uncertainty of many teachers, began to include in their curriculum minimal use of objective testing, some management protocols, and some goal statements that gave direction to efforts.

In this same manner, computer technology, in its initial stages can be designed in ways that crowd out the personal-social components of effective classroom environments. The challenge, then, is to find ways computers can serve to preserve and enhance the personal/social (humanistic) character of our schools.

   Issue #2. Control in the cybernetic relationship between learners and machines.

   WSCF Position: Computer literacy education has as its primary goal the education of the learner to assume control over the computer.

Two computerized toys represent the dichotomy in this issue quite well: SIMON and Big TRAK. On the one hand, I turn on SIMON. It shows 1 color, then 2 colors, then 3 colors and more colors in random sequence. I repeat just as they are shown: blue; then blue, green; then blue, green, yellow; then blue, green, yellow, green. This continues until I fail to repeat what SIMON has done. The computer is in control. On the other hand, with Big TRAK I push the button to go forward, then two lengths, then right turn, 15, forward five lengths. Now I push GO. Big TRAK makes a starting noise and goes forward 2 lengths, turns right and goes forward 5 more lengths. Just as I have directed it. I am in control. In the same manner, at the computer, a drill and practice program is designed to encourage me to do just as the computer tells me to. The computer is in control. On the other hand, in programming, I tell the computer to PRINT my name and the computer does so. I am in control.

It is important that we realize that computers can be used in at least these two ways as represented by tutor and tutee in the title of Taylor's book: The Computer in the School: Tutor, Tool, and Tutee (Taylor, 1980). As schools integrate microcomputers into their curricula, they have too seldom addressed this fundamental question about computer use. The position taken by the staff of the Wisconsin Summer Computer Fest was to make the predominant use of computers in the labs and in the CoRAL conform to their roles as tutee. The learners were to assume control. The workbooks were written to emphasize this goal, the software selected was based on this as a major cirterion, and the activities in the CoRAL were selected and organized with this purpose in mind.

    Issue #3. Physical environments and student experiences with computer technology.

    WSCF Position: Computers serve in support roles and their physical presence should appear subordinate to other aspects of the environment.

Still in existence are the remnants of early foreign language labs with the egg-crate style arrangement of listening stations for many learners. That orientation is repeated in today's computer labs when ten computers on as many tables are pushed against a wall creating ten identical stations for ten learners at a time. Such arrangements fail to meet the criteria of aesthetics, and the facilitation of communication among learners.

In WSCF, three things were done that seemed to substantially affect the impact of the physical environment on learners. First was the design of the tables. Tables were designed as rectangles in which one of the corners was curved in a concave shpae. The tables were covered with anti-static carpet on their top surfaces and on their pedestals. Each table was designed to serve two or three learner stations and they were pushed together, usually in the center of the room, to form a variety of attractive shapes. The second design feature had to do with the staging of the labs which was accomplished through furniture arrangements and partitions which had been painted in bright, harmonious colors. These were supplemented with wall hangings, prints, and in the CoRAL with stage blocks borrowed from the University TV station for the purpose of dividing the room. These blocks provided temporary stages that served a variety of purposes in the CoRAL. Finally, a variety of rather large potted plants completed the creation of an environment that served to embed the technology in a total environment in which children were indeed the central point of attention: an environment that invited sharing and communication among children and adults.

    Issue #4. The nature of computer literacy.

    WSCF Position: Computer literacy education assumes a broad range of goals associated with the development of understandings about the role of computers in our society and about the manner in which we can personally use computers to serve our purposes.

Two extreme positions that address this question are those of Luehrmann (1981), on the one hand, and Heller and Martin (1982), on the other. In the first instance, Luehrmann suggests that learning to program is the essence of computer literacy. His position is that "Computing belongs as a regular school subject for the same reason that reading, writing, and mathematics are there" (p. 686). The Heller and Martin book takes the position that computer literacy is learning about computers, their history, how they work, what they do, how they fit into the future, and how they affect our lives. In the preface, they say, "it contains all of the information needed by the teacher to become computer literate and can be used in the classroom with or without a computer" (p. x). They would expect teachers and children to go from such a study of computers and computing to an exploration of programming, but computer literacy, per se, is not dependent on programming skills.

The WSCF assumed a middle position here. One's understanding of computers is enhanced with programming experience and, hence, half of the child's time at all levels is spent in the computer labs. Equally important, however, are those activities that extend understanding beyond the programming technology of the computer that one experiences. Activities designed to extend one's understanding both inward and outward are needed. Those inward views help the learner appreciate what a computer is (INPUT, CENTRAL PROCESSING UNIT, MEMORY CAPACITIES, OUTPUT), electronic experiences acquaint the learner with chips and circuit boards and transistors. The outward experiences illustrate that toys contain computers, that business and research organizations use computers, that the weather station and the TV station depend on information transmitted in part by computers. All of these activities contribute to a broad scope of computer literacy objectives.

Issue #5. Computer literacy education for all children.

WSCF Position: Every effort must be made to see that computer literacy curriculum and instruction be equally appropriate for all social and economic groups.

It is expected that increasingly, throughout this decade, computer literacy, including programming skills, will be an important ingredient in career opportunities in all segments of the business community. The past two decades have witnessed in this country a growing concern for the provision of equal opportunities for three segments of our population: minorities, the poor, and women. Opportunities for minorities and the poor are frequently restricted by financial limitations. At the present time, there are many affluent homes in which computers are available for children. Clearly, many of our students from such homes will be computer literate and will continue to arrive at school with competencies exceeding other children and in many cases, exceeding that of their teachers. Unless schools assume the responsibility for the computer literacy of all children, the career opportunity gap between the affluent and the less affluent will widen.

Our women students represent a somewhat different problem. Though women have been shown to have an aptitude for mathematics comparable to that of men, their achievement is frequently less than that of the male counterparts. This difference is related to a number of factors: stereotyped sex roles that start in the home with very young children, peer pressures that too often put down high achievement on the part of girls, and girls' poor attitudes toward mathematics. These factors have contributed to girls' taking fewer high school courses in mathematics than boys and hence, their admission to many majors on college and university campuses is severely limited. Will these same limitations happen in respect to computer literacy? There can be no doubt that evidence already available points in this direction. In Computer Fest '82, girls comprised one-third of the enrolment at the primary level, one-fourth at the intermediate and junior high levels, and one-eighth at the high school level.

Issue #6. Protecting software copyright agreements.

WSCF Position: Computer Fest staff makes every effort to protect agreements on software use and to make students aware of the law in this respect.

Though such an issue would appear to have a clear cut solution, such is not at all the case. Indecision in this matter results from two factors. First, there is not a clear definition in the law about what can be done under what circumstances. Second, the contracts that frequently accompany purchased software differ from one another in their agreements made with the purchaser. At the classroom level, the teacher with several pieces of software has no way of knowing what agreements have been entered into concerning any given program. Indeed, because under some conditions, extra copies of software may be made, the teacher frequently does not make an easy distinction between locally created software and that which has been purchased and has been copied under a specific contract agreement. Though many users, young and old, make a hobby out of collecting software, schools are extremely vulnerable when they encourage such behavior. Indeed, they have a moral responsibility to see that breaking the law in this respect does not occur under their auspices.

These six issues are by no means an exhaustive list of those which continuously confront us. These six may not include the most crucial issues. There are many others that come to mind: selecting appropriate languages, violence and the potential to create an arcade atmosphere in the classroom; pornography and censorship; and involvement of faculty in all the disciplines.

THE SHAPE OF THE WISCONSIN SUMMER COMPUTER FEST '83

The Wisconsin Summer Computer Fest '82 was deemed to have been successful in its contributions to the five hundred children in attendance. It was successful in its demonstration of innovative curriculum practices and it was successful in increasing the competence and expertise of eighty graduate students. Many of these graduate students have assumed increased responsibility for the development of computer literacy programs and for inservice education in their local school districts for the past year. Others have served as consultants or have assumed other professional positions largely as a result of their participation in Computer Fest. Based on the successful experience in its first year, Computer Fest '83 will be extended and modified in a number of ways.

1. ESTABLISH A SET OF COMPUTER LITERACY EDUCATION OBJECTIVES.

As a demonstration center for curriculum development, it seems reasonable that we should provide an example of the manner in which an organization might proceed to develop such a set of objectives and provide additionally an example of what such a set of objectives might contain.

2. CREATE A CLOSER RELATIONSHIP BETWEEN THE COMPUTER LABS AND THE CoRAL.

In its initial year, Computer Fest functioned not so much by design as in practice, as a set of five separate labs. In '83, a distinct effort is being made to see that staff members of the computer labs and the CoRAL, work more closely together during the Spring seminar and, hence, during the summer program. How can assignments and experiences in the CoRAL lead to the development of related programming experiences in the computer labs? How will this relationship assist in the students' understanding of what is occurring in both places?

3. A SPECIFIC DESIGN TO SERVE INDIVIDUAL DIFFERENCES

Because of the high ratio of instructors to students, we were able in Computer Fest '82 to meet the individual needs of students with considerable success. Because the number of intermediate age children will be doubled in Computer Fest '83, the groups will be divided into four experience levels: the first to include those with little or no computer experience and the fourth to include those who attended Computer Fest '82 and other 'experts'.

4. INCLUSION OF PARENT-CHILD PARTICIPANT PAIRS

In part, as an effort to improve the contribution of Computer Fest to the education of girls, parent-child pairs will be included in certain sections of the program. Though it is anticipated that in most instances, these will include more mother-daughter pairs than father-son pairs, it remains to be seen if this proves to be the case.

5. EXTENDED CoRAL FOR SECONDARY STUDENTS

For Computer Fest '82, the CoRAL was planned for all students from grades 1 to 12. As it turned out, however, most of the activities of the CoRAL were more appealing to elementary than secondary students. For the second year, a separate secondary CoRAL is planned. Its emphasis will be on electronics, robots, communication networks and interface controllers associated with a variety of computer applications.

CONCLUSIONS

Computer Fest was a success in its first year and we have every reason to believe that Computer Fest '83 will continue that tradition. It is believed, however, that if it is to be successful in '83 and in following years, that it must be constantly changing. It must be changing if it is to serve as a demonstration site, for once one kind of experience is demonstrated to be successful or not so, one would hope we could move on to the demonstration of other curriculum ideas. Second, it must be changing because the field is moving so very rapidly. Robotics represent an excellent example of our need to be ever changing in our emphases. As Computer Fest '82 drew to a close last summer, several of us contemplating the nature of Computer Fest '83 began our discussion of the role of robots in instructional programs. There was a sense that we were early in our approach to this topic, that schools would not be moving in this direction quite yet, and that with the assistance of faculty from the UW Department of Electrical and Computer Engineering, we could get some things underway. During the past eight or ten months since the close of Computer Fest '82, however, much has been written about robots, some use in the schools has been reported, and several instructional robots are now available in the marketplace. The cutting edge seems to have passed through from the closing of one Computer Fest to the opening of another. Certainly, there are many unasked and unanswered questions about robotic curricula in the schools and we are pleased to join those who are beginning to ask such questions. The phenomenon of the robot, however, is characteristic of the whole field of computer literacy education. It is moving very fast and we are all challenged to do our utmost in each succeeding year of this decade to assure that the Wisconsin Summer Computer Fest continuously contributes to our understanding of issues and problems associated with curriculum development and teacher education in computer literacy education.

FOOTNOTE

[1] Contracts between the University of Wisconsin and Scott, Foresman Publishers has resulted in the publication of these four workbooks and editions for other computers at each of the four levels.

REFERENCES

[1] Fox, G.T. & DeVault, M.V., An historical perspective on individualized instruction, Programmed learning and educational technology 4 (1978) 271-283.

[2] Heller, R.S. & Martin, C.D., Bits 'n bytes about computing: A computer literacy primer (Computer Science Press, Maryland, 1982).

[3] Luehrmann, A., Computer literacy: What should it be?, Mathematics Teacher 74 (1981) 682-686.

[4] Taylor, R.R. (Ed.), The computer in the school: tutor, tool, tutee (Teachers College Press, New York, 1980).

STATUS REPORT: INSERVICE COMPUTER LITERACY TRAINING

C. Dianne Martin and Rachelle S. Heller

Department of Computer Science
University of Maryland
College Park, Maryland
U.S.A.

Fifteen years ago pioneers in the field of computer assisted learning predicted that by 1980 all American children would have access to computers in the classroom. Budgetary constraints prevented most school systems from obtaining the large-scale computer equipment previously needed to achieve this goal. However, with the advent of low-cost microcomputers the hardware problem has been solved. What remains is the human problem of preparing teachers to teach about and manage computer resources in their classroom. This paper will discuss several successful models for delivery of inservice computer literacy training to teachers.

INTRODUCTION

For the past five years leaders in the field of computer education have been calling for universal computer literacy as the major goal for the instructional use of computers in the 1980s. In the recent U.S. Office of Technological Assessment Summary Report (OTA, 1982), the importance of teacher training in bringing the new technology into the classroom was cited:

"Widespread use of technology in the classroom will require that teachers be trained both in its use and in the production of good curriculum materials. Too few teachers are so qualified today."

Both classroom teachers and administrators have identified computer literacy training as a real need.

Through no fault of their own, most teachers at the elementary and secondary levels have not been prepared to teach about computers or use a computer in the teaching of their own discipline. They are "BC" teachers, teachers who received their education Before Computers. Three years ago an Association for Computing Machinery (ACM) report (Taylor, et al, 1980) recommended the minimum literacy requirements for every teacher. The real issue has become the implementation of adequate training programs to provide this literacy level for teachers.

Whether the sponsoring agent for inservice training will be at the national, state, or local level, the commitment of administrative support and staff resources, not the least of which is financial, is crucial for success. School systems are going to have to be committed to spending the money it will take to provide teachers with the necessary skills in computer literacy. Administrators of school systems can demonstrate a commitment to computer literacy by offering professional days for inservice computer literacy training, by creating resource centers and by providing support staff especially in the areas of software and hardware, by devoting part of teacher meetings to computer literacy, by designating a resource teacher within the school, and by being generally supportive toward the teachers' efforts in this area.

In many cases the contextual setting will help determine the content of inservice training. Such factors as attitudes of teachers, availability of computer hardware, number of teachers to be trained, amount of time that can be dedicated to training, and the location of the training have a role in determining the content of the course.

For any inservice training to be effective, it has been shown (McLaughlin & Marsh, 1978) that participants should have input into the planning of the training. They should also feel that the training will meet their perceived needs. Teachers' attitudes are also affected by their classroom environment. The teacher who knows that the newly acquired skills are relevant and useful in the classroom will have a vested interest in the training.

The availability of hardware for the inservice training as well as for classroom use after the training has a definite impact on the content of the course. If there are sufficient numbers of computers, the course can offer hands-on experience to the participants; otherwise, the course has to be taught in a demonstration mode. The time commitment involved for inservice training can be from as little as the time needed for a one-day overview of the topic to as great as the time needed for a full three credit college level course.

SPECIFIC MODELS:

Three specific examples of computer literacy inservice training models to be described by this paper are a one-day seminar offered for educators by the Smithsonian Institution, a three-week summer workshop offered at the University of Maryland under a federal grant, and semester-long, after school course provided by a local school district, the Montgomery County Public Schools (MCPS), for its teachers.

Smithsonian Institution:

The Smithsonian Institution in Washington, D.C. provides a Resident Associates program committed to offering quality educational opportunities to its members and the general public. A one-day computer literacy seminar for educators was developed and presented in December, 1982. The seminar lasted six hours and included the topics: putting computer literacy into context, how a computer works, teaching problem solving, BASIC programming, LOGO tutorial, integrating computers into the classroom curriculum, evaluation of software, and teaching social impact issues. The thrust of the seminar was to teach the educator as much content as possible, as well as to demonstrate teaching techniques of the content. The course was held in a large auditorium and was presented in a lecture-demonstration mode. To help the participants assimilate all of this information, each one was provided with a textbook, <u>Bits 'n Bytes About Computing: A Computer Literacy Primer</u> (Heller and Martin, 1982), to be used as a reference book after the seminar.

It is difficult to draw conclusions about the impact that such a one-day seminar might have on the participants. It was intended to be a first step to encourage participants to seek more information and more training elsewhere. Based on the comments on the evaluation, it would appear that such a course could fulfill the goal of offering the first step in inservice training to teachers. Significantly, the most requested follow-up to this one-day session was for a hands-on programming workshop.

University of Maryland Summer Workshop:

A three-week computer literacy summer workshop was conducted at the University of Maryland for elementary school teachers at grade levels 4-6. The workshop was held July 6-24, 1981 under a U.S. Department of Education grant.

Thirty teachers of grades 4-6 were selected from two local school districts to participate in training sessions--each of which involved three hours of instruction and discussion, and three hours of supervised laboratory practicum--on Mondays through Fridays for a three-week period during the summer of 1981. The 30 participants were divided into two learning groups; each group spent half of each day in the classroom environment and the other half day in the laboratory environment. During the 1981-1982 school year, follow-up visits were made to help with any problems and encourage material development.

In addition to providing participants with a technical basis for understanding computers and their uses, the classroom was also used to illustrate the use of computer-related activities for grades 4-6. The participants were encouraged to "learn by doing" and had the opportunity to try out many of the activities that they would be using with their students later on. The teachers were able to discuss and to demonstrate how materials provided in the workshop can be incorporated into curriculum areas such as social studies, English, mathematics, history, science and art.

The laboratory part of each day enabled the participants to acquire hands-on experience with computers. The laboratory was equipped with eight PET microcomputers to be used by the teachers in teams of two per micro. Based on several studies which have been done and on the experience of this workshop, it would seem that putting the teachers in teams on the microcomputers was the optimum way to use the equipment. This lab experience was necessary and invaluable for teacher training. It deepened the teachers' understanding of computer concepts, gave them a better idea of frustrations and accomplishments their students will experience, and sharpened their understanding of what computers can and cannot do.

The project was evaluated in two phases. In the first phase the participants were given pre and post tests at the beginning and end of the workshop. These tests were of two types. One was the Minnesota Educational Computing Consortium (MECC) Literacy and Awareness Assessment, of which 53 questions having to do with computer literacy content were used, to test the basic computer literacy knowledge of the participants. The pre and post results of this test showed an average gain of 10 points out of 30 on content knowledge. The second test was based on the teacher competencies established in 1980 (Taylor, et al) by the ACM subcommittee and was used to test the participants' self-perception of their computer literacy against the eight competencies. On a scale of 1 to 10 their self-perception of computer literacy jumped on the average from 1.8 to 8.2.

In addition, a post workshop evaluation was given to elicit information about the structure, teaching techniques, and classroom arrangement of the workshop. While the overall reaction to the workshop was strongly positive, 10 out of the 30 participants expressed dissatisfaction when asked whether access to micros was sufficient to complete their work satisfactorily even though each participant had at least 36 hours of hands-on computer time.

The second phase of the evaluation was the assessment of the long range impact of the workshop on the teachers. Did it bring about any changes in their classrooms? This stage of the evaluation was conducted at separate inservice training sessions for the two school districts involved. The circumstances in the two school districts over the six month period were significantly different. One district had purchased six of the PET computers from the workshop. These computers had been placed in schools with six of the trained teachers. Two other teachers had received other computer equipment by the end of the school year. Thirteen of the original fourteen participants were able to attend the follow-up inservice day. Their evaluation of impact was very positive.

The leadership in the other district, on the other hand, had chosen not to purchase any of the PET computers from the workshop, had not yet purchased other computer equipment, and had directed that no PTA was to purchase computer equipment on its own.

Twelve of the original 15 participants were able to attend the follow-up session.

Their perception of the impact of the content of the workshop in their classrooms was considerably lower than their counterparts from the other school district. Of those who provided additional comments, most of them expressed frustration with their school district for not providing them with computer equipment.

MCPS Semester-Long Course:

In 1978 the move to microcomputers began in Montgomery County, Maryland. In addition, Montgomery County, like many school systems around the nation, was hiring few new teachers. Even those newly hired were not exposed to computers or computer literacy in college. "These two factors meant that curriculum improvements in computer literacy must be supported by local staff development." (Philip, et al, 1982). Change was deemed an important part of an inservice program. It was observed that computer literacy would be an evolving thing, what was literacy today will be obsolete tomorrow. A model for inservice was needed that provided a way to organize and think about change of this magnitude. The Concerns-Based Adoption Model (CBAM)(Hall and Loucks, 1978) was chosen.

A course was designed based on the components of computer literacy including procedural thinking skills, using a computer and programming, the knowledge of computer fundamentals, applications, impact on society and attitudes about one's confidence to control the computer, to enjoy using it and to respect its usefulness.

The course was designed to meet once a week for 15 weeks. Each session was three hours and began at 4:30 p.m. at the central office building. Each session had a literacy session and a hands-on component using a Commodore PET. Activities included group participation projects adaptable to classroom situations, visits to central computer operations, videotapes and films and speakers on topics of interest. The lab sessions were lecture/demonstration of BASIC and finally an hour of hands-on PET.

Evaluation took place during the course and at the end. Because it is a CBAM model, which stresses individual nature of change, the instructors monitored the participant's progress after each session. The Work Record was filled out by the teacher, read and commented on by the instructors and the class agendas were often adjusted. At the end of the first pilot year a three part evaluation form was administered. The first part asked the teachers to evaluate, checklist style, four categories about instructors, the instructional activities, the materials and equipment, and assignments. The scale was from 1 to 5. At the end of 1981 the overall rating was a 4.86 (Philip, et al, 1982). The second part of the evaluation was to have them complete a bar graph concerning their skill level on computer literacy and programming concepts. The self-rated growth at the end of 1981 indicated that many participants "owned most topics and could teach others" (Philip, 1982).

The inservice developers in Montgomery County feel that the greatest testimony to the CBAM model is when the teachers returned to schools to demand that they have microcomputers in their classrooms. Since the pilot course almost 400 teachers have received the training with a tremendous demand for continued offerings.

CONCLUSIONS:

In order to draw any conclusions about the different inservice models described, we need to consider their impact on the whole process of bringing computer technology into education. If such technology is viewed as an innovation, then we need to examine inservice training as an intervention designed to facilitate diffusion of the innovation. We have to examine inservice as it relates to the process of change in the school setting (Hall and Loucks, 1978).

We will look at these issues in relation to the specific models described. In the case of the one-day seminar the impact was immediate, rather than long-range. The word which describes the prevailing attitude among the participants at the end of the day was "more." They stated verbally and in evaluations that they wanted more hands-on computer time, more depth, more information, two days instead of one, etc.

In making an informal assessment of where these participants were in their level of concern in relation to the computer, we would conclude that most of them had passed from the awareness stage into the informational stage. They were ready to sign up for a computer course or go to a computer store to look at home computers. Many of them were starting to enter into the personal stage of concern where they were ready to examine the new information in relation to their own roles as educators. Although some of them would probably try the activities demonstrated in their classroom, most of them would not implement major changes in their teaching as a result of the seminar.

Our assessment of the three-week workshop is quite different. Those teachers did receive "more" of everything--hands-on computer time, information, interaction with their peers, and a chance to do the activities themselves. The impact of this model seemed to depend upon the follow-up environment of the participants. Those teachers from the one district who had computers were able to integrate what they had learned into their classrooms. Many of them moved up into the management level of concern about how to use, organize, schedule, and implement the innovation. Some of them went even further into the concerns of consequence and collaboration. They were concerned about training other teachers in the system and acquiring more computers.

An additional impact of this workshop was the adaptation and adoption of the model by the Madison Metropolitan School District of Madison, Wisconsin under a federal grant. During June, 1982, a facilitator from the University of Maryland spent one week teaching twenty teacher specialists how to present the workshop to teachers in the school district. This was immediately followed by two three-week pilot workshops conducted by the teacher specialists. Based on the evaluation and feedback from the two pilots, the model was to be refined and presented as a regular inservice course to be offered in the fall and spring of the next school year.

The impact of the MCPS semester-long course has been the most far-reaching of all the models discussed. It has evolved from the pilot stage to a regularly offered course which has gone through several refinements based on participant feedback. Almost 400 teachers have been trained in the course creating a snowball effect in the school system. This has created a natural support system and collaboration mechanism for new teachers who enter each offering of the course.

At the same time the school system is demonstrating its commitment to change by providing this inservice training, it is backing up that training with a further commitment to acquire additional computers in a systematic way. This serves to foster an equally high level of concern on the part of teachers to bring about change in their classrooms. Some of the early participants in the course are now at the collaboration and refocusing stages of concern, serving on committees and assisting in inservice training of other teachers. Much of the success of this model can be attributed to the concerns-based approach which has allowed participants to contribute to the refinement of the model in a dynamic feedback loop as the course was presented.

Michael Apple predicts that our definition of literacy will change as we approach the year 2000. It will encompass not only technical literacy but social, political and aesthetic literacy as well. We will want our students to have the skills to take an active part in our political system. To that end all students, not just the gifted, must be computer literate in all its aspects. This can only happen if our teachers are comfortable enough with the content to introduce the computer into the classroom with confidence. Teachers need to feel in control of their classrooms. Inservice must be the mainstay of this comfort, confidence, and control.

REFERENCES

[1] Apple, Michael W. "Curriculum in the Year 2000; Tensions and Possibilities." *Phi Beta Kappan*: January, 1983.

[2] "First Survey on State Governments and the New Techology." *Electronic Learning*, Vol. No. 1, 2, pp. 56-59: November/December, 1981.

[3] Hall, G.E. "Issues Related to the Implementation of Computers in Classrooms: Where to Now?". Research and Development Center for Teacher Education, University of Texas at Austin: February, 1981.

[4] Hall, G. E. and Loucks, S. "Teacher Concerns as a Basis for Facilitating and Personalizing Staff Development." *Teachers College Record*, Vol. 80, No. 1: September, 1978.

[5] Heller, R.S. and Martin, C.D. *Bits 'n Bytes About Computing: A Computer Literacy Primer*. Washington, D.C.: Computer Science Press, 1982.

[6] Hunter, Beverly. "Computer Literacy in Grades K-6." Human Resources Research Organization (HumRRO), presented at ADCIS Conference, Atlanta, Ga., March 1981.

[7] "Informational Technology and Its Impact on American Education (Summary Report)." Office of Technology Assessment Congressional Board of the 97th Congress. Washington, D.C.: 1982.

[8] Martin, C.D.; Heller, R.S.; Austing, R.H. "Computer Literacy: Structuring a Workshop for Elementary School Teachers." Proceedings of the Western Educational Computing Conference, November, 1981.

[9] McLaughlin, M.W. and Berman, P. "Retooling Staff Development in a Period of Retrenchment." *Educational Leadership*: December, 1977.

[10] McLaughlin, M.W. and Marsh, D.D. "Staff Development and School Change." *Teachers College Record*, Vol. 80, No. 1: September, 1978.

[11] Philip, C.C.; Muntner, J.; Cutlip, P. "Computer Literacy Education for K-6 Teachers." Proceedings of the 1982 AEDS Convention, Orlando, Fla.: May, 1982.

[12] Taylor, R.P.; Poirot, J.L.; Powell, J.D. "Computing Competencies for School Teachers." Proceedings of the National Educational Computing Conference, June 1980.

[13] Wolf, A.; Frechtling, J.; Tompkins, L. "Evaluation of MCPS Inservice Training." Montgomery County Public Schools, Rockville, MD: 1982.

Session 3 - Discussion

Rapporteurs: B. SAMWAYS, C.J. WATKINS

MARTIN completed her talk with reference to CBAM : Courses Based Adaption Model (Hall & Loucks). One word descriptions are used for each attainment level:

0   Awareness
1   Informational
2   Personal
3   Management
4   Consequence
5   Collaboration
6   Re-focus

VAN WEERT opened the discussion by asking MARTIN to elaborate on the "model"; how it works in practice. He further asked "How do you know, for example when they have reached level 5. MARTIN replied that at the beginning of each course the participants are asked "Why are you here? What do you expect from the course?" In this way they realise that we are concerned. At the end of each day they are invited to make comments. These comments can result in an explanation, or in a topic being recovered, the next day. In the Minnesota Educational Computing Consortium course those who attained levels 1 and 2 returned to teaching whereas those reaching levels 4 and 5 could be used to train other teachers.

WALDOW likened this to predicting the winner after the race had been won. He felt there was no basis on which these criteria can stand. MARTIN pointed out that the model described was used in one school only. All teachers entering the courses must be at zero level or level one. The "RAND" report recommends development models and not deficit models.

BONELLO-KUBATH commented that one hour or one day courses have two purposes in that they demystify computing and encourage teachers to take more advanced courses. However with longer courses teachers assimilated the materials and their questions get better and better. T. BONELLO-KUBATH asked V. DeVAULT whether the ideas from the Fest had filtered down into the classroom. It was answered in that all pupils came from local districts and that 50% - 60% of teachers have had one course. The schools on average have two or three computers and this year pupils came back with greater computer knowledge.

JONES asked whether CBAM could be used for the selection of teacher leaders for the Fest. V. DeVAULT pointed out that no selection took place as they accepted all teachers who applied. JONES then referred to the possibilities of using something similar to the Tutor Pack of the U.K. MEP Microprimer course which allowed course tutors to select their own material from a set of menu cards. Though interested, M. DeVAULT stated that he could not guess the effect of such a system in his country, and that the U.K. was better at distance learning.

BAUERSFELD raised the question of curriculum change, referring to Ron Havelock's idea of three types:-

1   Administration
2   Research, Development and Diffusion (RDD-Model)
3   Problem Solving

He gave most hope to the third type and pointed out that any change is difficult in the complex school situation and that it cannot be achieved in one day or even one week courses. To send the teachers back to school after one week is like "burning tomatoes with a hand held flashlight"

MARTIN pointed put that 400 teachers in Maryland schools have received such treatment whilst M. DeVAULT reflected on such changes having taken place before (viz New Maths). Even now there are more computers in the home than in the school - what chance does the school have?

BAUERSFELD replied by saying that computer manufacturers will continue to compete with different models and their individual success will depend on the software they offer. If we say that "the ability to use a simple system is literacy" then there are two kinds

1   The literacy of the scientist
2   The literacy of the pupil who addresses the computer.

Thus the computer language itself is not important. In the long term it is (1) that is important. We must consider its role in problem solving and the difficulties of using such systems. Is anyone able to justify which steps will achieve that aim in the long term?

LEVRAT pointed out that the group was discussing computer literacy in elementary schools as if secondary education did not exist. We must make sure that children leaving schools are prepared for society and that in terms of computer literacy this will become more difficult in future years. Can I ask both speakers what backup they give to teachers who have attended their courses?

MARTIN stated that in Maryland schools the follow up was well established, M. DeVAULT admitted that problems were left to the school district; and in some cases the electronic mailboard system. He then went on to define Computer Literacy as being "learning to live comfortably in a high tech society." For some it may be to get better jobs, but not for all. MARTIN used Beverly Hunter's definition of Computer Literacy: "whatever a person needs to know in order to function in our information based society". However it should appear in all disciplines.

WALDOW stated that computer literacy is what is required for a person to function in a computer-based society. However if this is to enable them to play games at home then he would rather not be involved. T.KUBATH proposed the idea of a discussion group that evening on "What is Computer Literacy" and this was readily accepted by the chairman. She then asked MARTIN what was a "specialist" in computer education. The reply was a teacher who can teach other teachers. BAUERSFELD then asked if we were not going too fast and in the wrong direction.

TAGG requested to know from the speakers to what extent they had collaborated with psychologists, sociologists and educational researchers. M. DeVAULT made reference to their advisory committee and to the contact with such people at the university in their curriculum work. With regard to the Fest there was very little collaboration with both educational researchers and psychologists. MARTIN reported that cooperation with Dr. Ben Schneidermann, University of Maryland, who is involved in Psychology and Computer Science Studies in human factors and Dr. Judith Kull, University of New Hampshire who is involved in educational research - particularly the preservice training of teachers.

VAN WEERT asked what should we teach teachers. If the only thing is computer literacy then there is nobody who can list the course context. V. DeVAULT answered in that we do not question what we teach. In Europe we think and do nothing: in America we do something but don't think enough.

SESSION 4

A TEACHER PERSPECTIVE OF COMPUTER LITERACY FOR CHILDREN

Margaret M. DeVault

MADISON METROPOLITAN SCHOOL DISTRICT
Madison, Wisconsin
U.S.A.

Rather than imposing an adult view of computer literacy on children, we should develop the uses of computers as children see them operating in their world at the present time. This approach lends itself to the child's ever expanding perspective on the computer's ever expanding technology. Hence, children are in no way limited by their inability to understand computer concepts and issues at an adult level nor need they seek to understand elements of a technology that will in all likelihood be changed as they reach adulthood.

THE COMPUTER AND THE CHILD

The child's world is action oriented. It requires involvement. Because the computer is an interactive device it has a natural attraction for children.

One means of developing computer literacy for the child is to take a broad perspective of the computer--What kind of action is available to the child?

The child's action can be that of:

-- a responder
-- an initiator

As a responder, the computer provides an opportunity to link experience with what is seen in the adult world. One responds with a name or number or selects a task. Essentially one is providing information. An example might be our electronic banking. One merely provides information, in response to questions from the bank, to accomplish a given task.

As an initiator, the focus for a young child is to gain a broader perspective, rather than expecting a high level of sophistication. What is it the computer can do? The objective is to see the computer as a tool to accomplish a task. Appropriate tasks might be accumulating scores, making lists or alphabetizing. The use of the computer to accomplish repetitive tasks can be illustrated.

As a responder, two categories commonly used are drill and practice and simulation. As an initiator, the the computer becomes a tool and general tasks are programming and using utility programs.

As children learn about the wide range of things a computer can do, they develop an understanding of how it is used. A gradual awareness of computers unfolds and they seek control.

Generally, the child's earliest work is drill and practice kinds of programs and a child 'feels' in control because the machine reacts according to the child's decision. Work on a computer, however, may not be what it seems to the child. The feeling is one of having made the machine produce a response. If children are given many pieces of drill and practice software they begin to realize they are merely responding and they begin to alter its use. It becomes a device for problem solving tactics:

What will happen if one selects wrong answers?

How large a number can one use in a response?

What will happen if one doesn't respond at all, or not with the choices offered?

This transition from a responder to one in control appears to occur at different levels--perhaps the earliest evidence is merely giving wrong responses to prolong one's time at a computer. This is probably the lowest level of taking control, but it is an attempt to move away from being merely a responder. A higher level might be that of analyzing what a piece of software might have in it's design and testing a hypothesis, such as, the size of the number that can be selected.

Simulation games are frequently the second type of material given to children. A good piece capitalizes on the child's curiosity to experiment allowing the participant opportunity for decision making with reasonable outcome. Lemonade, a stand from which children sell lemonade, and Trail West, a wagon train heading west are two popular examples of this kind of activity.

A third kind of responder activity is best described by movement and dexterity linked to decision making. These 'games' are generally found in arcades and less frequently in schools. Perhaps their absence in schools is because of the amount of time required to master games of this sort, or because of the prohibitive cost of a quality game. I suspect, however, we are not certain of the merit of this type of activity and if its proper place is in the academic curriculum.

Children, then, generally begin by assuming the role of a responder and move through pieces of software described as drill and practice, simulations, and games. This sequence may occur because of a philosophical belief that this is the best curriculum for the child, or it may occur because the teachers are learning as the children learn and this is where teachers feel successful in their management of a new technology and from their knowledge of computers and their potential uses in the classroom.

There are activities, however, that can be used to move a child toward the role of an initiator and simultaneously expand perspectives of computer applications. Computers and computerized toys can be seen to store a series of directions and respond to a series of commands. Rather than turning on a piece of technology and responding with a 'correct' response with these toys, a child selects an activity and determines the parameters of that activity. A computerized car or tank, for example, illustrates how a child can use a toy to experience control and decision making that can be developed with direct links to their experiences with microcomputers. They can also experience the frustration of the computer's doing exactly what it was instructed to do rather than what one had expected it to do. Similarly, a computer can be programmed to draw, make music, or print, and the child's world begins to intersect the adult world. Using the computer in the child's world can exhibit a wide variety of the uses of the computer. Perhaps not as extensive as the current adult uses, but at a more relevant level for the child's level of comprehension. An example of this is the use of the computer to generate a list of class members to be used for sending Valentine cards. The computer directing the printer to generate 25 copies and storing the list is the beginning of data management for the child. Using a computer with a modem may bring information into the child's classroom world. The experiences they have had with the telephone calling a friend or relative to share happenings, or calling for information, weather, time, etc., can easily apply to the computer using telephone technology to transfer information into the classroom. The concept of electronic mail is then easily perceived.

We have seen, then, that adult uses of computers have their parallel instances of use in the child's world. The interactive power of the computer in the adult world provides answers to our questions or initiates certain services. In the classroom, the child uses the computer to locate information. In the adult world, our names are listed in data banks which result in a flow of mail from sources that automatically include us in their mailings. In the classroom, the child's name on a computer-stored list results in the arrival of valentines. In the adult world, reservation clerks use the computer for information from distant places concerning the availability of rooms on a given date. In the classroom, a computer-modem-telephone brings information from a computer downtown. An analysis of adult uses of computers reveals a parallel set of uses that are appropriate for children in the classroom. One challenge, then, in the development of computer literacy education programs, is to identify more concepts about computer applications through the world that have their counter parts in the activities children enjoy in the classroom.

It is through continuous effort to present children with such computer activities that allow a demonstration of the broad use of computers that builds a child's understanding and demonstrates what computer literacy might be.

CONTINUING CONCERNS FOR THE FUTURE

As a broad curriculum is developed for children there is a tendency to take the current uses of computers (applications) and turn a study of those uses into the curriculum itself. The children are then expected to do this 'thing.' Learning or 'training' to perform this task becomes the emphasis. There occurs a shift away from learning about what computers can do in a broad sense to a learning of task-specific skills. All this, in spite of the fact those applications will in all likelihood change as the technology changes. A more appropriate focus might be on the resulting social impact of computer applications. What computers can do and what their social impact is now and what it will be, is the core of the computer literacy curriculum.

As Mike Apple (1983) indicates, "Given the important role of technology in the future, all students--not just a select few who are 'gifted and talented'--should be literate both in using computers and microcomputers and in analyzing their social implications." He continues, "If we approach computer literacy as a narrow vocational issue, we are bound merely to add one more relatively ineffective career education program to the many that already exist."

It is this continuous emphasis in the literature on the potential career uses of the computer that is perplexing. Catherine D. Tobin (1983) presented her position on computer literacy as, ". . .students learn by doing. What students are learning must be meaningful to them; must give them opportunities for exploration and creativity; and, in turn, provide them with a wide range of experiences." A beautiful, sensitive agreement with Piagetian philosophy. The focus remains on the child. She goes on to say, however, "At the same time students will be developing skills and understandings that they will need in the future." It is at this point the child is put into a career education perspective. She presents an advertisement for a writer to develop end-user materials and predicts "most of us will become 'nontechnical end-users' . . ." It is this temptation to predict future computer use that should be deemphasized in our work with children, particularly in an area of technology that is in a continuing revolutionary stage. Tobin continues, " . . .and we will be working as 'problem solvers.'" It is the child as a problem solver that must remain before us at all times.

COMPUTERS AND LEARNING TO LEARN

It is possible to describe a curriculum that allows children to experience what computers can do and, hence, to develop understandings about what they are doing in our society. It would be negligent, however, not to address also what computers are able to do for the child's learning style, or stage of developmental learning, that may occur most readily in classrooms with computers.

Henry F. Olds, Jr. (1983) summarizes Piaget's thinking, ". . .Piaget focuses on two subjects of major educational concern; what his years of research say about how education should proceed, and how young people can be well prepared for the world of the future. He argues that learning proceeds best when a person can actively engage in directly experiencing the world, and then have the opportunity to share that experience in a reciprocal relationship with other people. Such a process, he claims is critical to the health of both the individual and the society, because it establishes the proper balance between individual autonomy and social collaboration."

It is this opportunity to learn, analyze the learning, and share the experience openly that we must certainly include as a part of our computer literacy education. Olds sees combining Piaget's perspective with Papert. "Papert emphasizes that one of the most important benefits of using a computer is the opportunity to enter a 'what if' world and play in that world. There one can freely experiment and learn, without cost or penalty, from one's mistakes. The computer gently but firmly reminds us that human error is the most powerful impetus for learning that exists."

Again, perhaps the great function of the computer will be to teach us openly about learning as we learn.

Papert (1980) in his book, Mindstorms, spoke of his work in Geneva, "I began to see how children who had learned to program computers could use very concrete computer models to think about thinking and to learn about learning and in doing so, enhance their powers as psychologists and epistemologists. For example, many children are held back in their learning because they have a model of learning in which you have either 'got it' or 'got it wrong.'"

Papert sees the computer as changing this perspective of success or failure and using the computer as an 'object-to-think-with.'

Our concern might be whether we can demonstrate appropriate mental activities and can monitor their exercise and growth. Whimbley (1980) in writing about the potential for improving intelligence through education points out, "Training intelligence presents a special problem because the constituent mental activities are generally carried out covertly-inside the person's head. In order to train intelligence, it is necessary to bring these mental activities to the surface. The methods used to accomplish this include unison response, the model's introspective protocol, thinking aloud during practice, and one-to-one Socratic dialogue. Furthermore, individual or small group instruction seems to be a requirement--at least until some other feedback technologies are developed."

It appears the computer will provide not only the essential feedback described above by Whimbley but also the potential for the Socratic dialogue. It may be preferable to interact in a conversational manner with a human but given the student/teacher ratio in schools today, and preferences of some students, the computer technology allows a storing of interaction potential and also an opportunity for generating a creative dialogue which otherwise might not take place. It provides an opportunity to display (share) current mental activities.

As Whimbley describes earlier techniques developed by learning researchers, he states, "All these procedures externalize the thinking activities of problem solving so that they can be demonstrated and practiced in full view." If we assume, as Whimbley has, that intelligence can be taught through the development of problem solving skills and if it can be clearly demonstrated that problem solving skills are enhanced with the use of computer technology, then we need to view problem solving with computers as an important part of computer literacy. The computer is a revolutionary invention that can be used to aid in the development of problem solving skills and, hence, in the improvement of human intelligence.

BIBLIOGRAPHY

1   Anderson, Ronald E., Klassen, Daniel L. and Johnson, David C., In defense of a comprehensive view of computer literacy--a reply to Luehrmann, Mathematics Teacher 74 (1981) 687-690.

2   Apple, Michael W. Curriculum in the Year 2000: Tensions and possibilities, Phi Delta Kappan 64 (1983) 321-326.

3   Bacon, Stephen J. Syllabuses for the Future, In: Lewis, R. and Tagg, E.D. (eds.), Computers in Education: Proceedings of the 3rd IFIP World Conference (North-Holland, Amsterdam, 1981).

4   Johnson, David C., Anderson, Ronald E., Hansen, T. P., and Klassen, Daniel L. Computer literacy--What is it?, Mathematics Teacher 73 (1980) 91-96.

5   Luehrmann, Arthur, Computer literacy--What should it be?, Mathematics Teacher 74 (1981) 682-686.

6   Olds, Henry F., Jr. On understanding computers, Learning 2 (1983) 30-34.

7   O'Neill, Gerald K. 2081 (Simon and Schuster, New York, 1981).

8   Papert, Seymour, Mindstorms--Children, Computers and Powerful Ideas (Basic Books, New York, 1980).

9   Tobin, Catherine D. Developing computer literacy, Arithmetic Teacher 31 (1983) 22-24.

10 Whimbley, Arthur, Intelligence Can Be Taught (E.P. Dutton, New York, 1980).

COMPUTING IN BIRMINGHAM PRIMARY SCHOOLS

Colin J. Watkins

Primary Computing Coordinator
Birmingham Educational Computing Centre

This paper gives a chronological account of the development of computing activities in Birmingham primary schools since 1980, during which time the author has been attached to the Birmingham Educational Computing Centre (BECC). Many of the points in this paper are therefore biased towards a central point of view, and may be interpreted differently when viewed from a school.

The paper concentrates on a project which started during 1980 and is on-going; no final conclusions can be drawn from it as yet. However, the paper does indicate how closely its findings are meeting the original objectives. The project has met many problems, which are described in some detail in the hope that others may be able to avoid similar difficulties.

THE BACKGROUND

1 The Birmingham Educational Computing Centre (BECC)

BECC has influenced the development of computer activities in Birmingham primary schools and initiated and supported the project which is described in detail in this paper.

A decade ago, the use of computers in education was mainly in the hands of enthusiastic teachers in individual schools throughout the country. There was little general awareness of computers among educational leaders, but some were beginning to realise that Local Education Authorities needed to offer some central support. In Birmingham this led to the establishment in 1974 of an Educational Computing Centre to provide computer power to schools and continuous in-service training for teachers. The latter aim was pursued by recruiting a body of experienced teachers who were deployed into schools on a part-time basis to teach computer studies and at the same time to interest and train existing staff, so that eventually the schools they served might become self-sufficient. Some fifteen teachers of high quality have been attracted to Birmingham for this purpose.

2 The Author

The author is a primary school teacher, with Open University (OU) qualifications in computing. During his OU course he used a mainframe terminal provided by BECC, and in due course a Tandy microcomputer, to experiment with the use of computers in his primary school. In 1980 he was invited to be seconded to a year's course at the University of Birmingham, instituted by a consortium of West Midland LEAs and financed by the Microelectronics Education Programme to train fifteen teachers to be leaders in field of computers in education.

THE START

The original group of schools concerned with the project came together under its own impetus in the summer of 1980. The Inspector for Computer Education in Birmingham recommended that they organise a series of meetings to identify their needs and asked the author to become a member of the group to give advice and form a path of communication with BECC.

THE FIRST IDEAS

Discussion centred round a project to use a microcomputer to hold details of all teaching resources held in different centres around the city. This foundered after a realisation of the difficulty of collecting and processing the amount of information involved and, finally, the complete inadequacy of one microcomputer for access by some 5,000 primary teachers.

A further way forward to be explored was the specification of computer aided learning programs. This was also abandoned since only the author had programming expertise at this time, and in any case no school was equipped with a computer to use and evaluate such programs.

The group therefore decided to ask for a course to be arranged so that they could learn about computers and programming.

THE FIRST COURSE

BECC agreed to provide resources to mount such a course and nominated one of the centre's staff to organize it, with the author as his assistant to gain experience. Some twenty people were eventually recruited, such was the interest engendered. It was decided that course members must have "hands on" experience and learn to program in BASIC, the only language available on microcomputers at that time.

As no microcomputers were readily available, the course started in the Spring term of 1981 with four weeks spent using terminals linked to a Prime minicomputer at Birmingham Polytechnic. Later the course transferred to Research Machines 380Z microcomputers and changed its style to less formal workshops, in which individuals could proceed at their own pace and develop their own interests. The availability of graphics increased the interest, releasing programming from the strait-jacket of string handling and mathematical routines.

The course led to the development of regular workshop sessions for primary teachers, which are discussed later in this paper.

A CUL-DE-SAC

The author's participation in the Birmingham University course referred to above led to the initiation of a project to study the effects of stress on young children when taking a traditional form of test compared with the results of taking a similar test run by a computer, with a computer to keep records and eventually analyse the results. Two Birmingham schools were used for the trial, Heathmount Primary and Nansen Primary. The author wrote the necessary software and three microcomputers were loaned by a computer manufacturer.

The project never achieved its aim but three useful lessons were learnt from the reasons for this:
a) The estimated time for writing the software was too short
b) Teachers using the system needed more detailed briefing
c) The computers used were unreliable.

One important general conclusion was that hardware in schools must be reliable, otherwise months of hard work can be destroyed in a few microseconds.

THE PROJECT PROPER

During the academic year 1980/81 when the author was studying at Birmingham University and BECC, it became apparent that one way in which BECC could be ready to advise Primary schools in the future was to organise and run a project in which a number of primary schools would be equipped with microcompunters supported from BECC. This would have a number of effects:

> It would generate a group of schools who had experience of running microcomputers, which could then be used to help other schools.

> It would help BECC to understand the level of support which primary schools would need in the future.

> It would enable new software to be properly evaluated.

> It might give some guidance as to how the micro can best be used to enhance Primary Education.

> It might also have some benefits for the children in the schools!

A number of problems which had to be solved before the project could start:

> How many schools should be involved in the project?

> How were the schools to be chosen?

> What microcomputer should be used?

> Should the schools all have the same micro?

> Who should pay for the micros?

> What software should be used?

> Where should the software come from?

> What management system should the schools use?

THE NUMBER OF SCHOOLS

It was decided that initially the number of schools should be six. This decision was influenced by the amount of finance available, the background of the chosen schools and the resources available at BECC.

The schools were partly self selected and partly BECC selected. BECC asked schools who were known to be interested if they would like to take part in the project. When the schools were asked to take part, they began to question the cost of the micro and if there would be any help from Birmingham Education Authority. The answers to these questions determined their eventual acceptance. The offer was made to most of the schools who had been involved in the original group but was also made to other schools. In all about twenty schools were approached. The exact number is not on record as some schools who might have been approached said that they could not take part before they had been asked! When the project started, there were five schools taking part. They were:

Blakenhale Primary
Nansen Primary
Glenmead Primary
Wilkes Green Primary
Tame Valley Primary

These schools represent different areas of the city. Two are considered to be "inner city" schools. One represents a new estate in the city and two are from post war housing estates.

THE COMPUTER

As none of the schools had a microcomputer of their own and none of the teachers involved had any experience of computing other than the course which we had organised, it was left to BECC to decide which machine was to be used. There were a number of factors which influenced the final decision:

1. The Local Authority has a "Buy British" policy.
2. The standard secondary micro was the Research Machines 380Z.
3. There was a limited budget with which to buy the machines.

At the time this decision was being made, a number of new British machines were coming onto the market. Two of these were seen as being almost ideal for use in Primary schools. They were:

The Research Machines 480Z and the BBC Microcomputer (Acorn)

Very little was known about Acorn as a computer manufacturer. The only micro which they had produced at that time was the Atom, which was considered to be rather eccentric! On the other hand, the Research Machine 480Z came from a company which had a proven background in producing micros for use in education. The machines they had produced were robust and reliable and Research Machines had always given excellent support to users of its machines. Research Machines were also putting a lot of effort into making the 480Z compatible with the 380Z so that a BASIC program which ran on the 380Z would also run on the 480Z. For these reasons, the machine chosen for the project was the Research Machines 480Z. We also decided that at this stage it would be more useful to use the same machine in all project schools.

BUYING THE MICRO

The Director of BECC made some funds available to the project but not enough to buy all the required machines outright. The schools involved in the project were therefore asked to pay half the cost of their machine. Many of the schools originally approached could not raise this finance and only five schools started the project. Orders were sent off for the machines in the Autumn term of 1981.

Soon after this date the British Government introduced a scheme to support the purchase of microcomputers for all secondary schools. The effect of this policy is discussed in the paper by R. Jones on page 27 . The Birmingham primary schools project started two years before this financial support became available.

SOFTWARE

BECC was already running a library system for software based on the 380Z. As programs written for the 380Z would run on the 480Z this library was a good initial source of software for the primary project.

A search for other software from outside Birmingham showed that very little had been produced at that time for the primary sector with the notable exception of the I.T.M.A. Project. (Investigations on Teaching using Microcomputers as an Aid) based at the College of St. Mark and St. John, Plymouth. A description of the latest developments in the ITMA project is given on page 161. Most of the school software produced by local and national projects had previously focussed on the secondary sector.

MANAGEMENT

The schools involved were asked to develop their own classroom management system for the micros so that the different systems used could be compared. It was planned from the outset that the project teachers should decide which systems suited their particular school.

SCHOOL VISITS

Visits were arranged to all schools during the Autumn term of 1981 in order to establish the expectations which the schools had about the use of the computer and the management system which they planned to use. These visits were informal and made directly to the headteachers of the schools concerned. Some points which emerged during these discussions are:

> One school was hoping to buy three machines which assistance from BECC. The headteacher of this school was firmly convinced that the microcomputer was extremely important for the future of primary education. The school had raised a great deal of money through fund raising activities and was intending to use this money to buy the computers. This school had already invested a lot of money in other audiovisual aids and was the best equipped primary school the author had ever seen! Another school had raised the money from capitation by not buying as many pencils as they normally did. This had caused most of the staff at the school to view the computer

with a great deal of suspicion. In each school a class teacher was nominated by the headteacher to be the main contact for BECC. Three schools were intending to timetable the microcomputer to go round all of the classes each day. Another was planning to use it for a week at a time in each class. In other schools the microcomputer was to be fixed in one place, either the library or the classroom of the contact person.

In most cases the headteachers thought it reasonable that someone in the school would learn to program the computer so that they could develop their own programs.

THE INTRODUCTION

As there was going to be a delay between the ordering of the machines and their delivery we took the opportunity to ask each school if they would like someone from BECC to visit the school in order to introduce the computer to the rest of the staff. Two of the schools declined the offer but a visit was made to the rest. There were no 480Z machines available at that time so we used a 380Z but told the teachers that although the machine was different the programs we used could run on the 480Z. This was the first contact with the staff from each of the schools.

DELIVERY

As usual with new developments the 480Z systems took longer to be delivered than we first thought and it was February 1982 before the machines eventually arrived at BECC. We had hoped to bring a teacher from the project schools into the Centre and issue the micros after an introductory session. However, the computers arrived just before the half term holiday and we decided it would be better to get the machines to the teachers so that they could get used to handling the equipment during the holiday.

SOFTWARE

The weekly informal workshop sessions were continued in order to allow the project schools to get advice and to copy programs. No attempt was made to enforce the use of any particular item of software; instead it was left to the teachers' own judgement as to what to use.

INITIAL OBSERVATIONS

When the machines first went into schools it was apparent that the teachers who took on the responsibility for them were collecting every item of software which would run on the 480Z. Early visits to schools indicated that most teachers were trying all programs with all children. At this stage there was very little matching of children's ability to software. Management of the machine varied from school to school. In most cases the micro was timetabled to go into all junior classes (Ages 8 - 11 years). The general trend during the project was that a single session had to be at least half a day and not a single lesson as some had intended in their original plans. In most of the project schools, the teacher who took on the initial responsibility was the main user. Other teachers were reluctant to

use the machine unless they were timetabled to do so. This meant that
the use of the microcomputer spread slowly throughout the school. In
one school the headteacher decided that he wanted to use the machine
himself. This meant that no other teacher has used the machine out
of school hours. Under these conditions the use of the machine has
been limited to the headteacher and to the teacher who initially
became interested. The other teachers have shown little interest and
in some cases have shown aggression towards the micro!

LATER OBSERVATIONS

The machines have now been in the project schools for over a year
(July 1983). Some of the initial observations still hold but some
changes have been noted.

Initial excitement now seems to have died down. Some reasons for
this are:

> Most schools tried to write their own programs when the
> computers first went into schools. No school is attempting
> to do this now.
>
> The software which was originally given to schools was
> "collected" from a number of sources. Quite often the
> documentation which came with this software was poor. This
> caused the schools to stop using the software. When the
> documentation improved, either by writing it ourselves
> or by getting it from the authors, the use of those programs
> went up and the schools became more self reliant.
>
> Over the year of the project software sources have improved
> and schools have been using published software more than
> "home brewed" software. Again they have become more self
> reliant.
>
> The initial expectations of the schools have become more
> realistic. For example, two schools initially saw the micro-
> computer as being used to help with school administration.
> Although this is possible, they have seen how difficult it
> is to write the software to do this job, and have appreciated
> that their cassette based micro is not the best computer to
> use. They have also seen how much time must be given to
> managing the machine in the school and to developing the
> curriculum in order to make best use of the facilities which
> the micro offers.

The use of software has changed. Whereas at first all programs were
tried with all children, it seems that most teachers involved in the
project are now being more selective. Either the children are being
matched to particular programs in order to develop particular skills
or more programs are being used which cater for a wide ability
range.

Teachers are changing their attitude to the computer. At the start
of the project I was asked if I could write a spelling program. No
other specification was given! Recently the same teacher brought a
spelling program to me and asked if I could adjust the spelling
program so that it keeps data files on cassette so that he could
use whichever file is appropriate.

There has been a noticeable shift from simple test/reward programs to programs which demand more teacher involvement. This matches the observed uses of the micros, which at one time were left running in the corner of a classroom but now are a much more integrated part of classroom activities.

CONTINUING DEVELOPMENTS

The project has given us valuable experience which we can put to good use during the next two years when the number of machines in Primary schools will increase rapidly thanks to the Government's new scheme which provides half the cost of a microcomputer. The Education Authority has decided to help Primary schools to buy these by offering to pay the other half of the cost. This has caused BECC a number of problems:

> How will all the teachers be trained?
> What software needs to be developed?
> How will the machines be distributed?
> Which machine should be bought?

Our solutions to these problems are:

TRAINING

In September 1982 we advertised a course called "BASIC programming for Primary Teachers" which was designed for 20 teachers. We had one hundred and fifty applications within two weeks. We have just (March 1983) finished the fourth run of the course and took twenty five teachers on each. We have not yet exhausted the original waiting list. This gave us some idea of how large the in-service training commitment was going to be. A total of nine primary teachers have been seconded on to two full time courses for the year 1982/83 at local colleges which have experience in educational computing.

With these nine teachers we will be able to train two teachers from each of Birmingham's 344 primary schools. This is the minimum in-service training to which we are committed under the Government scheme. Each teacher must attend at least a two day training course. In order to fulfil this commitment we will have to run eleven courses each term until the end of the scheme. This could mean that we have few resources with which to support current users or to develop software. There have been some discussions as to how the teachers can be replaced while they are being trained because it is seen as important that the teachers are available in the working day so that the training course is not additional to their normal work load.

We soon realised that running such courses on a cassette based machine is not very efficient. A great deal of time is wasted waiting for programs to load from cassette. We have therefore worked with our local Microelectronics Education Program (MEP) Centre on a networking system whereby a number of 480Z micros can load programs from a single 380Z disc based system. This network has now been successfully used on three courses.

SOFTWARE

The teachers involved in the project have now realised that they are not capable of writing advanced educational software. We have also realised that our resources will be stretched in running the in-service training which the Government project needs. We are therefore setting up "specification groups" in order to ensure that software is written which will be used by Birmingham teachers. These groups are already in existence in the secondary sector and we believe that they offer a sensible way of using teachers expertise without them having learn how to program. We hope, through these groups, to guide publishers who are new to the field into developing good educational software.

DISTRIBUTION AND SUPPORT

We could not distribute all 344 machines in one go. We have decided to bring schools together into groups of about ten. Each group will be attached to a "satellite" school which will become the first point of contact for each school within the group. These satellite schools will have extra equipment in order to fulfil this role. There are currently (March 1983) 19 satellite schools and 32 groups. All of the original Project schools are now being used as satellite schools. Other satellite schools are those from which a teacher has been seconded to the local colleges.

WHICH MICRO?

Our experience with the first microcomputers showed us the importance of using reliable equipment and our primary school project has reinforced this lesson. Many educational programs now use large amounts of memory. It was therefore essential that whatever machine we used was not limited to small memory size. We also saw the need for standardisation of equipment across Birmingham if we were to make the best use of our limited resources. For these reasons we have decided that all primary schools in the city will use the Research Machines 480Z. This machine has 64k of user memory, RGB (Red Green Blue) colour output, Extended BASIC in read only memory, and a robust and reliable case. The package comes complete with a cassette recorder, RGB colour monitor and documentation.

THE FUTURE

Having been forced to be pioneers in the field, it is encouraging to see the support which is now coming from government sources which can be channelled through BECC to our primary school teachers. Major efforts will be made to encourage the development of good educational software and to provide an easily accessible software library for Primary schools. This may mean arranging for the "satellite" schools to interrogate the Authority's mainframe computer. This could make the use of local "telesoftware" commonplace in Birmingham primary schools. The skills we may have acquired in the past years will help us to give Birmingham primary schools the encouragement and support they will need in the years to come.

Session 4 - Discussion

Rapporteurs: P. GORNY, F. KUBATH

JONES asked M. DeVAULT to describe her three simulation programs. DeVAULT replied that she used the only available simulations for her hardware: Lemonade Stand, Trail West and Gold Miner. These programs in basic economics engaged the students in some problem solving activities.

BAUERSFELD asked for clarification regarding the role of the child as an "initiator". DeVAULT responded that she did not have a formal definition. She was concerned more about the error of organizing her teaching toward the expectations parents had for their children's future jobs, rather than toward the children's desires.

BAUERSFELD, referring to the design of the minimum programming group, asked WATKINS which member was concerned about the overall goal. WATKINS replied that the teacher, a curriculum development specialist from a university or publisher, was the guide.

WALDOW suggested that programs should be more interesting than normal textbooks for children. In the minimum programming group (teacher, software coordinator, programmer), where, he wondered, was the child's position? WATKINS responded that the programs were evaluated in the classroom by children and teachers.

VAN WEERT returned the discussion to the direction we want to take in software development. WATKINS replied that an educated teacher is necessary as the guide for the minimum programming group. VAN WEERT rephrased his question to ask how we ensure that the minimum programming group doesn't simply develop a momentum of its own to determine the direction it will follow. WATKINS replied that he didn't know.

JONES cautioned against the centralized producer approach and offered the National Curriculum Plan as an alternative. This organization informed members of available software from other members that could be shared.

MARTIN wanted a definition of a software coordinator. WATKINS indicated that managerial skills and the ability to establish and support communication between teachers and programmers were the essential features.

KLOTZ supported teaching programming to teachers to maintain their traditional sense of control of the learning situation and thereby maintain their sense of confidence. They must be cautioned not to overestimate their programming ability, but stay open to new ideas. WATKINS pointed out that teachers' confidence went down after his twelve-hour course. He explained that their new programming ability did not match their expectations. Using available software, however, had the advantage of adding new ideas to the situation. He cautioned against the hope that teachers will become expert programmers. KLOTZ still felt it necessary that teachers should have a headstart on the children by learning some programming.

M. DeVAULT remarked that teachers in her course found programming relaxing and were unconcerned about philosophical directions. They enjoyed programming so much that many bought their own computers after the course.

SESSION 5

INTRODUCING COMPUTERS TO PUPILS
IN A
NON-TECHNOLOGICAL SOCIETY

Erling Schmidt
DAKS, Aalborg Skolevaesen

Niels Tovgaard
DOS, Odense Skolevaesen

These days the Greenland society experiences a
series of upheavals, partly because of the new
technology. The introduction of the micro
computer as an aid in instruction in Greenland
brings special challenges to be met. But on the
other hand, the computer may turn out to be a
valuable aid which might solve some of the
problems special to education in Greenland.

BACKGROUND

Greenland is the world's largest island with an area of 2,175,600 km^2 and extending 2,670 km from the north to the south, which corresponds to the distance between Denmark and the Sahara. All of Greenland has an artic climate, which means that the mean temperature for the warmest month does not exceed 10 degrees Celsius. Only one seventh is ice-free coast, the rest barren sheet ice with an average thickness of 1,5 kilometres.

Approximately 50,000 people inhabit Greenland, distributed in about 140 small and a few larger towns, of which Nuuk (Godthaab) is the largest with about 10,000 inhabitants. Approximately 4/5 of the population were born in Greenland, while the rest are Danes staying in Greenland for varying periods.

The relation between Greenland and Denmark goes far back and has been formalized in different ways through the ages. At present, Greenland - like the Farøe Islands - has a home rule arrangement within the Danish realm. The Home Rule Executive Council has already taken over the administration of and responsibility for many areas, e.g. the educational area as from January 1st, 1980.

EDUCATION IN GREENLAND

There are 9 years of compulsory schooling in Greenland (ages 7 to 16); elementary school comprises a preparatory part (grades 1 to 3) and a "primary" part (grades 4 to 9). After this, the pupils may continue up to 4 years on a voluntary basis. In principle, the language of instruction is Greenlandic, but because of the lack of native teachers and educational material in Greenlandic, the Danish language is extensively used. Otherwise, Danish is the first foreign language, which may be taught already from grade 1, but is compulsory from grade 4.

There are approximately 850 teachers in Greenland, of whom about 350 talk Greenlandic. And there is still quite a number of teachers, especially in the outer districts, who have not attended a teachers' training college. But lately, the intake of students at the "Grønlands Seminarium" has increased considerably, and the teachers' education has been restructured so as to fit into the new schooling. A sufficient coverage of native teachers is expected to be reached about 1990.

Naturally, the geographic conditions have an immense influence on education in Greenland. For instance, distribution of educational material from the Center of Educational Aids in Nuuk (Godthaab) to the distant settlements is very problematic. It takes place by helicopter, ship, dog sledge etc., according to place and season and can take months. This is one of the reasons for the growing interest in how telecommunication can be of assistance in this respect which naturally leads the interest towards the prospective application of educational programmes. Of great importance is the fact that most of the West Coast of Greenland is covered by a radio link, which can easily handle great amounts of telephone, TV and data, and furthermore, there is satellite connection to the East Coast (and to Denmark). Thus, the technical base is ready.

EDP IN GREENLAND

Development in the edp* field has been relatively slow in Greenland, and there are few processing installations which are in the hands of the authorities, "KGH" (The Royal Greenland Trade Company), and a few other companies. Often an isolated word processing ssstem is the closest approach to the "edp age". A number of companies have data processing carried out for them in Denmark, either as batch-operation or - increasingly - on-line.

Quite a number of special technical problems are also connected with the use of edp in Greenland. The power supply, for instance is not stable everywhere, and sometimes static electricity creates big problems, partly because of the very dry air, partly because it can be very difficult to establish adequate earth connection. Only in one respect it is easier to introduce edp in Greenland than at any other place, as was mentioned at the edp conference in Greenland: "the cooling problem can be solved by opening a window ..."

CONFERENCE 1981 EDP ON GREENLAND PREMISES

In November 1981, the Executive Council had the first conference about edp in Greenland. The purpose of the conference was to get a survey of the activities already taking place or on their way in the edp area, in order that co-ordinated and rational development could be ensured.

Particularly, it was pointed out from the beginning to the end of the conference that the application of edp in Greenland will be made on Greenland premises, so that to the widest possible extent consideration is made for the special Greenland conditions, and so that the Greenland people are fully involved in the development from the very beginning.

* edp stands for "electronic data processing"

At the conference, the role of the elementary school in relation to
the introduction of edp in Greenland was discussed. It was the general
attitude in this respect that informatics and CAI should be dealt
with at the elementary school level, partly in order that everybody
could be informed of edp, and partly in order that prospective
education can take place more functionally in this area.

FIRST EXPERIENCE WITH COMPUTERS IN SCHOOLS

In connection with the conference, Erling Schmidt was invited as a
guest lecturer, but at the same time the opportunity was taken to
introduce micro computers for the very first time in the schools of
Nuuk (Godthaab).

There are three schools in Nuuk (Godthaab) and each of these received
one day's visit. Also a guiding meeting was arranged for all of the
teachers prior to the visit, and furthermore a presentation was
given at the "Grønlands Seminarium" (the teachers' training college).

In practice three RC700 Piccolo micro computers were at our disposal,
one of which had been transported in a bag from Aalborg/Denmark without any damage. The programs used were various training programs for
the subjects Danish, Mathematics, English, etc., as well as calculation and simulation programs from other subjects such as Physics,
Geography, Biology etc. Most of the programs were made in Danish, but
a few had been translated into Greenlandic, and more were translated
in the course of the visit.

It turned out that problems, experiences, prejudices, advantages and
all other aspects in connection with a first presentation of edp at
a school in Greenland were more or less similar to those experienced
in Denmark.

The pupils learned to operate the equipment very qucikly, and there
was an obvious and immediate motivation for working with the micro
computers. Groups of pupils formed quickly at the Piccolo's, discussing between them the tasks given and the replies to be made. The fact
that the majority of the programs were in Danish did not cause any
trouble, as there was always at least one in each group knowing
enough Danish for solving the problems. And the few programs in Greenlandic created much amusement among the pupils - also due to spelling
errors.

The pupils accepted the micro computers and the programs immediately
and showed in general a relaxed attitude. There was no special confusion or awe of the devices, but rather a general acceptance of the
fact that problems could be presented on a screen with a follow-up
treatment of the reply. Furthermore, the pupils accepted immediately
that the computer could make mistakes, and this fact resulted in a
tolerance towards programs sometimes reacted unexpectedly to replies
given. In fact it was found that the computer was not regarded as
such a big authority, as pupils in Denmark sometimes regard it.

The teachers' attitudes were more varied. They realized quite many
possibilities of applications of the computer as an audio-visual aid,
for instance there would be many advantages in having identical programmes in Greenlandic and Danish. With this tool at his disposal, a
Danish-speaking teacher could help pupils better who were not so
good at Danish, and vice versa. But at the beginning the teachers
also showed a general hesitation, which is only natural, taking into

consideration that they were presented with quite new possibilities which might involve great changes. This hesitation may also be explained by the fact that most of the teachers were seeing a micro computer for the very first time, not to mention the use of the computer in education! But on the other hand, the teachers immediately recognized the motivation and the interest which the equipment and the programs created with their pupils, and that this might be utilized in a positive way.

This first - and very short - presentation of the possibilities in connection with the edp conference turned out to have created such an interest that a follow-up was made from part of Greenland.

THE SECOND ROUND - MICROS PROVE TO BE USEFUL

In April, approximately 6 months later, an approach was made to the school authorities of Odense, one of the cities in Denmark where pioneer work is going on in this field, asking for assistance in an experiment in the application of micro computers in education. In fact, the problem had arisen that pupils who had left the elementary school and had started further education, had such "holes" in their mathematical skills that the instruction was discontinued.

Now it was hoped by means of CAI, corrections of the pupils' knowledge could be obtained, so that instruction might continue.

The school authorities of Odense responded positively to the approach and released Niels Tovgaard from his daily instruction, so that he could go to Greenland for 14 days as a consultant for the start of the CAI activities. At the same time, "Regnecentralen" had showed the good-will to provide three RC700 Piccolo micro computers at disposal, and "GIO-tele" (Greenland's Technical Organisation - tele) assisted with the practical aspects and also in many other ways.

During Niels Tovgaard's visit, there was made a more systematic approach to the presentation of the micro computer and its possibilities. E.g. a mini-course was held for the teachers in order that they yould get an idea of the possibilities and limitations in the field. Not all of the teachers were interested in participating, but among those present several became so interested that they continued to use parts of their spare time to work on with these matters.

As experienced during the first visit, it turned out that there was no problem in getting the pupils to work at the computers. Although many of the pupils came from very small outlying settlements and had grown up in a society without any technology at all, there were no problems in working with the computers. The interest among the pupils was so great that they often carried on working with the problems after the end of the lesson - and this was something which had NEVER happened before!

Also it was found that the period of 14 days of consultant assistance was far too short. It is easy to get started, but soon various problems arose, e.g. the wish for minor changes in the programmes and after 14 days of assistance the teachers are not capable of carrying out this kind of operation. But since then, the contact has been kept between Greenland and the pioneer institutions of Denmark, so that the consultant assistance is still functioning indirectly.

THE FUTURE

So far, the experience in applying CAI in Greenland has turned out to be extremely positive, and systematic work in this area is carried on. As a consequence of the positive results, some equipment has been procured, both for schools and for the further education institutions. By now, about ten RC 700 Piccolo computers have been bought, mainly for Nuuk (Godthaab), but other towns will follow.

Lately, there is a growing interest in utilizing tele-communication for the distribution of programs in Greenland. As already mentioned, a radio link is established, which could easily transfer the programs requested to wherever is wished. In this respect, a series of decisions is expected before long.

Finally, the conclusion can be made that there have been no serious problems in connection with the introduction of micro computers and CAI in education in Greenland. In fact, it rather seems that there will be a number of obvious advantages, and under all circumstances, development is fully active.

COMPUTERS AND EDUCATION

OPINIONS BASED ON MY EXPERIENCE OF
TEACHING JUNIOR HIGH SCHOOL (12-14)

Satoru Yoshimura* and Ryo Kuroda**

In this article we first explain the general situation in
computer-based education for junior high school students
(aged 12-14) in Japan. Next we describe the actual conditions of computer-based education at Keio Futsubu Junior
High School were S. Yoshimura works. From our teaching
experience, we should like to explain computer-based
education, especially its significance, methods, notable
points, plus some ideal forms for the future of programming education. What we call computer-based education here
does not mean a so-called Computer-assisted Instruction
(CAI) system: we want to consider it as the education in
which we teach the students how to use computers and what
we can do using the computer. Although on a simple level,
in this report, we tell mainly of the experiences the
students had in the learning of computer programming, what
impressions they had and what they knew about using
computers.

CURRENT CONDITIONS IN JAPAN

With the spread of electronic calculators, from the time they came
to be used in ordinary homes (about 1970) a topic of discussion among
specialists in mathematics education at the primary and secondary
levels has been how to make use of these efficient appliances in the
classroom. However, even now electronic calculators are not in
general use in the classroom nor is their use generally taught.
The reasons for this are the lack of experience of the teacher, the
problems caused by different types of calculators, and the fact that
they have no connection with entrance examinations for senior high
schools. The same thing could be said about computer-based education.

Apart from the business classes at senior high school, computer
education at high school level is not common in Japan today. Just
like electric calculators, computers will first have to become widely
used in homes and offices and finally will come to be used in the
classroom.

However, "Computer-based Classes for Junior High School Students"
were started about 10 years ago as one of the events of "Information
Dissemination Week" organized by the industry world, and some of the
computer makers started the same kind of class as one of their
publicity activities and began to teach junior high school students
how to make programs.

---
 * Keio Futsubu Junior High School, Yokohama, Japan
** KENGAKUSHA CO., LTD., Tokyo, Japan

The widespread use of personal computers has reinforced this development.

COMPUTER CLASSES OF KEIO FUTSUBU JUNIOR HIGH SCHOOL

A computer class for teachers and clerks was first held at the Faculty of Engineering of Keio Gijuku University in 1966. During the discussion it was decided to hold computer-based classes for junior and senior high school students in the summer of the same year.

According to the reports for 1970, an Assembler (machine language) was used in the computer class. At that time, the university students also used the assembler language, and learning about the computer was based on practice rather than lectures.

Participants, No. of Days

	Beginners	Experienced	No. of Days
Junior high	29	27	6
Senior high	33	14	5

It was reported that the number of programs run on computer was 1772, about 20 programs per person, using about 40,000 punched cards. This class was continued in approximately the same form until 1982, and the number of junior and senior high school students participating amounted to over 1,000.

Aroung 1970 a Computer Club was set up at Keio Futsubu Junior High School, and some students began studying for themselves. Some of them subsequently took the Grade 2 test for information processing engineers at the Ministry of International Trade and Industry, and seven of them passed it being the youngest ever to pass the test. At about this time programming contests for junior and senior high school students were held.

OUTLINE OF INSTRUCTION FOR THE COMPUTER CLASS AT KEIO FUTSUBU JUNIOR HIGH SCHOOL

In 1977 at our school we began teaching all the seniors how to write programs in the following way:

i) Text: " How to Use a Computer. How to Write Fortran"
  1. Writing names: WRITE statement, FORMAT Statement, H-notation.
  2. Reading number values: READ statement, INTEGER, COMMENT Statement.
  3. Calculating: How to write assignment Statements, REAL
  4. Getting an arithmetic mean: IF Statement, GO TO Statement
  5. Making tables: DIMENSION, X-notation.

ii) Cost: about $ 2 (including the punch card and textbook)

iii) Teaching Method: We do not treat the class as a formal one but the students train and advise each other.
  1. From each class we receive as assistants about five students who are interested in computers.

2. These assistants are given a total of six hours introduction to the computer in their own time after school and gain an understanding of the practice of computer use.
3. After distributing texts, punch-cards, program coding sheets, etc., we explain how to use the computer. This required one hour for the whole class.
4. The students get the instruction from the assistants, in their class, and they receive a JOB card (permission for computer use). After school they go to the computer room and punch the cards and start up the computer.
5. After five or six programs the level goes beyond the assistants' knowledge, then the students check their reference books, ask for guidance from university students and thus they go on to a higher stage.
6. After about three months we have them submit a report together with the best program that they have written.
7. The assistants give a preliminary grade to the program submitted and report the results.
8. Those who use up their allocation for the rental of the computer have to open their own accounts and use them for their individual studies (about 30% of the students open their own accounts).

iv) Student reports: The report submitted after the program practice can be classified as follows:

1. Simple calculation of the cubic volume and surface area (20%)
2. Making numerical tables and/or graphs. (30%)
3. Mathematical problems such as linear equations with three unknowns and/or prime number tables. (30%)
4. Programs dealing with everyday life and hobbies such as the calendar and RANDOM-BOX. (20%)

Here are some of the students' impressions:
1. Wonder for and/or attraction for computers.
2. Annoyance at errors made and delight at successfully computing the program.
3. Enjoyment of the practice and hopes of using computers in future in many cases.

Thus, we may say that we have reached the goal of our computer class.

OUTLINE OF INDEPENDENT RESEARCH (Free Studies)

In our school we hold an exhibition once a year, in which each student submits one piece of work connected with his favorite school subject. Computer related works among these are as follows.

Our school has about 710 students, of whom 18 students submitted a work related to mathematics, and 8 of these were related to the computer. There were also 5 works by the students who chose some other subjects which were related to the computer, thus giving a total of 13 related to the computer. (2%)

The projects had a wide variety, from a study of using a personal computer like the PC-8001 (NEC) and the basic programming for using it to a study of BASIC taking three years, making a music synthesizer, and the work of the program itself. And also from the results of the sports test in the first and in the second year they estimate what results the students will get. We believe they make the best use of the computer when they apply it to their immediate environment.

AIMS OF COMPUTER-BASED EDUCATION AND ITS PLACE IN THE CURRICULUM

First, we have a lot of opinions from our students saying that computer-based education should separate from the other subjects like "reading education" or "library eudcation". University graduates tell us that more than 80% of them are required to have some knowledge of the computer in some form or other in their business. They point out the following as characteristics of computer-based education.

logical	methodical	planning
creative	applicable	linguistic
informative	expressive	game-like

They suggest that computer-based education should be planned taking these characteristics into consideration.

Those who devoted themselves to computer programming when they were in junior high school expressed the opinion that through their experience of programs, flow charts and system flow they now thought in terms of these and therefore developed the abilities to plan and criticise.

What elements of computer-based education will become important is not clear. However, it is certain that whatever will be important for those who are in the position of leading the complicated society of the future, we as persons who educate children, should concentrate on the educational aspect of the computer rather than consider it as a hobby or game.

ARITHMETIC INSTRUCTION PROGRAMS USING A MICRO-COMPUTER

A lot of educational programs using the computer (CAI) are being written, but none of them aims at accuracy and speed in calculating.

Next, we are going to present a paper aiming at remedial work based on analysis of student error which we are sure you'll find interesting.

Outline of the Programs

These learning programs are developed as an arithmetic learning tool. They are used for Pupils about 7-9 years old (in Japan) to be used to prepare a lesson on calculation.

These programs type out basic arithmetic problems on a micro-computer display and wait for an answer to be typed in on the keyboard. If the answer is correct, the program types back the correct mark, and types out the next problem. If the answer is wrong, it types back the bad mark, and gives helpful advice about solving the problem.

Program 1: Problems are ADDITION, SUBTRACTION and MULTIPLICATION
which are generated at random. (Fig. 1)

    ADDITION (carrying up): A + B = ?
    range: $1 < A < 10$, $1 < B < 10$, $10 < ? < 19$

    SUBTRACTION (carrying down): A - B = ?
    range: $10 < A < 19$, $1 < B < 10$, $1 < ? < 10$

    MULTIPLICATION (multiplication tables): A x B = ?
    range: $1 < A < 10$, $1 < B < 10$, $3 < ? < 82$

Example of SUBTRACTION

    13 - 4 = ?   waits for answer

    13 - 4 = 8   x (bad mark)

    ⎡13 - 4 = 8   (parsing of 13)
    ⎣10 + 3 - 4 =

    10 - 4 + 3 = ?   (commutative law), waits for answer
      6↓

    13 - 4 = ?   waits for answer

Program 2: Problems are high level integer DIVISION (calculation
by writing, which are generated at random. Also, these
are classified into two types. The first type is exactly
divisible, the text indivisible.

In this program, emphasis is laid on the temporary quotient, not on
the exact solution.

Example of DIVISION

       ?
    160) 800   waits for answer

       1
    160) 800   (bad mark sound)

       ?
    160) 800   advice: Estimate the temporary quotient digit.

       4   Mentally round off 160 to 200
    160) 800   advice: The temporary quotient digit is less
                                than the true qotient digit.

       ?
    160) 800

    find the exact solution loop.

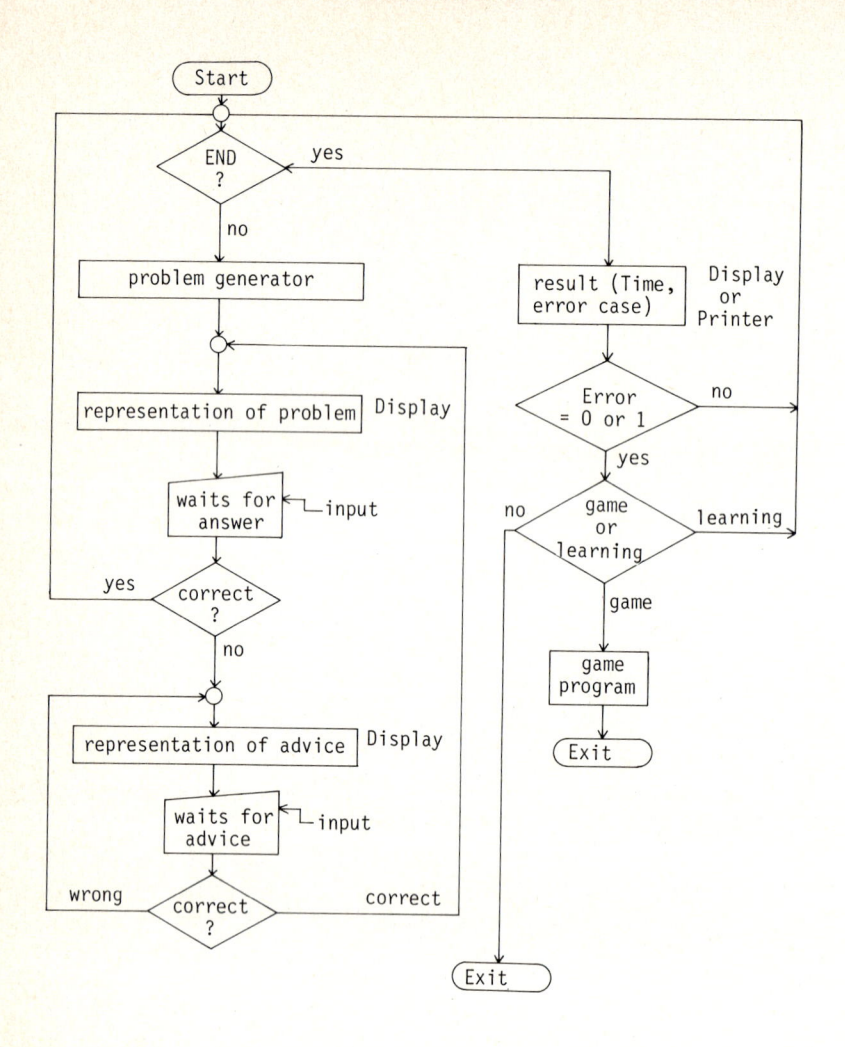

Fig. 1 Flowchart for ADDITION, SUBTRACTION and MULTIPLICATION

"DATALAERE" IN ELEMENTARY SCHOOLS
EXPERIMENTS IN GRADE 5

Niels Tovgaard
DOS, Odense Skolevaesen

Erling Schmidt
DAKS, Aalborg Skolevaesen

Through the last 10 years there have been increasing activities in the field of "datalaere" in the Danish elementary school system.

So far, this "datalaere" instruction has very often been given in form of a voluntary subject in grades 8-10. But in recent years accelerated technological development has raised the question whether the "datalaere" instruction should be compulsory. For reasons of time, this can hardly be carried out through in grades 8-10, therefore experiments have been started at a number of schools with "datalaere" as a compulsory subject in grade 5 in order to see whether the themes can be treated on this stage.

BACKGROUND

In Denmark, we have 9 years of compulsory education (7 to 16); apart from a few private schools, this course is covered by the local school authorities. Almost all pupils, however, start with one year's voluntary attendance in a nursery school class, and furthermore, our school system offers a 10th form after the compulsory course. From primary school you can continue in the educational system, or you can start having an occupation. The primary school system works under the respective local authorities, but with regard to subjects, examinations, etc., it is governed centrally by the Ministry of Education via legislation, implying that the schools all over the country have the same list of subjects.

The first experiments with "datalaere" started at the end of the sixties, and since then this subject has had an agitated life. In 1972 a departmental report appeared which clearly emphasized the importance of starting up "datalaere" in the school system. 1976 we had a new Education Act without "datalaere" in the list of subjects, however, and with a few exceptions this prevents the subject being introduced in the primary school system.

Some of these exceptions have come about by the utilization of a paragraph in the Education Act concerning experimental work, others by connecting "datalaere" with other existing subjects. This instruction in "datalaere" is rather unevenly distributed over the country, as it concentrates in regions e.g. Odense and Aalborg.

Over the latest years, the Ministry of Education has been pressed in order that the Act might be changed to comprise "datalaere" in schools all over the country. A discussion has been going on concerning the placing of the subject, which most people wish to be compulsory. So far, the subject has normally been put in grades 8 to 9, but the number of weekly lessons at these grades does not give adequate room for more compulsory lessons. This is the reason why the lower grades, where more time is available, are being considered. In order to get some experience in "datalaere" at these grades, experiments are going on in the Odense and Aalborg school systems.

WHY "DATALAERE" IN THE SCHOOLS?

From the very start it has not been the purpose of "datalaere" in Denmark to educate young edp specialists or programmers, but to give the pupils sufficient knowledge and understanding in edp matters to get on in a society where edp is already present.

New technology is applied in almost all areas of our life, and to a still increasing extent. To all people, the impacts of new technology will have an immense influence on everyday life.

If "datalaere" is not taught at all levels of education, right from the primary school, the power of knowing something about new technology will be limited to a very narrow elite of technocrats.

Therefore, knowledge of new technology should be possessed by everybody. Only in this way can all the citizens of our democratic society be able to participate in the debate of the many advantages and disadvantages implied in the use of new technology.

WHAT IS "DATALAERE"?

The subject should contribute to demystifying and dedramatizing the use of micro processors and computers. The object of the dedramatization is not to eliminate critical attitudes towards the application of edp and new technology. On the contrary the instruction should replace mystery, myths, misunderstandings and rumours by knowledge, understanding, skills, experience and attitudes.

How are words like "knowledge" and "understanding" to be interpreted? You may know something without necessarily understanding it. Knowledge in itself is not always valuable. Therefore, concepts such as "knowledge" and "understanding" should belong together in the formulation of the aims. If both knowledge and understanding of a phenomenon is possessed, then this knowledge may be transferred to other situations and be applied there. If, for instance, you understand how a computer operates in principle, you will regard many phenomena in your everyday life as understandable. It will contribute to structurising your comprehension of the surrounding world.

What then, should the pupils know and understand in relation to "datalaere"? They should learn about the "new technology" - in its widest sense. Machines are produced to solve problems, to put it very simply. In short, the pupils should know something about these machines and the problems they are capable of solving. And they should understand how they operate, how the problems they can solve have been prepared by people, before the machines can handle them. They should know what types of problems cannot - and can probably never be - solved by machines. The pupils should also know and understand that what comes out of the machines is totally depending on what has been put into them.

Based on this knowledge and understanding together with skills in problem solving and the application of computers, the pupils should be led to taking attitudes to some of the problems, advantages and disadvantages arising when new technology is applied in society.

THE PURPOSE OF "DATALAERE"

Formulated in items, the aims could be described as follows:
1) That the pupils obtain a knowledge of the method of operation of computers and of the historical, social and cultural background of computers.
2) That the pupils obtain such skills in programming that they are able to produce simple programs and to test these themselves.
3) To inspire the pupils and give them a possibility of using edp in their everyday life.
4) That the pupils obtain a knowledge of society's use of the edp-technology.
5) That the pupils obtain a knowledge and understanding of some important sets of problems in connection with edp-technology and its impact on society and the individual.
6) That the pupils see and understand the connection between the various social changes created by edp-technology (in working, family, and spare time activities).
7) To prevent alienation from edp-technology and to give the pupils the understanding that it is manageable.
8) That the pupils acquire the ability to evaluate financial, political, ideological, and cultural statements concerning edp-technology.

THE CONTENTS OF "DATALAERE"

The contents of "datalaere" can be divided into two main areas:
1) Data and problem-solving
2) Edp and society

In the first main area the following subjects are treated:

the computer, algorithms, programming, etc. - and it must be emphasized that instruction in programming is not a goal in itself but a necessary instrument intended to provide the pupils with a better understanding of the possibilities and limitations of the computer.

In the latter area, social aspects in relation to edp are treated, but based upon the actual knowledge and understanding given through instruction in the first main area.

It goes without saying that it would be unrealistic to imagine that pupils of 11-12 years can have the above-mentioned aims fulfilled completely. This is the reason why work is going on with a model where the subjects from "datalaere" are resumed at a later grade, however, with an amended weighting. Roughly, the allocation will be as follows:

	Data and problem-solving	Edp and society
Grade 5 - 6	two thirds	one third
Grade 8 - 9	one third	two thirds

EXAMPLES OF THE INDIVIDUAL INSTRUCTION COURSES

In all instruction courses it has been intended to make things as concrete and relevant to the pupils as possible. Therefore, the computer and its possibilities and limitations are illustrated by phenomena which are known by the pupils, and which are part of their everyday life. If, for instance, a subject like "automatic control" is going to be treated, a device as simple as a traffic light is chosen for illustration.

CONTROL OF TRAFFIC LIGHT

For this subject, models of 6 crossroads and approximately 100 small traffic lights were procured. Furthermore, interface was established so that the traffic lights could be switched on and off via the parallel port of the micro computer.

Here we met the first problem: It would be inadequate and far too time-consuming if the pupils were to program the traffic lights in COMAL80, and therefore a special "language" was constructed, for control of traffic lights, only. In fact, this "language" was a small-scale interpreter, written in COMAL, and it proved to be highly suitable for its task.

Because of the simplicity and clearness of the "language", the pupils could concentrate immediately on the actual tasks and make the many different algorithms for control of the various kinds of traffic-light controlled crossroads.

The difference between using COMAL80 and the dedicated language can be exemplified as follows:

COMAL80 version

```
0010 OPEN FILE 1, "/17/PORT", Write    // parallel port opened as a file //
0020 REPEAT                             // blinking loop
0030    PRINT FILE 1: CHR$(8);         // bit 3 goes high: light on //
0040    EXEC pause(0.5)                // pause for half second //
0050    PRINT FILE 1: CHR$(0);         // parallel port low: light off //
0060    EXEC pause(0.5)                // another puase //
0070 UNTIL ORD(KEY$)=32                // hitting space-bar exits loop //
0080 END
0090 //-----//
0100 PROC pause(time)                   // procedure to pause //
0110    starttime:=SYS(3)/50            // SYS(3) is the clock //
0120    REPEAT                          // dummy loop for 'time' //
0130    UNTIL (SYS(3)/50)-starttime>=time
0140 ENDPROC pause
```

"TRAFFIC-LIGHT-LANGUAGE" version   (English version)

```
1: TAEND RØD(1)                         1: ON  RED(1)
2:       PAUSE(0.5)                     2:     PAUSE(0.5)
3: SLUK  RØD(1)                         3: OFF RED(1)
4:       PAUSE(0.5)                     4:     PAUSE(0.5)
5:       FORFRA                         5:     AGAIN
```

The work with the traffic light gave excellent results, and the pupils obtained understanding of how various sequences can be controlled by means of a micro computer, a program and attached equipment.

FROM TRAFFIC LIGHTS TO ROBOTS

Besides, this was extended in another course, where a working model was constructed, showing a conveyor belt with a magnetic crane which could move iron objects from one place to another. For this model a special "language" was also developed, in which the movements of the conveyer belt and the crane could be programmed.

From the work with this model, the pupils were given a good illustration of the possibilities in new technology for e.g. industry by the application of industrial robots.

This subject was followed up by visits to various works, and the pupils were highly motivated for the many good discussions they had around the whole field of aspects concerning introduction of new, micro processor-based technology in society.

INFORMATION RETRIEVAL

To illustrate the possibilities of data-bases and information retrieval, the starting point was taken in the telephone book, which of course was known to all of the pupils.

They worked with this subject with great interest, and soon all of them had obtained a good understanding of the basic organisation of data implied in the production of a telephone book.

Naturally, all of the pupils also knew how to use a telephone book, and thereby knew its limitations. If, for instance, you know a person's address, profession, and first name, you cannot possibly find his telephone number in an ordinary telephone book. But if you call the information office, you get his number immediately. Therefore, their edp-system must contain more search possibilities than the telephone book. (This is only true in some countries).

(As a matter of form it should be mentioned that there is an edp telephone information retrieval system, named "OP-system", which can find a subscriber in a few seconds by means of any kind of criteria.)

A special "mini-OP-system" written in COMAL80 was made for the treatment of this subject. Here, the pupils themselves were able to establish, keep, and search a data-base for subscribers.

This project, by the way, is now being extended by the possibility of connecting the micro computer directly with a telephone exchange, so that the information retrieval system can switch through the telephones directly.

CONCLUDING REMARKS

The experiment with "datalaere" as a compulsory subject at grade 5 with 2 lessons per week started at the beginning of this school year. Therefore, it would be too early to draw definitive conclusions. But it may be stated that in general, it seems to be a success in that it is actually possible to give relevant and substantial instruction at this grade.

As the experiments are taking place at the request of and with permission from the Official Education Council for Experimental Work under the Ministry of Education, they will be concluded with official reports, of which the first one is already on its way and more will follow after the end of the school year.

Session 5 - Discussion

Rapporteurs: C. BERDONNEAU, T. BONELLO-KUBATH

LEVRAT suggested that the morning's speakers outlined experiences based on concrete situations. The speakers who had mentioned LOGO emphasized creativity rather than an understanding of society. He asked if they were mutually exclusive. TOVGAARD responded in the affirmative, but added that they could be studied in parallel. LEVRAT questioned that if both were pursued simultaneously, an emphasis on one might make the other harder to pursue later. SCHMIDT commented that his work with models prompted creativity - lots of ideas/solutions. He added that in some cases students arrived at ideas/solutions which proved valuable to real-life institutions.

MARTIN objected to the suggestion that LOGO was not a concrete experience. Compared to BASIC and PASCAL, she felt that LOGO was indeed more concrete, more relevant for young children. It allowed them to move from the concrete to the abstract and it offered different things to children of different ages. LEVRAT pointed out that LOGO was not related to society in any of the papers which he had read.

BAUERSFELD expressed interest in the crane which TOVGAARD had shown in an overhead transparency and its movement by a child. He wondered how understanding in such an area could be developed, adding that models were helpful in the development of scientific understandings. He supported, therefore, the use of simpler models to develop computer literacy (such as those SCHMIDT and TOVGAARD described) rather than big systems models.

LOETHE returned to the question of LOGO and society. He spoke about work with some children involving LOGO and an elevator, and referred to their ability to build up different language levels. He felt convinced, however, that issues relating to computers and society, such as privacy or administration, should be dealt with at the secondary level. YOSHIMURA commented that LOGO was not used in Japan.

TOVGAARD noted that the Danish programs in grades 5-6 (two-thirds data and problem solving and one-third EDP and society) and grades 7-9 (one-third data and problem solving and two-thirds EDP and society) were to be seen as a unit, which in turn prepared students for a later level. For TOVGAARD, working with models was preparing students to talk about more complex things at a later level. SCHMIDT concurred, adding that the effort was made to put subjects in grades where students were ready for them.

V. DeVAULT pointed out the distinction between public and private schools in Japan and asked whether computers were used extensively in the private sector. YOSHIMURA replied that in general there was little difference because computers were not much used in the elementary and junior high schools but some curious, eager and diligent teachers used computers in their classes. Teacher training in computer use is, however, included in many courses.

MARTIN asked YOSHIMURA whether the interest Japanese girls expressed in computers was equal to that of Japanese boys. YOSHIMURA perceived no difference. SCHMIDT added that one reason why they had moved computer use down to the fifth grade was to hopefully catch girls before they discovered their difference from boys, and before they "threw away" the world of physics and mathematics. STEWART proposed that all children are interested in computers, some more than others, and sex differences are irrelevant. She cautioned, too, that we may be writing software that creates differences.

V. DeVAULT indicated that there appeared to be an interesting contradiction in Japan. On the one hand, it was a country making impressive use of computers in business and industry, while on the other hand, it appeared to be doing the least in computer education. YOSHIMURA explained that two reasons might be teacher resistance and financial restraint. If more computers were acquired for the home, he felt that this would pressure the schools to do more.

LEVRAT returned to the issue of boy-girl computer interest, noting that computer options were filled by more boys than girls (approximately two-thirds boys), though opportunities seemed equal. BERDONNEAU asked LEVRAT how many female instructors were in his informatics department. He replied few (one in ten).

AHLSTROM asked for a translation of the term "datalaere". SCHMIDT talked about a government document published in 1972 which recommended the introduction of "datalaere" in all school levels. AHLSTROM felt that the term "datalaere" had a broad scope and referred to computers in society. BOLLERSLEV clarified that besides computer science, "datalaere" includes the influence of computers on society.

PETTY requested more detail regarding the networks in Greenland. TOVGAARD said they do not exist yet. SCHMIDT pointed out, however, that the technical system (radio and satellite connections) was already in place. He further postulated that computers would soon link schools to the network in the main town of Nuuk.

MARTIN commented that we tend to develop the technology and then consider the ethics. In America, she suggested, the term computer literacy had a strong problem solving emphasis, while in the last five years, a social aspect was added. Furthermore, computer literacy is now an essential outcome of contemporary education in America. SCHMIDT commented that problem solving was a tool to prepare children for life in a computerized world. In Denmark they are not trying to produce computer science specialists -- their scope is much broader.

SESSION 6

PROBLEM SOLVING USING THE MICROCOMPUTER

W. George Cathcart

Department of Elementary Education
University of Alberta
Edmonton, Alberta
Canada

Polya's four-step model for problem solving can be used in a microcomputer environment. When a computer program is being written to solve a problem, some of the specific activities that need to be engaged in at each of the four steps are somewhat different from those engaged in when solving a problem in a nonprogramming context.

INTRODUCTION

In 1977, the National Council of Supervisors of Mathematics (NCSM), published a position paper on the basics in mathematics education in which they stated that "learning to solve problems is the principal reason for studying mathematics" (p. 20).

An Agenda For Action published by the National Council of Teachers of Mathematics (NCTM) in 1980 reinforced the NCSM position by stating, as its first recommendation, that problem solving was to be the focus of school mathematics in the 1980s.

A problem, in contrast to an exercise, is any situation for which a solution is not immediately apparent. The path to the solution is blocked. No formula or algorithm comes to mind that will immediately solve the problem. Problem solving, then, is the process of removing the blockage. This is done by applying one or more heuristic processes such as breaking the problem into subproblems and applying previously learned knowledge to the solution of the subproblems.

A second major thrust in school mathematics in the 1980s is clearly the use of the microcomputer. The number of microcomputers in classrooms has been increasing exponentially during the past few years and will continue to increase for some time to come. The NCTM also strongly recommended in An Agenda for Action that we take full advantage of the power of calculators and computers. (Recommendation Three.)

MICROCOMPUTERS AND PROBLEM SOLVING

Gress (1981) identified four areas in which the computer can be used to develop problem solving skills:

- as an instructional delivery system,
- by enabling students to construct models of a problem or a situation via programming,
- by enabling students to explore a computer environment by manipulating variables, and

- by enabling students to develop problem-solving skills and make decisions through running an interactive simulation of a real-world situation. (p. 41)

While the microcomputer can be used in all of these ways to develop problem solving skills, this paper focuses primarily on the second with minor references to the third. Subsequently this will be referred to as using the microcomputer as a "tutee" (Taylor, 1980).

PROGRAMMING AND PROBLEM SOLVING

Kantowski (1982) implies that programming solutions to problems helps students refine their understanding of the structure of mathematics and mathematical processes. Children are often not satisfied with algorithms that are slow and proceed to look for ways to revise the algorithms to improve the efficiency of the computer program. Kantowski also implies that programming motivates children to generalize their routines. A program which can be used to solve a number of similar problems is more satisfactory and useful than one which will solve only one specific problem.

> A person who knows how to express thoughts in a computer language has a new way of talking, writing and thinking about the ideas that he or she wants to embody in the instructions to the computer. And any time you discover a new way to think about something, or a new language for describing your thoughts and setting them down for a closer look, then you have a new tool for solving problems.
> (Luehrmann & Peckham, 1981, p. 7)

Programming a computer to solve a problem is an excellent way to meet both recommendations one and three from An Agenda For Action. To use the computer as a *tutee* to enhance problem solving skills requires some programming expertise on the part of the problem solver. Teaching programming in a problem solving setting is a powerful way to teach both because one contributes to and reinforces the other.

While LOGO, PASCAL and other languages are receiving considerable attention as problem solving languages, all examples in this paper are in BASIC. Except for LOGO, BASIC is probably the easiest language to teach to elementary school children because they can learn to do things with it very quickly with a minimum of background information.

POLYA'S MODEL AND PROBLEM SOLVING WITH THE MICROCOMPUTER

Polya's (1957) four-step problem solving model has been widely promoted in mathematics education and is generally accepted as a useful model for problem solving. The four steps in Polya's model are:

1. Understand the problem.

2. Decide on a plan of action.

3. Carry out your plan.

4. Look back.

As one would expect, this model can also serve as a useful model for solving problems using the microcomputer. However, some of the specific activities and questions that are normally used at each step are different in a programming context than in a nonprogramming setting. Some of the necessary modifications are described below.

Step one, understanding the problem, is just about the same whether one is solving a problem with or without the computer.

In devising a plan, step two, an overall plan of attack has to be chosen such as "act it out" (simulate), make a table and look for a pattern, solve an equation, etc. In addition, more specific strategies need to be chosen. This usually involves determining small steps or the solving of subproblems. Computer scientists refer to this procedure as stepwise refinement. Moursund (1981) says that,

> In stepwise refinement, one systematically breaks a problem into smaller, more manageable pieces. . . . If one can solve Subproblems 1, 2, and 3, then the original problem can be solved. If a particular subproblem is not immediately solvable, further stepwise refinement is necessary (p. 19).

Moursund diagrams this as shown in Figure 1.

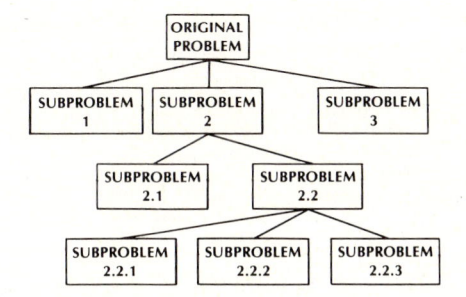

Figure 1. Stepwise Refinement (Moursund, 1981, p. 19)

These steps must be organized into a logical sequence and a flowchart or other structure set up to establish the logical sequence. Algorithms may need to be developed or even small programming procedures or subroutines written for some of the steps. A final check needs to be made that all the conditions of the problem are met through the plan decided upon.

At step three (carrying out the plan), using pencil and paper, one did the computation, made the table, drew the graph or did whatever the chosen strategy required. To solve a problem by programming it on the microcomputer, step three becomes writing the computer program. If some small routines were written to solve subproblems as a part of step two, these need to be incorporated into the main program at this stage.

When using the computer, the looking back at step four will involve an examination of the program to see that it did correctly what was intended. In addition you may ask whether the program could be simplified. This could involve a refinement of the algorithms to improve efficiency, the combining or elimination of some steps, or other modifications. Furthermore, the program should be reexamined to determine if it can be generalized to handle different but similar problems. Another step four activity is to revise the program to produce a more aesthetic display or printout by organizing the text and results in an appealing and easy to read format. Text should be double spaced and not too much on the screen at one time. The results should be in chart form with headings when appropriate.

Figure 2 (adapted from Reys and Krulik, 1980) summarizes the problem solving process in a programming context.

HOW TO SOLVE IT

First.
YOU HAVE TO UNDERSTAND THE PROBLEM.

Second.
CHOOSE AN OVERALL PLAN, THEN ORGANIZE THE STEPS (SUBPROBLEMS) INTO A SEQUENCE (FLOWCHART OR SIMILAR FORM) AND WRITE ALGORITHMS FOR EACH STEP OR SUBPROBLEM.

Third.
WRITE A COMPUTER PROGRAM USING THE SEQUENCE AND ALGORITHMS.

Fourth.
EXAMINE THE SOLUTION OBTAINED. GENERALIZE IT IF APPROPRIATE.

Figure 2. (Adapted from Krulik and Reys, 1980)

EXAMPLE 1: HANDSHAKES AT A PARTY

The "handshake problem" has become somewhat of a classic by now. For this reason it may serve as a good example of the above process.

> There are ten people at a party. If each person shakes hands with the other guests, how many handshakes will there be?

The following paragraphs describe the four steps in the problem solving process, assuming a computer program will be written to solve the handshakes problem.

Step 1: Understanding the problem.

The following questions may be asked to help the problem solver to understand the problem:

- How many guests are at the party?
- If Jim shakes hands with Carol, does Carol need to shake hands with Jim?
- If you were at the party, how many people would you shake hands with?
- Can I restate the problem in my own words?

These same questions could be asked whether or not the microcomputer was being used.

Step 2: Decide on a plan.

The first part of step two is to decide on an overall strategy. Suppose we choose to simulate (act out) the problem. We could line the ten people up and have them shake hands one-by-one with each other and count the handshakes.

Jim   Trevor   Carol   Nancy   Trina   George . . . Mavis

Jim leaves the line and shakes hands with Trevor, then with Carol, and so on to Mavis. Jim then stays out of the line because he has shaken hands with everyone else.

Trevor now leaves the line and shakes hands with Carol, then with Nancy, and so on to Mavis. Trevor then stays out of the line because he has shaken hands with everyone else.

We can now make a chart to show this.

PERSON	SHAKES	WITH					NO. OF SHAKES
Jim:	Trevor	- Carol	- Nancy	- Trina	....	Mavis	9 (10-1)
Trevor:	Carol	- Nancy	- Trina	- George	....	Mavis	8 (10-2)
Carol:	Nancy	- Trina	- George	- Mark	....	Mavis	7 (10-3)
Nancy:	Trina	- George	- Mark	- Lesley	....	Mavis	6 (10-4)
.		.		.			.
.		.					.
.		.					.

The observation that the number of handshakes for person J is $10 - J$ is reasonably apparent from the above chart.

The second part of step two is to plan some more specific strategies. For this problem we might make the following notes.

- Handshakes initially is 0.

- For each person, P, increment the number of handshakes by 10 - P.

- This suggests a loop: For P=1 TO 10
    HS = HS + (10 - P)
    NEXT P

The next step is to organize the strategies or subproblems into a logical sequence. This is usually done by means of a flowchart or other structure. Since BASIC is generally not considered to be a structured language, the flowchart will be used.

Since there are not many steps in the program for this problem, it is probably not necessary to design a flowchart. However, it is a good idea to have children design a flowchart for most problems. Designing a flowchart for the handshakes problem is left as an exercise for the reader.

Step 3: Carry out the plan.

Write the program. A program to solve the handshake problem might look something like this:

```
10 REM --HANDSHAKE PROBLEM--
20 HOME
30 PRINT"10 PEOPLE AT A PARTY.  HOW MANY HANDSHAKES?"
40 HS = 0
50 FOR P = 1 TO 10
60 HS = HS + (10 - P)
70 NEXT P
80 PRINT:PRINT "THERE ARE ";HS;" HANDSHAKES WITH 10 PEOPLE."
90 END
```

[Of course, if a student noticed that each person shakes hands with nine other people, but each handshake is a double (when Trevor shakes with Trina then Trina also shakes with Trevor), so there are 10 x 9 / 2 handshakes, the program becomes simple. The student now has a formula, HS = (N*(N-1))/2, and needs only substitute numbers into the formula to solve the problem. The student may be inclined to use a calculator to find the answer rather than write a computer program.]

Step 4. Looking back.

Are the results reasonable?

Can the program be generalized so that it will work for a different number of people? First, the number of people at the party will have to be accepted as input. Line 30 can be modified to do this. The number of times the FOR/NEXT loop is executed will have to be changed to account for the different number of people. Also line 60 will need to reflect the new number. Finally, line 80 will need to be altered slightly to print out the number of people rather than 10. The following program incorporates these changes.

```
10 REM --HANDSHAKE PROBLEM--
20 HOME
30 INPUT"HOW MANY PEOPLE AT THE PARTY? ";N
40 HS = 0
50 FOR P = 1 TO N
60 HS = HS + (N - P)
70 NEXT P
80 PRINT:PRINT"THERE ARE ";HS;" HANDSHAKES
   WITH ";N;" PEOPLE."
90 END
```

Another looking back activity is to reexamine the generalized program to see if there are some changes which could be made to improve the visual appearance of the display? The inclusion of some vertical and horizontal tabs would accomplish this. Rewriting the above program to achieve a more aesthetic display is left as an exercise for the reader.

EXAMPLE 2: COLORED DIE

Elementary school children may gain a more intuitive understanding of the laws of probability by solving the following problem. For older children this would not be a problem, although writing a computer program to simulate it may be.

> A 12-sided (dodecahedron) die has one blue face, two red faces, two white faces, three yellow faces and four green faces. If this die were tossed 50 times, how many times would it turn up blue? red? white? yellow? green?

The four steps in the problem solving process to solve this problem are described briefly in the following paragraphs.

Step 1: Understanding the problem.

To help understand this problem one may simply ask what it is that has to be done in the problem or restate the problem in his/her own words.

Step 2: Decide on a plan.

Given that a computer program will be written to solve this problem, the most obvious overall strategy an elementary school student would probably use is to simulate the shaking of the die.

Four major subproblems are immediately apparent.

1. How to simulate the shaking of a 12-sided die.

2. How to assign a color to the face showing.

3. How to keep a record of the color showing.

4. How to report the final results.

Given adequate instruction, the first subproblem is not difficult. A student will soon recognize that this requires the random number generator. To generate a random number from one to twelve requires:

> INT(12*RND(1))+1.

Subproblem two may be somewhat more perplexing as the correspondence between subproblems one and two is not often made. With a little prompting, an elementary school pupil will probably end up assigning colors to numbers in sequence something like the following:

```
BLUE    = 1
RED     = 2, 3
WHITE   = 4, 5
YELLOW  = 6, 7, 8
GREEN   = 9, 10, 11, 12
```

A decision with regard to subproblem three may be to store the cumulative results in five different counters and then print the final totals in chart form (subproblem four).

A slower but more interesting solution to subproblems three and four would be to print the results as they occur in a continuously changing digital display. Elementary school children prefer this kind of display and it is probably the one most of them would choose. Both approaches are within the programming expertise of most elementary school pupils who have been given adequate instruction.

With these decisions made, it is now possible to design a flowchart for this problem. Figure 3 presents the more generalized flowchart that may result after changes have been made in step four, looking back.

Step 3: Carry out the plan.

A program can now be written to solve the specific problem stated above. A program listing appears below after changes have been made in the next step.

Step 4: Looking back.

Do the results seem reasonable? The probability is quite high that the number of red and white faces is quite different. Even without formal instruction in probability, an elementary school pupil will intuitively believe that these should have occurred about the same number of times. The simulation could be repeated by rerunning the program. This may or may not improve the results. At this point, the teacher may be tempted to suggest that the number of shakes could be increased. The program can be generalized to accomplish this. Children could be encouraged to try simulations of, say, 100, 200, 500, 1000, 5000 and 10 000 shakes.

Finally, at step four, the student should pay some attention to the aesthetics of the display. Modifications to the program may be needed to accomplish this.

The following listing is one possible version of the final generalized program.

```
100 HOME
110 VTAB 8: PRINT "   A PROGRAM TO SIMULATE"
120 PRINT: PRINT "    TOSSING OF A 12-SIDED DIE."
140 VTAB 16: PRINT "HOW MANY TIMES DO YOU WANT"
150 INPUT "     TO SHAKE THE DIE?  ";S: HOME
160 B = 0:R = 0:W = 0:Y = 0:G = 0
170 VTAB 8: PRINT "  BLUE   RED   WHITE   YELLOW   GREEN"
180 PRINT "  ----   ---   -----   ------   -----"
190 FOR J = 1 TO S
200 K = INT (12 * RND (1)) + 1
210 IF K = 1 THEN B = B + 1: GOTO 260
220 IF K = 2 OR K = 3 THEN R = R + 1: GOTO 260
230 IF K = 4 OR K = 5 THEN W = W + 1: GOTO 260
240 IF K = 6 OR K = 7 OR K = 8 THEN Y = Y + 1: GOTO 260
250 G = G + 1
260 VTAB 11: PRINT TAB( 3)B TAB( 9)R TAB( 14)W TAB( 21)Y TAB( 29)G
270 NEXT J
```

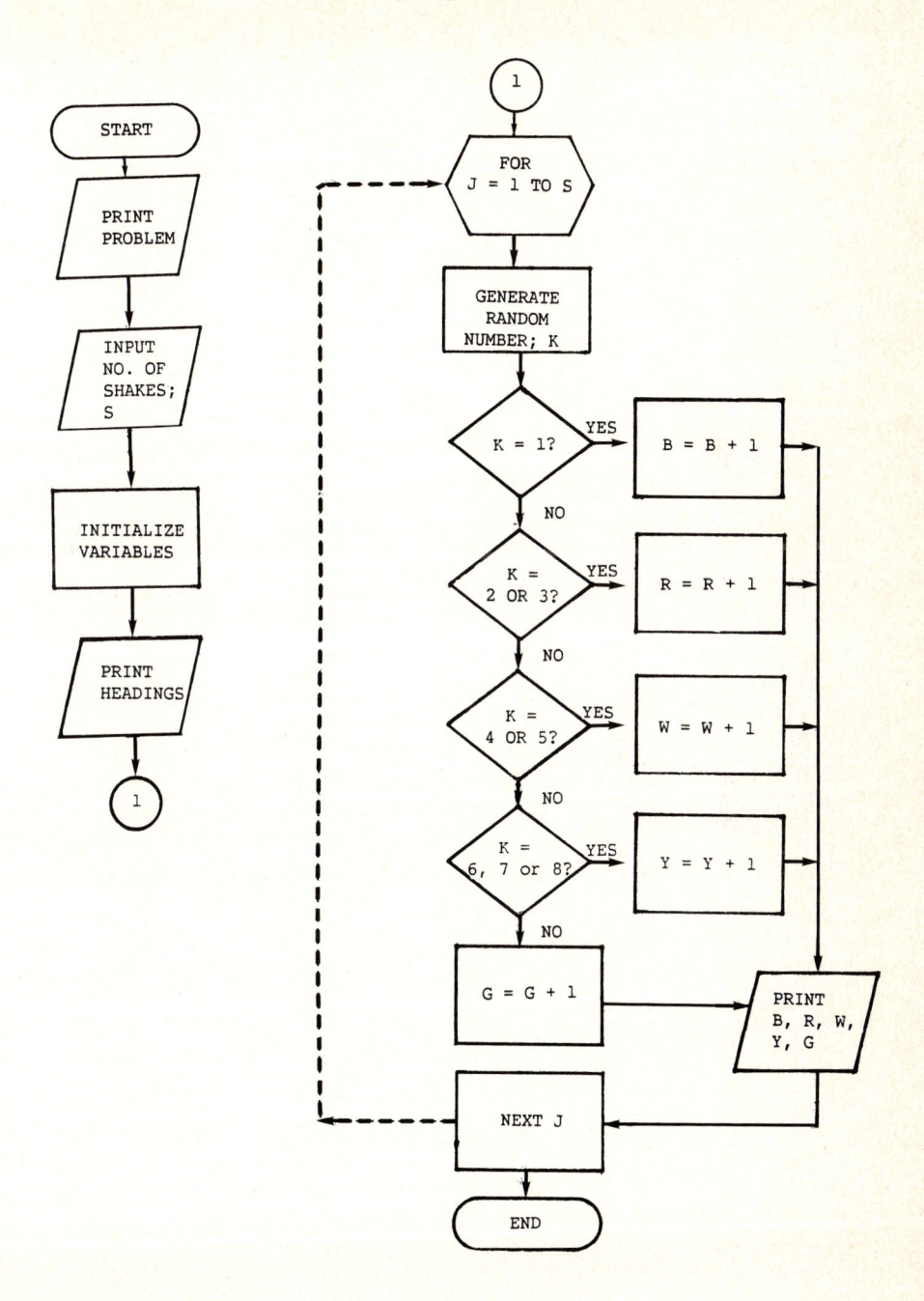

Figure 3. Flowchart for colored die problem

SUMMARY

The teaching of problem solving and an imaginative and productive use of the microcomputer are two major challenges facing elementary school teachers today. This paper demonstrated that Polya's four-step approach to problem solving could be used to solve problems by programming a solution. The activities that the problem solver engages in at each step are somewhat different when using a programming approach than when using nonprogramming techniques.

Two examples were used to illustrate the approach. Additional problem solving exercises can be found in Cathcart and Cathcart (1983).

References

[1] Cathcart, G. M. and Cathcart, W. G. Programming Exercises in Basic for Microcomputers (Gage, 1983).

[2] Gress, E. K., The future of computer education: invincible innovation or transitory transformation? The Computing Teacher 9 (September 1981) 39-42.

[3] Kantowski, M. G., The use of the microcomputer in instruction for problem solving, in: National Council of Teachers of Mathematics, Problem Solving Concentration Papers (National Council of Teachers of Mathematics, 1982).

[4] Krulik, S. and Reys, R. E. (eds.), Problem Solving in School Mathematics, (National Council of Teachers of Mathematics, 1980).

[5] Luehrmann, A. and Peckham, H., Apple Pascal: a hands-on approach (McGraw hill, 1981).

[6] Moursund, D., Introduction to computers in education for elementary and middle school teachers--chapter six: problem solving in a computer environment, The Computing Teacher 9 (September 1981) 15-24.

[7] National Council of Supervisors of Mathematics, Position paper on basic skills, Arithmetic Teacher 25 (October 1977) 19-22.

[8] National Council of Teachers of Mathematics, An Agenda for Action (National Council of Teachers of Mathematics, 1980).

[9] Polya, G., How to Solve it. 2d ed. (Princeton University Press, 1957).

[10] Taylor, R. P. (ed.), The Computer in the School: tutor, tool, tutee (Teachers College Press, 1980).

INTRODUCING COMPUTERS IN LONDON PRIMARY SCHOOLS

Bryan Weaver

Inspector for Computer Education
Inner London Education Authority
County Hall
London SE1 7PB

This paper details the introduction of computer work, over a two year period, into a group of 22 Inner London primary schools, and the first stages of supporting such work in the remaining 780 schools.

1. Background

The Inner London Education Authority (ILEA) has approximately 800 primary schools for children between 5 and 11, and 160 secondary schools catering for children between 11 and 18. There are over 30 colleges, including a number of a specialist nature. In addition, there are 10 general purpose teachers' centres which provide a range of support services for schools in their locality.

The Inner London Educational Computing Centre (ILECC) has a staff of approximately 30, including programmers, clerical staff and technical support staff.

2. The Beginnings

The decision to undertake a pilot project investigating the potential of microcomputers in the primary classroom was taken during 1980, at a time when three or four ILEA schools had used a computer for short periods of time, but when the majority of primary schools in the country were still unaware of the possible effects of the new technology.

£25000 was provided to equip a number of schools with equipment, and schools which had previously expressed an interest in using computers were approached with a view to their being part of the scheme. 11 schools were selected (referred to later as 'original' schools) and, since a further 11 schools (referred to later as 'extra' schools) were able to provide their own funds to purchase similar equipment the scheme eventually included 22 schools.

The aim of the pilot scheme was to:

2a. identify the needs of schools in terms of in-service training and technical support

2b. identify areas of the curriculum likely to gain from use of computers

2c. collect examples of good practice

2d. define software which should be produced

2e. form a basis for later expansion into the remaining schools in ILEA.

3. The Pilot Schools

A number of criteria were defined when selecting the 'original' schools:

3a. that a genuine interest had been expressed by the school

3b. that the Headteacher was committed to supporting the scheme, if possible being personally involved in the work

3c. that at least two teachers would be trained, and would share their experiences with colleagues in the school

3d. if possible, that there was some technical expertise in the school

3e. that the school would contribute £500 towards the cost of the equipment

3f. that it was generally agreed that the school provided a good education for its pupils, and would be likely to integrate the computer into its current curriculum.

In the event, of course, some schools scored more highly on some criteria than others. The 'extra' schools in particular did not always meet all the criteria.

The criteria were important to ensure that the pilot scheme, in the short time available before commercial pressures and government schemes created a very large demand, could concentrate on schools likely to succeed in this work, and likely to provide experiences which would be relevant to other schools.

4. The Equipment

It was important that schools' activities were not restricted by inadequate computer technology. Consequently it was decided to provide disc storage, large memory, good colour graphics and a printer. The computer selected was the Research Machines 380Z, which was well tested in our secondary schools and colleges and for which a certain amount of software was available.

A selection of software was provided for the schools, including that for text processing, information retrieval, a cloze procedure package, LOGO, various drill-style programs, and programs such as SEEK, PIRATES, EUREKA and JANE from the ITMA team (see accompanying paper by Petty and Stewart). A deliberate decision was taken to issue as much software as possible, with a view to teachers selecting those programs which fitted into their present teaching styles.

5. The training

Starting in September 1981 one teacher from each school was given one day's training per week for 5 weeks. During the next 5 weeks the second teacher was given a similar course. In January 1982 both teachers attended a three-day residential course, and in the following 5 months attended various half-day seminars on particular topics. Each teacher therefore received the equivalent of 3 weeks' training during a 9 month period.

Because the schools were intended to become, as far as possible, self-sufficient, it was necessary to convey a certain amount of technical knowledge as well as to consider curriculum implications. During the 5 days, therefore, teachers were taught skills such as how to copy discs and how to set up particular groups of programs for convenient access by pupils, and only a small number of programs - including text processing and information retrieval - were studied. This enabled teachers to develop confidence in using the computer and to feel that they were to some extent in control of its operation, and at the same time begin to consider how they would organise the use of the machine in their school.

The three-day course concentrated solely on curriculum issues, taking most of the requisite technical knowledge for granted. Sessions were devoted to particular programs or categories of programs, and discussion groups were formed to encourage teachers to exchange ideas. Two demonstration sessions involving children were set up, with teachers who had experience of particular programs showing possible classroom approaches.

The subsequent seminars served the dual role of enabling teachers to try out ideas and then combine experiences, and of allowing further programs to be considered in some detail.

6. Support Services

Most of the training was given by a small group of advisors, with technical support provided by ILECC. In the early stages in particular it was necessary to make visits to the schools, partly to discuss how the computer could be used in that particular school, but partly to allow teachers to raise individual problems which had occurred. Many enquiries were dealt with by telephone, and the seminars provided an opportunity to share problems. Many more visits to schools would have been preferable, but staffing did not permit this.

7. Comments on criteria for selection of schools

Certain conclusions can be drawn from schools' performances under these criteria. Comments are related to the criteria given in section 3.

7a. In a world where the press and television constantly refer to computers and their importance, and where (in some countries) government schemes encourage schools to obtain equipment, it is difficult to distinguish between genuine interest from a school and a natural curiosity, or desire to 'keep up with the crowd'. While it is important that the wish to explore new ideas is not stifled, it is equally important that schools do not misjudge the importance of computer use compared with other curriculum matters - for example, the quality of its mathematics teaching or the encouragement of scientific enquiry.

Some of the pilot schools had not accurately formulated their reasons for obtaining computers, and less constructive use of the equipment has been noticeable.

7b. Headteachers cannot be expert in all areas of school life, but are normally in a position to make informed judgements on curriculum matters. This is not, however, in general true of computer-based work. Less than half of the Heads became deeply involved in the work, and in some cases full responsibility was delegated. This meant, unfortunately, that some Heads became unrealistic about what could be achieved in a given time, and were unable to contribute fully to discussion at staff meetings.

It appears to be very important that Headteachers gain at least a general expertise in areas of work involving the computer, and preferably participate fully in at least one area.

7c. Two teachers in a school will be much better placed to combine their efforts, discuss experiences and contribute to staff discussion. Many teachers - indeed, many adults - are hesitant about involvement with computers, perhaps fearing displaying ignorance or foolishness. For one teacher to be isolated in a small school, unable to deal on equal terms with any colleague, would have been unproductive and potentially harmful. In all schools the involvement of more than one teacher ensured that nobody was totally isolated or without a second opinion or constructive help.

Many teachers found that they required an extended period - perhaps even a whole term - using the computer themselves and exploring possibilities, before feeling fully prepared to use the computer with children.

7d. Even after the relatively extensive training given, many teachers found difficulty in some of the technical aspects. In many cases, for example, no attempt was made to produce discs tailored to particular needs of children or classes, the original discs simply being used as supplied.

It cannot be expected that many teachers will develop a personal interest in the technology itself, and it would anyway not be desirable if teachers attempted to interfere with the operation of complex technology. It might reasonably be expected, however, that confidence would gradually develop in handling the system at a 'system manager' level. This has proved not to be the case, and the problem still remains of how to provide sufficient time and tutorial support to enable at least one or two teachers in each school to master the system manager role.

7e. The financial contribution expected of the 'original' schools was included mainly to test the level of their genuine interest. No school involved felt this was unreasonable, although it did exclude a few schools who had made a general enquiry prior to the scheme beginning. It seems natural to expect schools to contribute financially to the cost of equipment, and it is worth noting that the British Government's assistance scheme for schools involves a contribution from each school.

7f. Using a computer in a school places severe burdens on some staff and can have a disrupting effect. If in some major way a school is not making adequate provision for its children, ownership of a computer can only add to its deficiences.

It is judged important that advice to schools on computer purchase takes into account the possibility that the school should not proceed with a purchase at this stage.

8. Comments on the aims of the pilot scheme

These comments relate to the 5 aims given in section 2.

8a. To provide a teacher with a good overview of activities possible with a computer, the confidence to use the equipment and the opportunity to share problems and experiences requires a minimum of 3 weeks of training. This should be spread over a period of some months to allow work to be undertaken with children and experiences to be shared.

Any scheme of training which fails to recognise the magnitude of the task does a disservice to the teachers involved. Where for practical reasons - for example, lack of finance or training staff - it is necessary to reduce the time, great care should be taken to ensure that teachers appreciate what can realistically be achieved in the given time, otherwise teachers may set unrealistic targets for themselves.

It seems clear that support services, such as those provided by ILECC, must expect to carry the main burden of technical support and, up to a point, fulfil the role of system manager. This has major implications for national or local government schemes, since it means that short courses conducted outside the sphere of local support are not likely to solve one of the major problems encountered by teachers.

8b. The range of software available for use with primary pupils at the time of the scheme was small. It is possible however to draw one or two general conclusions from the kind of software selected by the schools.

Although many schools made some use of the short programs, each designed for one particular purpose - for example, to practise a skill or solve a strategy problem - it is widely felt that there are often equally satisfactory, and less inconvenient, ways of doing the same work without a computer. It is sometimes said that it is the novelty value of such programs rather than their educational content which is their main attraction.

It is obviously dangerous to over-generalise from a small selection of experiences, but it is nonetheless true that unless teachers see definite benefits from the new technology the sheer effort of getting to grips with it will be too much.

The software most widely used in the pilot schools, and by general agreement that which fulfils the most obvious need, is often very flexible and in some cases content-free. The most obviously beneficial, and most widely used, have been information retrieval (with some excellent local studies work involving census returns, and collection of scientific data inviting formulation of hypotheses); turtle graphics LOGO, used as a problem solving language, with geometrical activities being very much to the fore, but including children cooperating in the solution of problems; and text processing, with the computer offering a very powerful way of children editing and combining their work.

Particularly noticeable has been the degree to which such complex activities encourage children to discuss and collaborate in their work. Equally noticeable is the fact that much of the work undertaken with these packages would have been difficult, or impossible, without the aid of the computer.

8c. Even schools which normally based work around a resource centre preferred to have the computer in the classroom itself, for long periods of time so that its use was seen as natural rather than simply occurring because it was there. Some schools operated a system of allocating the computer to each teacher for, say, one day a week. This was however usually felt to fragment children's work, since the wait until the computer appeared again often broke the flow of the work. Sharing of this nature also tended to encourage the view that the computer was a special machine, at which children took a turn for a given period of time, and led to the use of trivial programs which could easily be completed in a very short space of time.

It seems very likely that each school will require a number of computers if teachers are to have use of a machine for sizeable periods of time. In fact, after only one year in the scheme, 6 of the schools had 2 or 3 machines, and one now has 6, all of which are very heavily used.

8d. The scheme failed to produce many really original program ideas. This is felt partly to be because the programs supplied - particularly the flexible ones mentioned above - were sufficiently worthwhile to satisfy the initial needs of the teachers. And partly because, with only one computer, a school could make complete use of it with perhaps only LOGO and information retrieval work being undertaken.

When, even in 1983, one looks at the very small range of powerful programs available, one must wonder if production of new software ideas will be as simple or as regular as many seem to believe.

9. Expansion into the remaining schools

In October 1982, as had been expected for about 18 months, the Government launched a scheme to assist primary schools to purchase one microcomputer each. The scheme offered a choice from three computers, but the experiences with the pilot schools made it clear to ILEA that only by standardising on one computer would it be possible to provide sufficient support for the large number of schools expected to take up the offer. The Research Machines 480Z was selected, and in the first six months of the scheme 300 ILEA schools applied for a computer.

The work done with the computers in the pilot schools had shown that any machine used had to offer a range of facilities. Unfortunately, presumably because of the cost involved, the Government scheme only provided cassette systems to schools. ILEA therefore provided its schools with extra funds to purchase a printer and a disc to add to the system, so that no school would find itself unnecessarily restricted in its use of the technology.

Because the Government scheme will only operate for 7 terms a very large amount of training has to be provided in a very short space of time. Although the Government scheme provided some training materials for schools they are widely regarded as being of limited value, and would not solve the main problems experienced by teachers in our pilot scheme.

Two teachers from each ILEA school which buys a computer are given a 4-day course to introduce some of the major concepts of computer assisted learning. The courses include:

- use of LOGO
- use of information retrieval software
- use of text processing software
- use of computers in primary science
- use of computers in primary maths
- use of computers in primary language development
- organisational implications for the school

Practical work on a computer is included, and the teachers are expected to practise further on the schools' own machine. Compared to the three weeks' training given to the pilot scheme schools 4 days is very little. However,

800 schools x 2 teachers = 1600 courses.

If each course caters for 15/20 teachers (which is the absolute maximum for any tutored practical work to take place) this requires up to 100 courses in 7 terms, or one course every week.

It is small wonder that many people question the wisdom of encouraging schools to acquire equipment without making adequate provision for training the teachers, or for providing the readily accessible support services which are so necessary.

Fortunately teachers, as a profession, are likely to take whatever support is available and do their best to cope. How many computers will be gathering dust in two years' time remains to be seen, but if schools concentrate on the accepted curriculum, taking advantage of the computer but not being ruled by its existence, there is evidence that children's learning can be greatly assisted — and that, when all is said and done, is what it is all about.

Session 6 - Discussion

Rapporteurs: M.V. DeVAULT, E. SCHMIDT

VORBECK expressed appreciation for comments and frankness about realities, but was shocked to hear that so little of the supported software development resulted in real programs. Who is going to evaluate these programs? Are programs to teach history or computer use? Who defines the objectives? Who defines strategies for evaluation? WEAVER stressed that there had been an attempt to spread the money around and that too little expertise has resulted in useful material. There is no external evaluation, unfortunately.

JONES reported that he had brought 36 programs that have been developed by MEP. Though he agreed that 400 programs do not exist at the present time, documentation and validation of many of these programs is underway. This does take time. At an early stage a "buckshot" approach was used and some good programs resulted. He suggested that perhaps too much of the effort was going to the big cities which may not use the same computer as do smaller districts.

GORNY reported that the Association for Teacher Education in Europe has assumed responsibility for locating and evaluating programs that are available from other countries. It is very difficult to make a European pool of programs. While much needs to be done to transmit programs from one country to another, much rewriting will still need to be done.

JORGENSEN asked for more information about the practical criteria about the way decisions about the use of computers in primary education. WEAVER resonded by saying that the energies of some faculties may be better given to something other than working with computers. It is a question of priorities. Pastoral views may be of a higher priority. van WEERT asked "What is a pastoral view?" WEAVER responded that a school has a social life which must be attended to before one can get on to curriculum innovation. These social needs of individuals and of facilties represent the pastoral view.

Concerning CATHCART'S paper according to GORNY the four- step model by Polya is designed perfectly for an educational environment, but it seems important to point out that the professional systems analysts have independently developed models with six and seven steps. Thereby they differentiate the two steps "writing an algorithm" and "writing a program" into algorithm/program design and testing. Thus the importancve of the logical-semantical and syntactical testing is stressed.

We begin with Polya, CATHCART said, because teachers are familiar with the model. Nonetheless, continued testing of the model to see about its usefulness will be of continuing importance. BOLLERSLEV suggested that in problem solving you are usually on your own. Does the Polya model serve only in a classroom setting? Does it serve individuals solving problems? Is it the final step 4, "looking back", that is the important check to determine if the right problem is solved? CATHCART responded that it is. LOVIS questioned the choice of the Polya model in that it might at a later time cause problems because of a flaw in logic. BASIC is not structured for the model. It would be better to have a top-down design. Using BASIC, someone will have to provide the structure.

LOETHE said this problem solving model is coming out, in his view, of a special working context; in case of Polya it is the context of working with paper and pencil. In the other case the algorithm and BASIC style of working is involved. Also the speaker's remark concerning the demarcation line between the engineering and research style can be explained by the fact that the tool used makes the working style and not vice versa. In ourcase the programming language and the embedding system encourages or even forces a special working style. What working style is actually used will be decided by the student intuitively. A working style grows out of working with tools and not by an intellectual decision. But the teacher should be aware of the working style which is encouraged by a specific programming environment.

LEVRAT suggested that the speaker's sceptism feeds a tendancy all too common with politicians. It is dangerous in view of the time it takes political decisions to be made. A computer in a school is a powerful ferment of new ideas not only about using the computer, but teaching other disciplines. In the example of history teachers, the speaker assumed they will design courseware although I don't see how they can do it without being aware of the possibilities of the computer. If you just allocate programming resources and do not interact with the teachers, your job could possibly be done better by a properly designed program on the computer. In service courses provide the history teacher with a view of the computer and its potential according to WEAVER. He thought one must accept that politicians will expect us to achieve what we say we will do.

PLANCKE-SCHUYTEN indicated that when you are doing problem solving in a programming situation you can use one of the cognitive models of problem solving (eg Polya, Dewey) to teach problem solving. These models are based mostly on introspection. The computer provides us with another method for studying the process of problem solving. When you put two children before a computer, and they start to work on a problem you get verbal interaction between the children, and between the children and the computer. Our hope is, while observing children, to learn a lot about the problem solving process.

WIBE said it seems we are still in the stone age in creating instructional programs. We stop thinking of the subject and think only of computers. We must set program creation in the context of curriculum content. We need some conferences on how to make programs in mathematics, in history, in geography. According to CATHCART we need the help of psychologists and entertaiment Hollywood types, but WALDOW suggested the first didn't believe in computers and the second cost too much. TOVGAARD reported that there are international groups working to produce software useful across country borders.

WEAVER concluded the session saying that his realism is a positive realism. Let us take an approach in which we are not expecting too much before we begin.

SESSION 7

PROGRAMMING TRAINING
FOR CHILDREN OF 11-14 YEARS OLD

Masakazu Nakanishi   Akira Aiba

Department of Mathematics
Faculty of Science and Technology
KEIO University
3-14-1 Hiyoshi, Yokohama 223
JAPAN

This is the report on our experiences of teaching of various languages, especially LISP, to children of 11-14 years old. We describe salient points and obstacles in teaching LISP to pupils of primary schools. It is said that LISP is hard to teach even if it is taught in the university. We tried to teach by three methods in order to know what method is the best to teach an abstract programming language like LISP. And we also consider human factors in programming training which have been obtained from our experiences.

1. Introduction

We had an opportunity to teach computing to children who belong to lower secondary schools attached to KEIO University. In the summer of the year before last, we held a course in programming languages on microcomputers. Microcomputers nowadays have as many facilities as older large scale computers. But a person often believes incorrectly that a microcomputer may be much easier to learn than a large-scale computer because it is small in size. It tends to be believed that the principles of microcomputers are different from large-scale computers. Our motivation in holding this school came as a consequence of having taught computer organisation capabilities and limitations.

The first computer course was held in the summer of the year before last, and it has been held semi-annually. Thus we have held four courses. The purpose of this course is to teach various languages, and it is not a "BASIC only course." We report some interesting results in our courses.

2.   Experience on the keyboard --- The present condition of JAPAN

Since Japanese is not a Western language and consists of many characters, almost no Japanese use a typewriter with a Japanese keyboard. There is no general-purpose computer with a complete Japanese keyboard. So, a novice using a computer in Japan must begin with the alphanumeric keyboard. Since a Japanese does not usually use the alphanumeric keyboard, he may feel fear of the computer.

We adopted a way to avoid this possible fear for children. The way was to use video games, which are very popular in Japan. Demonstrations of video games on a personal computer can surprise many people, because they are under the impression that the principles of video games are different from that of general purpose computers. At first, they were taught to enjoy video games with colourful displays. We expected that they might become familiar with a keyboard if they had enjoyed computer games.

We discussed the advantage and disadvantage of this method before starting our trial. The advantage is that children would then feel familiar with computers. The disadvantage is that they might only play games, or that they might fear they could not make such marvellous games. In the event, our conclusion is that this method is good. They never enthused over playing games. They became interested in making game programs by being shown how to make simple graphic demonstration programs.

During their experiences of the course, we found that younger children showed an interest in pictures, and older ones showed interest in sounds rather than pictures. Thus, we pleased younger children by games with elaborate graphics and we pleased older children by intelligent games with sounds. This must be an effective way to introduce children to computers.

3.   Education about various languages

In our courses we have employed the following languages: BASIC LISP, Pascal, Prolog and Assembly languages (6502, and Z-80). We do not adopt a "BASIC only policy" because we think some students will go on to specialise in information processing. Since we cannot forecast the next generation of languages, we prefer to teach a variety of languages. These languages have the following characteristics: BASIC and Pascal have concepts of traditional procedural programming. LISP and Prolog have concepts of functional programming and the predicate calculus, respectively. So far as Prolog is concerned, we could not get such interesting results in this course, but we got some interesting results in using LISP.

4.   Teaching LISP to pupils of 11-13 years old

It is said that LISP is one of the most difficult languages to learn. In particular, the concept of recursion, and a large number of parentheses make the learning difficult. In fact, these two difficulties have arisen in teaching university students. In our university, KEIO University, we are teaching LISP using a processor which can accept a meta-language in order to introduce it easily (1). At the second course which was our first experience of teaching LISP to children, we applied this experience in teaching of LISP to children of 11-13 years old, and we taught it using a meta-language. We had a feeling that the teaching of LISP would be difficult. Fortunately, teaching LISP to children was much easier than to students of the university. The concept of recursion and a large number of parentheses proved not to be so hard for children to understand. But there were some children who understood the concept of the "hypothesis" with difficulty. That is, the concept of the hypothesis that a program can call itself when it is coding as if it were completed. But this is a problem common to children and to students of the university not simply a typical problem for children.

We also faced the difficulty that we could not use the terms "function," "variable" etc., because children did not know these terms. This was solved by a rephrasing such as "black box", "name", etc. Apart from these problems, teaching LISP to children was very easy.

4.1   The second course

In the second computer course (which was the first time LISP was used) four pupils took a course in LISP.

The course of study of LISP was as follows. The first day: The syntax of S-expressions as data of LISP. Calculations of car, cdr, cons, atom eq, and null. The second day: Conditional expressions, the definition of various functions (including recursive functions), and utilising graphic functions. The last day: Reviewing lessons, and playing games.

Two pupils had already learned BASIC in our previous course eight months ago, and two other pupils were computer beginners. But all pupils could easily accept the concepts of LISP because they had no chance to touch a computer for eight months and had forgotten any knowledge of BASIC.

For the recursive function, they accepted the concept even if we used the term "recursive." Actually, they could trace evaluations of recursive functions. The main reason for this may be that they had not already learned about the concept of iteration or recursion. Students of the LISP course in our university have usually been taught FORTRAN. So, they have an established concept that a programming language is iterative. This may be one of the barriers to learning LISP.

Pupils did not know about a "function" because they had not been taught it in their school. We succeeded in teaching the concept of it using the idea that a function is a black box.

As result of our course, we concluded that the difficulties caused by the advanced concepts such as a "large number of parentheses", and " a specialised subject of the computation of LISP" could be ignored.

4.2.   The third course:

On the third computer course, five children took a course in LISP. Two pupils had experiences with BASIC, three pupils were beginners, and none of them had experience with LISP.

The course of study of LISP was as follows. The first day: The syntax of S-expressions as data of LISP. Calculations of car, cdr, cons, atom, eq and null. The second day: Conditional expressions, definitions of various functions (recursive functions only), exercises of a programming and playing games. The last day: Utilising graphic functions, and introduction to the PROG feature.

In this course, we settled the target that they could make programs without our advice. As we could not anticipate the reactions of pupils, we tended not to teach enough programming. We got their different reactions as follows.

We utilized many examples, but they could not write programs without our help. Though they could understand individual points such as recursion, a conditional expression, and the concept of a function, they could not make programs by relating them. For example, we tried to make them write a program to calculate the product of two natural numbers, say A & B, using zerop sub1 and plus which were already introduced. Of course, we taught them the outline of this program such as "if A is equal to 1 then B, otherwise (a-1)XB+B." But they could not write this program in LISP using them. They could not translate the notation in a natural language to the program in the LISP language. Even after some experience of these translation processes, most of them could not do it alone. Only pupils who had experience with BASIC did these processes positively. These processes seemed to be difficult for children.

On the third day, we introduced the PROG feature to use graphic functions. Programming using the PROG feature were affected by previous experiences of BASIC. That is, pupils who had experienced BASIC could easily write a program using the PROG feature. However, the cause of this was not in translation

processes, but in the process of making an algorithm. So, after making an
algorithm, they could translate to a program easily.

For us, it is difficult to make enough meaningful examples for children.
If we showed them meaningless examples, they lost interest. We need to take
steps to meet this situation.

4.3. The fourth course

On the fourth course, twelve children took a course in LISP. Three of them had
learned LISP, and the others had not. We divided these pupils into three
classes. In class-A, we taught them LISP in a traditional way. That is, we
started by teaching primitive functions (CAR,CDR,CONS,ATOM, and EQ). The next
step was to teach a conditional expression, and recursion. In class-B, we taught
them to draw pictures using LISP. This method originated from our experience
that younger children had been interested in pictures rather than sounds. In
class-C, we taught by making them write actual programs, because three out of
four pupils of this class had already learned LISP. In class-A and B, we taught
LISP by using S-expression rather than Meta-expression. In class C only
Meta-expressions were used.

In class-A we taught LISP using S-expressions as programs, and the ordinary
method of teaching LISP in the university. This introduction to LISP was
fairly easy. Of course, they did not understand the term "function" - they
rephrased a function to a command, and regarded "quote" as a signal for data.
(QUOTE is the function whose value is its argument). But the concepts of these
functions were accepted by pupils. In this class, there was a concept that they
did not understand easily. It was COND. The form of COND, which consists of
the pair of a predicate and a function, was thought to be an obstacle to
understanding. Therefore, almost all programs written in this class were made
from function compositions.

In class-B, we taught LISP using S-expressions as programs and by drawing pictures
in LISP. By introducing LISP by drawing squares, triangles etc., the language
was very easily accepted. We also taught them the method of drawing a circle.
As the course of study of this class proceeded, we did not teach a function
except graphic functions, equal and some numerical functions such as add1, plus
etc. Also we did not teach S-expressions as data. All programs written in this
class were made by using multi-body cond, and multi-body lambda expressions.
Thus, we did not teach exactly the concepts of recursion. But programming
without our help and reading programs without our help were very difficult.
One of the reasons may have been their poor experiences with LISP and its
programming.

In class-C, since three out of four pupils have had experience with LISP in
the second or third school, the introduction was very easy for them. About the
concept of function, half of them seemed to understand, but the rest of them
seemed not to understand. Only in class-C did we teach LISP by Meta-expression.
Because it has the feature that there is distinction between program and data,
they could easily understand S-expression as data. But they were not
accustomed to list processing rather than numerical processing. They could also
trace how the recursive function worked, but they could not easily make recursive
functions for themselves.

Overall, we gained the following results from this school.

class	introduction	concept of function	S-expressions as data	recursion	programming
A	easily accepted	accepted	easily accepted	"COND" was not easily understood	function composition only
B	easily accepted	only "equal" taught	do not teach	only iterative programming	very difficult
C	easily accepted	almost understood	understood	accepted	difficult

5. Conclusion

In addition, pupils of 15-18 years of age had lessons in some kinds of languages such as BASIC.LISP. etc., at this school. The main distinction between senior pupils and junior pupils was their relative ability at abstract ways of thought. (That is, the ability to imagine or assume what does not really exist.) Senior pupils were generally suprior to junior pupils at this. As far as a creative ability is concerned, there seemed to be little difference between the two groups.

What is most important in teaching programming to children is to teach them to set out the aims of their program and then to create a program to satisfy these aims. But the younger they are, the less able they are to state their aims and the programs we can teach are restricted to a few. We made various trials such as to contrive an editor program so that they could edit as if they were playing video-games.

References

(1) APPLE-LISP Reference Manual, Nakanishi Lab., Dept. of Mathematics, Keio University, Yokohama 1983.

APPENDIX: Attendances at the Computer School

The Second School

| | High School ||| Junior High School || Elementary School | Others | TOTAL |
	KEIO High School	KEIO Shiki High School	KEIO Girl's High School	KEIO Futsuhbu Junior High School	KEIO Chuhtohbu Junior High School	KEIO Youchisha Elementary School		
BASIC	6	1 3	2 2	4 6	1 6	5 0	1	1 5 4
LISP	1	1	1	0	0	4	1	8
Z-80	6	8	0	8	6	5	0	3 3
6502	1	0	0	5	0	4	0	1 0
TOTAL	1 4	2 2	2 3	5 9	2 2	6 3	2	2 0 5

The Third School

| | High School ||| Junior High School || Elementary School | Others | TOTAL |
	KEIO High School	KEIO Shiki High School	KEIO Girl's High School	KEIO Futsuhbu Junior High School	KEIO Chuhtohbu Junior High School	KEIO Youchisha Elementary School		
BASIC	3	4	1 4	1 6	1 1	1 7	1	6 6
LISP	7	5	5	0	2	4	1	2 4
Z-80	6	0	1	1	5	4	1	1 8
6502	1	1	1	1	3	0	0	7
PASCAL	0	1	1	0	1	3	0	6
HARD-WARE	2	0	0	2	1	1 3	0	1 8
TOTAL	1 9	1 1	2 2	2 0	2 3	4 1	3	1 3 9

The Fourth School

	High School			Junior High School		Elementary School	Others	TOTAL
	KEIO High School	KEIO Shiki High School	KEIO Girl's High School	KEIO Futsuhbu Junior High School	KEIO Chuhtohbu Junior High School	KEIO Youchisha Elementary School		
BASIC	3	8	4 7	1 3	7	3 6	4	1 1 8
LISP	2	4	2	0	0	1 4	1	2 3
Z-80	4	2	1	3	1	9	0	2 0
6502	2	0	2	0	0	0	0	4
PROLOG	1	0	2	0	2	NOT OPENED	0	5
HARD-WARE	1	0	0	2	1	NOT OPENED	0	4
TOTAL	1 3	1 4	5 4	1 8	1 1	5 9	5	1 7 4

Informatics in Elementary Education
J.D. Tinsley and E.D. Tagg (eds.)
Elsevier Science Publishers B.V. (North-Holland)
© IFIP, 1984

INTRODUCTION TO INFORMATICS:
AN EDUCATIONAL APPROACH TO A SYLLABUS FOR MIDDLE SCHOOL

Julien Fonjallaz

Cycle d'Orientation de l'Enseignement Secondaire
Centre de Recherches Psychopédagogiques
Geneva, Switzerland

For younger pupils and for a generalized initiation to informatics, a set of factors is imposed. To avoid passive consumers of informatics, one must look forward to create a comprehensive approach. Consequently, the educational strategy must amplify human potentiality (autonomy, creativity, communication abilities) and favour a good social use of this new technology for information processing.

This paper shows the global concept of teaching this introduction in a comprehensive school (12 - 15), and then focuses on the part relevant to the conference field. Up to now trials have been carried out in optional classes but experiments on a larger scale are about to start involving all pupils.

"The less we are taught, the more we learn"

An anonymous pupil

INTRODUCTION

The fast expanding invention of the microcomputer is the main factor making this introduction necessary. Using a micro becomes commonplace. Who would have thought, seeing these strange people driving their frightening automobiles in the beginning of the century, that now everybody would use a car. For micros, more than their fabulous technology, their accessibility is incredible. The image of strange people operating on mysterious machines is over. Deliberately, economical and political factors will not be treated.

The introduction to informatics will bring new means:
- for the pupils (methods of resolution, tools for calculations, texts and images processing, etc.)
- for the teachers (like the pupils PLUS a new pedagogical means).

This introduction will bring a new and rich pedagogical means. It brings the best hopes as did the audio-visual means. Our educational strategy must include this potentiality. To avoid the audio-visual poor assessment, we realize that the importance is not to bring computers into the classroom but to train teachers. A syllabus must link all these aspects. Teachers need multimedia abilities.

We can see it is impossible to brighten up the educational contents but it is necessary to imagine and improve a new educational approach. Pupils, parents, teachers and school systems are concerned.

The important problems and the basic conditions of success will be briefly explained:

1) For the pupils: what is known about cognition shows that, around the age of 12, children go from the concrete operations stage to formal operations stage (1). In computer science, one faces the problem of manipulating variable quantities. These variables have a mnemonic and a value. The comprehension of the notion "variable", the fundamental distinction between the variable's symbol (signifiant) and the variable's value (signifié), belong to the formal operation stage abilities. That implies an appropriate educational strategy otherwise the learning process stops. Support classes will be necessary. Many benefits, for instance in learning mathematics, will be brought by that successful acquisition. Another condition is to give access to an EDP workshop, under a teacher's supervision, outside normal classes.

2) For the parents: first, much information and then evening classes. A Parent School exists already. It allows the parents to follow the same courses as their children in order to help them out and to help their own self-training. This year, a course named "L'enfant, l'école et l'ordinateur" has started.

3) For the teachers: to favour interdisciplinarity, informatics will be taught by other subject teachers. To reach this objective, important training is necessary. This way informatics will not be only for scientific teachers. Two courses: the first one for those who will teach informatics, the second for those who will use computers as a new educational means.

4) For the school system: to assure training resources and experiments, in order to integrate informatics among other educational means, the school system must adopt a general policy.

THE GENEVA STATE EDUCATIONAL SYSTEM

A short survey shows which is the population involved. Compulsory school attendance goes from 7 to 15 years old. It is split in a primary cycle of 6 years and in a lower secondary cycle of 3 years which is subdivided into sections (scientific, latin, modern, general). This school is named "Cycle d'Orientation" (Comprehensive School) because possibilities are given or imposed to change sections according to performances. According to the section followed, it may open or close opportunities: either follow up in a higher secondary school or a full time apprenticeship. So there are different curricula for some subjects in the different sections. To belong to one section or another depends mainly on the difficulties in formal operations and in verbal communication. As our hypothesis is that the introduction to informatics should reduce these difficulties, this syllabus is constructed for all pupils. This will be one of the main points to check.

CONCEPT OF INTRODUCING INFORMATICS TEACHING

1) Our ten years experiment

From the year 1974, an adaptation of teaching materials, named Computer Education in Schools (CES) and made by ICL, is taught. Around 500 pupils followed this optional class and about ten teachers got a special formation. The main points were:

- to understand computers uses by survey and visit.

- to understand information processing by programming in a language having an Assembler logic. Works were made in batch with cards. Pupils got personal access to the computer.

2) Our present objectives

They come from that first experience and take into account the following facts:
- the easier access due to micros.
- the help of elaboration processes in the cognitive field.
- the importance of not learning a language but programming methods.
- the management of the double status of informatics either as a <u>means</u> of teaching or an <u>object</u> of teaching.
- the favouring of a real interdisciplinarity.

These objectives have to make the pupils able to:
- understand informatics like a tool for problem-structuring/solving.
- understand applications of informatics in other subjects.
- make out the importance and the value of informatics in society.

To carry out these general objectives, a set of 5 learning modules have been created. Three are obligatory and two optional. These modules assure a continuous training.

3) Obligatory modules

First Module: using a micro

In our 7th grade, pupils are 12 years old.
Ten two hours classes.
To reach this objective, practical studying of a language having these following properties (2)

Features	Educational grounds
- interactive	to allow an heuristic approach: attempts, errors, discoveries*
- procedural	decomposition of the problem solved at a specific level.
- algorithmic	description of action sequences
- symbolic	formal manipulation.

The language will be LOGO.

At the end of the module, pupils must be able to:
- use alone software organized in a menu.
- realize limited projects following their own interest or according to their teacher's recommendations.

These abilities allow Computer Aided Learning and integration in other subjects.

---

* It means that errors are a natural part of a learning process. The question is not to give guilty feelings but to give working methods and "debugging" knowledge (3).

Second Module: understanding the system structure

In our 8th grade, pupils are 13 years old.
Ten two hours classes.
This objective will be reached by:

- the study of the system configuration, a computer + devices
- the functional description of the devices.
- the notions of network, remote or local processing.

At the end of the module, pupils must be able to:

- identify the different parts of a system and describe their function.
- explain in a critical point of view the different ways to use information processing. They will be aware of potential misuses.

Third Module: exploiting a computer

In our 9th grade, pupils are 14 years old.
Fourteen two hours classes.

At the end of this module, pupils must be able to:

- realize the influence of informatics on the working methods in professional and private life.
- use general public applications.
- know their civil rights about information processing.

4) Optional Modules

   One may start after completing the first module.

   ### Fourth Module: understanding of the computer's functioning

   To satisfy the pupils' curiosity over the general laws of the computer's functioning, we propose the study a language closer to the working logic of the computer than the human way of thinking. That implies a language like ASSEMBLER simple enough to be understood, and having the following properties:

   - a small set of instructions
   - a single accumulator
   - memory and operation codes made by mnemonics.

   Moreover, the functional analysis of an operating system is taught to understand the general information flow.

   ### Fifth Module: operating his own computer

   To allow pupils the best use of their computer
   The program will be according to their needs.

DESCRIPTION BY OPERATIONAL OBJECTIVES

1) The method

   The modular decomposition of the general objectives describing the concept is still used in the analysis of the operational objectives. Every module is split up into sequences of operations, forming steps. Every step is ended by the description of abilities reached by the pupils. This way, a better control of the learning process is possible both for the pupil and the teacher. Due to a lack of space, only the first module will be described.

2) <u>First Module: using a computer</u>

   Step 1: A short introduction to operate the micro

   1) Micro-system display
   2) Starting/ending
   3) Running an existing program
   4) Presentation and use of the keyboard, control keys, editing commands
   5) Presentation of the six basic commands of the TURTLE geometry.

   At the end of this step, a pupil must be able to:

   - start and end, in safe conditions, the micro-system
   - show its elements and explain their function
   - run an already made program
   - run commands in prompt mode
   - distinguish the simple commands from the parameter commands
   - understand the language restrictions when giving orders.

   Step 2: Programming

   1) Notion of command sequences, procedures. A program is defined as a nest of procedures
   2) Editing and running simple procedures
   3) Saving and re-using his work
   4) Notion of prompt mode and procedural* mode.

   At the end of this step, a pupil must be able to:

   - create a sequence of orders, edit it in a procedure
   - run his procedures
   - make a program by nesting procedures
   - save his work on a floppy disk
   - distinguish prompt and prodedural* mode.

   Step 3: Operators - Operands

   1) Presentation of arithmetic, logic, list operators and their syntax
   2) Use of operators for constant operand
   3) Notion of variable and value
   4) Notion of link:
      - between a variable and its value
      - between variables
   5) Presentation and use of input/output procedures.

---

* A command sequence is defined in a procedure and then run

At the end of this step, a pupil must be able to:
- understand the notions of operator and operand, and distinguish the action from the object affected
- use operators over constant operands
- make the transition to variables and distinguish the mnemonic of variable from its value
- give a value to a variable:
   a) by assignment
   b) by link between variables
   c) by acceptation
- have access to the value of a variable by display

Step 4: Work Structure

1) Procedures with parameters, functions
2) Nesting procedures
3) How to use a library of procedures

At the end of this step, pupils must be able to:
- understand the causality between using variable operands in a procedure and the necessity to parameterise it
- use procedures with parameters
- use functions
- understand the distinction between a procedure and a function (one returns a value but not the other) and see that they are made the same way
- break up a task into a set of easy problems realized by procedures
- make a program by nesting procedures so that every step is made and run separately
- use recursion

Step 5: Communications man/computer/man

Making or/and using package (program + documentation)

At the end of this step, pupils must be able to:
- know how to documentate their own program in order to use and maintain it
- communicate their programs with a documentation
- use a package knowing how to extract from its documentation what is necessary to be able to run it.

Remarks: programs will be made in geometry (4), arithmetic and word processing. The importance is to show that informatics is not only to make calculations.

CONCLUDING REMARKS

A top-down analysis has been used from the general motives to pupils' activities described in detail. Before setting the official syllabus and producing teaching materials, an experiment is necessary. We will find out if cognitive difficulties are solved and if our syllabus is clear enough to be taught even by non specialist teachers. One realizes that introduction to informatics interferes in:

- the cognition
- the working methods
- the communication abilities

for both teachers and pupils and it is not easy to handle all the side effects.

Experiments made in optional classes allow us to be optimistic. Pupils are open minded. It is easier to acquire a new way of thinking than to change an old one. That is why it is most important to find a strategy interesting to teachers. We do not mean those who already have a computer but those for whom informatics may be beautiful - but only for other people. We do not have to persuade these teachers to become informaticians but to use informatics as a new pedagogical means. This way the introduction will be successful and a poor assessment of audiovisual means will be avoided. We are faced with a new tutorial function.

A question to end with: why do we have to teach programming nowadays? It is possible to find a lot of software which runs with simple command statements. This way of using computers will increase. We think that the answer doesn't belong within Informatics. It is a social problem arising from the fact that in every school system selection is based mainly on two abilities:

- formal skills
- verbal communication.

Teaching programing, in a real educational approach is an excellent medium for increasing these abilities. This way, Informatics might be the Latin of modern times.

REFERENCES

(1)   Piaget Jean, La naissance de l'intelligence chez l'enfant (Delachaux et Niestlé)

(2)   Papert Seymour, Mindstorms: Children, computers, and powerful ideas (Basic Books)

(3)   Sleeman and Brown, Intelligent Tutoring Systems (Academic Press)

(4)   Abelson and diSessa, Turtle Geometry (MIT Press)

Session 7 - Discussion

Rapporteurs: M. DeVAULT, G. PLANCKE-SCHUYTEN

In the discussion on the paper from the Japanese authors, VAN DE WOLDE asked how the students knew what the languages meant when they selected their courses by programming language. NAKANISHI responded that the children know what the languages generally imply: PASCAL is structured, BASIC is not, Z-80 is used for game playing.

VAN WEERT asked if the children did not have trouble with the algorithms. The response was that there is no difficulty in defining the algorithm because they think in computer language; but in coding it there are many difficulties.

GORNY asked if there are uses of digitizers and menus to make Japanese letters available. The response was that there is available a light pen or touch pen to be used on a board but not on the keyboard. BOSLER questioned why the Japanese do not develop a special input system. The response indicated that work is being done but it is not yet available.

VAN DE WOLDE questioned whether recursion is not a conceptual problem. How do you introduce the concept? NAKANISHI responded that recursion begins from an assumption. The child assumes his program is already finished (actually it is not) and then uses the beginning assumption.

BERDONNEAU questioned whether in recursion they used
   1) symmetry loops
   2) recursion with parametric programs
   3) piling and unpiling

NAKANISHI responded that in LISP the basic concept is recursion using a meta language and demonstrated the assumption statement. BERDONNEAU replied that this is recursion with parametric programs.

On the paper from Switzerland, BOSLER noted that the presentation stated that teachers need multimedia abilities and questioned whether teachers might think best in their natural surroundings using natural materials. His thesis: teach with media as little as possible; rather teach with things in the environment. Fonjallaz's response indicated that there is no good tradition, we want to have the ability to choose the best medium. VAN DE WOLDE indicated that BOSLER might be taking a narrow view of the word medium. BERDONNEAU felt that the media would depend on intent. If you want to reflect, for example, upon music you would need a medium to store and return the sound. The simpler methods do not allow this.

WATKINS questioned whether verbal communication will increase with the use of the computer since verbal communication will be limited by the keyboard. The response indicated that two or more people would use the keyboard and therefore there would also be man-to-man communication. LAUTERBACH commented that the computer is not necessary to improve communication. WATKINS agreed that teachers could provide the experience that would initiate improved communication without reliance on the computer.

BERDONNEAU reported that research in France has indicated that children working with LOGO have more precise communication than other children. However, the non-LOGO children embellish their communication and are more prolific in their communication though the additional details they provide are of little relevance to the situation.

SESSION 8

SPRITES WITH FIRST GRADERS

Catherine Berdonneau

Institut de Recherche sur l'Enseignement des Mathématiques
Université Paris 7
Tours 55-56 - 2 Place Jussieu 75005 PARIS
France

A new micro-world has recently become available in LOGO environments, providing facilities for color and animation. Sprites offer attractive features for young children, and have been used with first graders in the usual LOGO approach: pupils, generally working in pairs or small groups (up to four), create the shapes they will assign their sprites and imagine stories to be produced on the computer screen. This micro-world proves as relevant for youngsters as floor turtles or "Instant Programm" with a screen turtle, but seems less restricted. It provides interesting classroom activities, dealing with story writing, counting and spatialization, and offers a new set of situations for research on math education. These experiments are still on an exploration basis, which means that no structured evaluation was intended. It is yet too early to document case studies precisely. The aim is not to teach children programming, but to use a new pedagogical device for multidisciplinary motivation, somehow similar to Freinet's press.

INTRODUCTION

Before any further presentation, it must be stressed that since our first [1] experiments with LOGO in primary education, our aim has never been to teach children programming. We use computers as a tool for research on mathematics learning, and as a pedagogical device among others. It is assumed that the reader is familiar with general ideas about LOGO. Otherwise, please refer to [2]. Sprites are a rather recent micro-world in LOGO: they first became available on the T.I. 99/4 and 99/4A and have been widely used at the Lamplighter School in Dallas (Texas) since 1980. This version of LOGO provides facilities for color and movement, thus leading to activities inspired by arcades games and animation. Such a micro-world obviously offers attractive features for first graders, but also nicely fits the curriculum general and mathematics objectives at this level. Rather little information seems to be presently available about this micro-world: none of the M.I.T. LOGO Group memos deal with this subject so far, and no report was published on the work conducted at the Lamplighter School -only a few short papers in various computer and/or education magazines [3] [4]. In France, T.I. 99/4 or 99/4A micro-computers have been commercially available for about one year, but the French version of T.I. LOGO is just beginning to be marketed. We were offered the opportunity to participate in the design of this version, and thus we could start the first experiments on Sprites in a school context, in France.

WHAT ARE SPRITES, AND WHAT DO CHILDREN DO WITH THEM ?

Sprites are beings which live on a CRT, but won't show if they are not decently dressed. Up to 32 Sprites can be used, each one of them having to be assigned a shape and a color before being called to the center of the screen where it becomes visible. They can be put at any place on the screen, either using "turtle commands" such as FORWARD, RIGHT... or X and Y coordinates: to the surprise of turtle users, the sprite shape does not rotate with a RIGHT or LEFT command, though the movement direction does change. For instance:

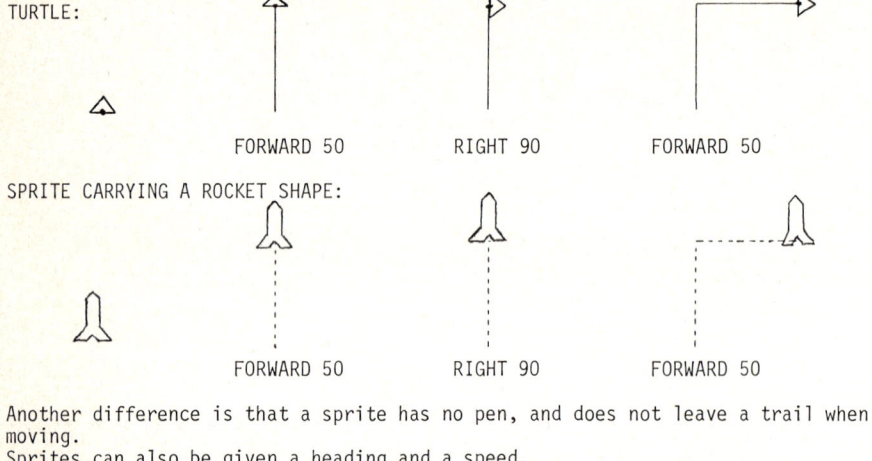

TURTLE:

                 FORWARD 50   RIGHT 90   FORWARD 50

SPRITE CARRYING A ROCKET SHAPE:

                 FORWARD 50   RIGHT 90   FORWARD 50

Another difference is that a sprite has no pen, and does not leave a trail when moving.
Sprites can also be given a heading and a speed.
Five pre-defined shapes (a plane, a truck, a rocket, a ball and a box) are available, but we deliberately choose not to mention them, thinking that children would be more strongly involved with shapes of their own.
Shapes are designed by the user on a 16x16 grid, each square being either given no color or a color to be specified later on: this is achieved using arrow keys alone or together with the function key. Of course first graders are not used to drawing pictures on a grid, and the first shapes were copied from paper models created by the teachers. After a while, the students gain some ideas on how to draw a shape on a grid, but generally produce very tiny designs, which are almost invisible when carried by a sprite.

As anticipated, children developed a strong feeling of possession on these shapes, and we almost experienced a real drama when we displayed posters with the different new shapes available on each micro-computer (we had two of them for the very first experiment), one of the children proving quite shocked: "why do they have my frog!"

Taking inspiration from the shapes exhibited on the posters, the children imagined a tale (some new shapes were created at that time, according to specific needs expressed by the pupils for their own story) and "drew" it on the computer. Some expressed the idea that "it would be nice to have some sprites move", and were told how to give a heading and a speed to the corresponding sprites.
Most of the tales were rather peaceful and friendly (flowers and animals were abundantly used) but a few groups produced war stories, suggesting two planes crashing each other in flight.

PROBLEMS AND WEAKNESSES.

The most unpleasant constraint is the present schedules: we had some short experiments (two weeks with daily practice) which is a little frustrating both for the class when the machine goes away and for the observer. A one year experiment offers more sessions, but they take place only once a week, at a fixed period in the week. A few teachers begin to use the same micro-computer and version of T.I.-LOGO in a much more informal way: the machine is available to the pupils all day long, most of the classroom activities being organised as workshops. They report of a very quick adaptation of children, and mutual teaching spontaneously taking place. Unfortunately, the teacher being at the same time the only observer has very little time to gather precise information on how this works. He/she is a good witness of what has been achieved by the kids, but knows too little about how they did it.
Since we wish to collect similar observations about all the pupils in the class, we can't let them completely free to explore the system. We also have too little confidence in their capability to master the various tasks required for designing sprites (especially for those who are considered as low ability students) and we usually worry much too much on how to make it easier for the children.

WHAT IS BEING LEARNED THROUGH SUCH ACTIVITIES ?

Children learn very little about computers and programming, but, as stressed at the beginning, this was not our goal. First graders only "drive" their sprites, but do not write procedures. |5|
Preparing new shapes provides many activities related to counting:
- counting squares on the model and on the grid. This is not as simple as one might imagine, since counting squares is not the same as counting their sides (the old problem about trees and intervals). Besides, the counting rhyme is not yet stable at this stage (omissions, flips...)
- adding -and sometimes even subtracting - several numbers in order to make sure that the sum always comes up to 16 on each row and each column.
Spatialization is also intensely practised:
- paths on a grid
- right and left, up and down, above and under...
Symmetry is intuitively used by the pupils as a help to draw their shapes: symmetrical shapes are much better reproduced than non-symmetrical or nearly symmetrical ones. Spontaneous square-grid drawings are produced by the children, brightly colored and showing evidences of their sense of symmetry (reflection, rotation symmetry or translation).
The fact that "right" is always on the same side (as opposed to the turtle's own right, which sometimes is your left)

        △   ▽

   The turtle's right   The turtle's right
   is the same as mine   is <u>my left</u>

makes the world of sprites better able to meet the needs of first graders.

CONCLUSION.

Besides offering a very relevant classroom activity for first graders, the world of sprites enables numerous observations on children's activities and strategies. We still have too few reports (two short sessions and a one year experiment have been observed on a research point of view; a few other observations are available from teachers working on their own in their classroom) to be able to document precisely different profiles, though this is one point we wish to focus on. We also hope to have the opportunity to continue this experiment for a second year with the same children, which should lead them to writing procedures for sprites. A few sessions with third graders showed a much more rapid adaptation to the machine and its constraints, and a very efficient team work leading to writing procedures within a rather short time; but all the general observations we made on first graders remain true.

REFERENCES

|1| Berdonneau C., and Dumas R.-M., Des enfants, des nombres, et une tortue, in: Pratique Active de l'Informatique par l'Enfant, Recherches Pédagogiques n° 111 (I.N.R.P.-S.E.V.P.E.N., Paris, 1981)

|2| Papert S., Mindstorms: Children, Computers and Powerful Ideas (Basic Books, New-York, 1980)

|3| Musha D. R., Levis C. L. and Overall T., T.I.-LOGO Curriculum Guide (Texas Instruments, 1981)

|4| several papers in Byte, Vol. 7 n° 8 (August 1982)

|5| Berdonneau C., Lutins au Cours Préparatoire (G.R.E.P.A.C.I.F.I.C., Paris, 1982)

Editorial footnote

In France, first graders mean children of age 6 years.

MICROS IN THE PRIMARY CLASSROOM - THE ITMA TRAINING MATERIALS

Jan Stewart, Rosemary Fraser, Jane Petty, Hugh Burkhardt

The ITMA Collaboration

The College of St. Mark and St. John, Plymouth.

Shell Centre for Mathematical Education, The University of Nottingham.

The MICROS IN THE PRIMARY CLASSROOM course consists of five modules. Each provides an exploration of computer based materials centred on classroom activities. Although each module can be used independently, the set is written to provide a structure aimed at gradually developing the teacher's confidence and awareness. Programs such as CLUE, SLYFOX and SEEK show how teachers and pupils can create their own materials without needing computer expertise. As new programs emerge from various sources they can be incorporated easily into the classroom explorations that are timetabled in the Course Readers.

The introduction of microcomputers into primary schools offers great potential for future teacher training provision. In particular it could form a focus for reviewing classroom activities in terms of both content and teaching style bringing a new challenge to the integration, management and use of resources within one or several institutions.

For training courses to succeed, however, they need, like all good educational activities, to involve teachers actively and practically in their own learning. Far too much money has already been wasted on the mere provision of quality materials or the isolated, passive lecture. Teachers need to learn by doing.

Let us listen in on two teachers using Module I. They are browsing through a program called PIRATES. Before them is a 'Course Reader'. This has guided them through making their timetable for the evening and they are now following suggestions for simulating a lesson with PIRATES, a supporting program which involves the location of hidden treasure based on clues from the micro.

Teacher 1: (Reads from screen) Another problem? Now, we make our choices here don't we.

Teacher 2: Press 'Y' for yes and let's leave the clues the same but go on to a bigger grid.

Teacher 1: 'Y' and 'G'?

Teacher 2: Yes and then 'Return'.

Teacher 1: How big shall we make the grid?

Teacher 2: Well, 100 by 100 would challenge my lot. They'll cope with the 9 by 9 grid but I'd like them to see if they can use the same strategies on even bigger grids.

Teacher 1: How big can the grid be?

Teacher 2:	Let's get the Program Notes ......mmm (browses) Gosh, you're not going to believe this!
Teacher 1:	(Laughs) Why?
Teacher 2:	You can go up to 99,999 each way AND on to negative axes (Laughs).
Teacher 1:	Well, let's do this (points to Course Reader). It says "enter - 1,000, 1,000 for x and - 1,000, 1,000 for y" and, oh I like this! (reads) 'Pupils now begin to perform at a level much above the 8-9 year stage'. You bet they do!
Teacher 2:	Well, we can always 'quit'! Press Return and I'll guess 0, 0.
Teacher 1:	Why?
Teacher 2:	Well, it's roughly in the middle and it will cut out a lot of the chart.
Teacher 1:	(Reads from screen) Ah! - Go NE 500, 500?
Teacher 2:	Good idea ....

Micros in the Primary Classroom - the course being used - aims at meeting the needs for teachers who are confident with the basic running of the new technology and have tried out a range of ideas in their classroooms. It would provide an ideal extension to the Micro Primer packs provided by M.E.P. (see paper by R. Jones, p. 27).

Based on five modules, the first two - 'The Classroom, the Micro and You' and 'The Curriculum and the Micro' - create opportunities for considering the place of the microcomputer in the learning environment of the primary school.

At first the teachers are simply asked to browse through the materials, explore them with their classes and observe. Each will use them in a significantly different way (a fact often ignored by program designers) and yet patterns will probably emerge. First, they may begin to understand some of the roles a computer may play within the classroom. Secondly, they may experience some effect on their own teaching style - perhaps with some programs a move from the authoritative didactic posture so often imposed in some classroom relationships to the role of consultant and counsellor for the solution of computer set problems. Also, they may even observe interesting changes in behaviour or attitudes in their children.

By the end of Module II it is hoped that teachers may begin to appreciate the potential of the new technology for widening the range of activities within a school. Several recent reports have, for example, suggested that factual recall and skill exercises of an imitative kind feature largely in some classrooms and many computer programs met by teachers will also fall into this category. Others, like PIRATES, however, encourage the development of strategic skills and the application of knowledge by presenting open investigative situations to the children. Normally such a 'problem solving' approach is very demanding on the teacher as it requires styles of working that most find too difficult to employ. Research by ITMA has shown, however, that one of the most important single contributions of the micro could be in supporting and encouraging teachers to adopt such an approach.

As Modules I and II progress the course programs themselves are critically examined as to their potential for learning and teaching. This is done by the filling in of the matrix (Fig. 1). Note here how the teachers must imagine how the materials might be used in a range of schools (filled in by X's) as well as in

Micros in the Primary Classroom 163

Program matrix	Module 1				Module 2			Module 3						Module 4			Module 5
	PIRATES	BIGALF	BURGLAR	COUNTERS	WORDWORM	JANEPLUS	BARSET	BARPIC	AUTOSUM	OOPS	BLOK	AIRTEMP	EUREKA	EDDY	CLUE	SEEK	THINK	INTREE	SLYFOX	SCENE
Skill learning			▓																	
Concept learning			✕																	
Concept reinforcement			▓																	
Skill practice																				
Strategy development			⊠																	
Problem-solving																				
Investigations																				
Computer-managed activity			▓																	
Teacher/child/computer activity			✕																	
Large-group activity																				
Small-group activity			✕																	
Individual activity			▓																	

○ indicates probable use by you;
✕ indicates possible use by other teachers;
|||| indicates that you actually achieved this in class.

Figure 1

their own situation (marked by 'O's). The subsequent blocking in of a section (with vertical lines -||||) would indicate the teacher's actual progress in using the program with the children. As an example you can see on Figure 1 that one teacher thought that she might use BURGLAR (a Module I program in which children must discover the number the computer has thought of) for skill learning, concept reinforcement and strategy developing as an individual activity managed completely by the computer (O's). She envisaged, however, that in addition the program COULD be used for concept learning and be managed by the teacher with an individual or small group (X's). When she finally tried out the program, however, she used it as she had planned but did not exploit the strategy-developing potential of the program (||||'s).

By the end of Module II it is hoped that teachers will not only be discussing the place of the microcomputer in the curriculum but, indeed, the primary curriculum as a whole. Material within the Course Reader of Module II is aimed specifically at stimulating this.

On reaching Module III teachers will have already experienced a range of managerial constraints presented by introducing the new technology and its supporting software into their classrooms and schools. They will also have begun to consider on their matrices (Fig. 1) a range of different forms of organisation that may be used even for one program. This whole question of 'management' is now taken further. Module III gives advice on a range of problems - even such fundamentals as the arrangement of classroom furniture for clear viewing of a screen by a large group or points to consider when formulating a school policy for movement of the machine around the school.

A great emphasis is also placed on the need for teachers to provide non-computer supporting materials and activities for most programs - a collection of which can form an important section of any school resources library. This is clearly indicated by the module's supporting programs. BLOK, for example, a logic program using multi-attribute materials, cannot be successfully used without considerable pre-knowledge of logic games by the children. The availability of suitable concrete materials is also crucial. BLOK can, however, make a valuable contribution to learning when part of a carefully planned group of logic activities.

Similarly, EUREKA (Fig. 2), a program which develops skill in the interpretation and sketching of graphs, can lead to some valuable work away from the computer.

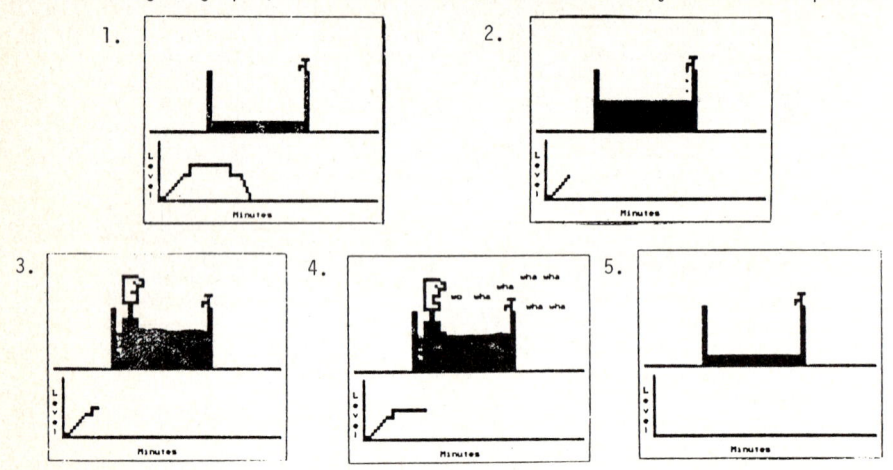

EUREKA simple entries (T = taps on or off, etc.) allow the construction of scenarios for taking a bath; the cartoon illustration of what occurs is matched by a graph of water-level against time, either of which can be suppressed if pupils are to sketch the curve or interpret the graph. A replay facility allows the results to be described and discussed.

Figure 2

Look, for example, at the work of Suzanne (Fig. 3). Having built up 'story-lines' with the man in the bath and then guessed the 'story' of a graph produced by the computer without supporting pictures, Suzanne produces a story of her own in three ways - words, pictures and graph. Folding the top section down she presents the latter to Jonathan who writes his 'version' of events. In checking, Suzanne reflects on her own efforts and comes to some perceptive conclusions. Thus as much valuable work can result after 'turning off' the EUREKA program as when it is in use - something which must be given considerable thought by teachers when using any computer materials.

Further managerial problems are presented in Module III through two 'film mode' programs, AUTOSUM and OOPS. Both randomly produce 'sums' with a content and level set by the teacher, but in OOPS an occasional wrong answer is included to be spotted by the children. At first the continuous nature of these materials may puzzle or even alarm the teacher. Valuable managerial tactics are developed, however, through discussing and evaluating their classroom potential. The additional facility to 'control' the content of the problems presented gives some support to this otherwise unusual and less familiar type of program.

Finally, another 'different' use of the microcomputer is introduced through EDDY - a simple word processor for use by children or teachers. This has created great

Suzanne

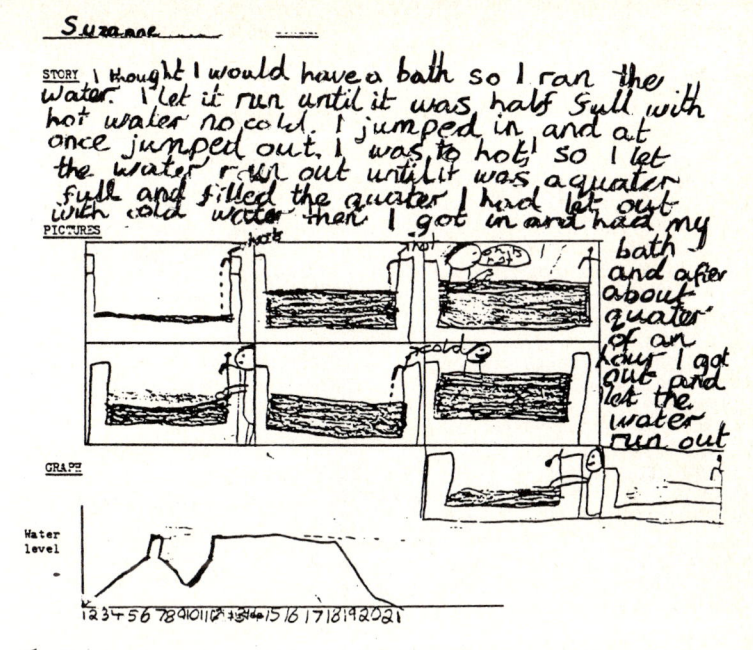

STORY I thought I would have a bath so I ran the water. I let it run until it was half full with hot water no cold. I jumped in and at once jumped out. I was to hot, so I let the water run out untill it was a quater full and filled the quater I had let out with cold water then I got in and had my bath and after about a quater of an hour I got out and let the water run out

PICTURES

GRAPH

Jonathans story of my graph Puts the plug in, turns water on, rises and then gets in stays for a little while and then gets out, and it goes down, and gets in again, then it rises, and then stays in for a long time and pulls the plug out.

My comments This was quite good but Jonathan said that the first time I stayed in for a little while but I was meant to have jumped striaght out again but my graph may have decived him

After EUREKA has been 'switched off', Suzanne writes a story in three ways. Jonathan makes a suggestion about the 'story' described in her graph and Suzanne uses this to review her own efforts - with some interesting conclusions.

Figure 3

interest and, although requiring a printer, extends the teacher's view of the potential of the new technology. Files created on EDDY can then be 'marked' in CLUE (its supporting program) and these 'marks' (which we call 'flags') allocated different functions. For example, a text created on EDDY could have every tenth word flagged and deleted on CLUE. The same text can be jumbled for a sequencing exercise - simply achieved by flagging the beginnings of sections and using the 'print/jumbled' CLUE option. Thus, printed materials are produced for use by groups in school. Checking of 'results', e.g. finding the actual missing words in a text can be checked on the screen by allocating those words to be a colour, (e.g. red) instead of deleting, but the main purpose is to generate quickly useful non-computer materials for the higher reading skills.

Module III concludes by dealing with a further management need - that of evaluating the quality and potential of any computer materials. This is done through a detailed twenty-eight point check list. Here, some points can be answered by simply browsing through a program; others require careful observation in the classroom. In the early stages such an evaluation is laborious. The task does, however, place a structure within the teacher's mind to enable ultimately a rapid and skilled assessment of new materials - hence its inclusion in the course.

By Module IV and V teachers are ready to explore some specially designed systems, SEEK, THINK and SLYFOX, for which they can create their own materials. INTREE and SCENE enable the rapid execution of these original ideas without any prior knowledge of programming by the user. SEEK and THINK, two binary classification systems, develop observation and language skills and may be used for a wide range of tasks from simple identification of slugs or unknown white powders to an exploration of the feelings of Napolean as he fights the battle of Waterloo. SLYFOX develops the skills of logic, language, visualisation and problem solving as children search for a fox in a farmyard or an alien invader on their space ship (Fig. 4). The power of all systems becomes most apparent as teachers and children generate their own 'searches' which fit in with their individual interests and curricula.

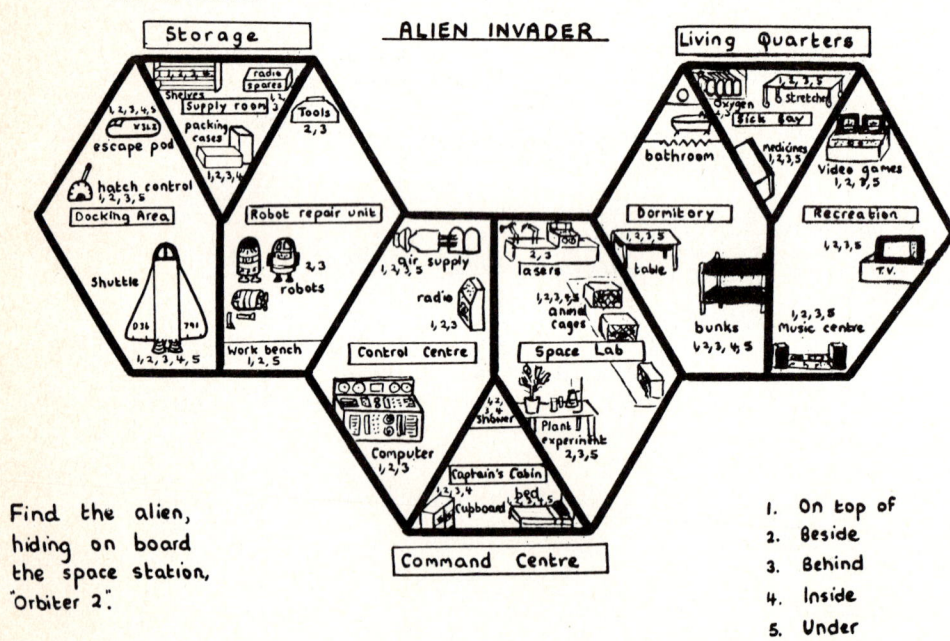

Pupil support materials for SLYFOX 'scene' created by a teacher without any computer expertise. Other 'teacher-authorship' materials of this kind include BARSET (Mod. II), CLUE (Mod. III) and SEEK (Mod. IV).

Figure 4

'Micros in the Primary Classroom' therefore aims at providing a very practical course for examining some sophisticated aspects of using the new technology in schools. Being flexible it can be used by lecturers working from a centre such as a College, for a 'school-based' course or even as a distance learning pack by teachers themselves. To cope with the different expertise of users each Module contains a 'Course Reader' suggesting suitable timetables for exploring the materials, plus valuable supporting information. The activities in a module vary - some occupying three or four weeks, others, e.g. Module IV, requiring a whole term. Also, they may be tackled in any order or Modules bought separately according to the teacher's interests and needs.

Several of the programs can be used across the whole age and ability range. The discussion in the staff room over coffee of teachers' experiences and explorations of the same material at different levels, should promote a healthy sharing of ideas and an enjoyable way of reviewing the primary curriculum both with and without a computer.

Burkhardt, H. et al (pending) Human Interactions with Computers in Complex Situations I.T.M.A. Plymouth/Nottingham

D.E.S. (1982) Mathematics Counts: Report of the Committee of Inquiry into the Teaching of Mathematics in School (Chairman: W. H. Cockcroft) H.M.S.O.: London

Fraser, R. et al (1983) Micros in the Primary Classroom Longmans: London

Fraser, R. et al (pending) Learning Activities and Classroom Roles I.T.M.A. Plymouth/Nottingham

Editorial footnote

In England, the term 'Primary' usually refers to the age range 5-11 years but sometimes extends to 12 or 13 years old.

SOFTWARE FOR THE ELEMENTARY SCHOOL

Glenn Fisher

Alameda County Superintendent of Schools Office
685 A Street, Hayward, CA 94541 USA

ABSTRACT

Software is the determinant factor in how a computer is used. The essential issue of computer use in elementary schools is the availability of appropriate software. Software available for instructional use at the elementary level in the United States consists mainly of drill and practice materials of a widely varying degree of instructional sophistication. Much of the recent highly regarded software is not drill, but problem solving and simulations. These types of software are more difficult to use in the classroom, and their use has serious implications for curriculum development and teacher training. Most schools curricula do not support extensive use of this type of software, and teachers are not trained in these areas.

Many schools and districts are developing evaluation processes and creating procedures for selecting software. There are 17 major evaluation projects with federal or state funding in the United States. Some states are considering treating software like textbooks for state evaluation and adoption. This has drastic consequences for the software market.

The issue of integration of computers into the curriculum affects software use, yet it has not been addressed by most schools and districts. Will the future hold sophisticated uses of computers in elementary schools - word processing, the use of spelling and grammar checkers, extensive simulations and problem solving - or will the major use be as a supplement to instruction through computerized drill?

SOFTWARE EVALUATION

ISSUES IN EVALUATION
     Most evaluation forms and procedures divide the process into three areas:
          ** content
          ** instruction
          ** technical aspects
Content judges the accuracy of the factual content of the program. Instruction focuses on the pedagogical design of the program. "Is it effective in providing for student learning?" is the major question. The manner of response to student entries, the format, the manner of providing feedback, and the sequence of the program are considerations. Technical aspects reflect the programmer's competence in writing the program.

Clearly, the important issues are the content of the program, and the ability of the program to effectively help students learn. There are two critical problems:
(1) inherent bias in much software and
(2) the lack of a sound pedagogical basis for software design.

Many educators at first glance feel there is no bias in available software. However, there is often considerable bias in the format of the program, and in symbolic or image elements. Often the graphics used for rewards involve symbols of more appeal to a particular group (boys) than to others. In one math program, for example, after you get ten problems right you get to fly a rocket ship and try to blow up asteroids. This type of violent, aggressive action, and the images of rockets, tend to appeal more to boys than to girls. Thomas Malone found that there were significant differences between what elementary school age boys and girls liked best in a program.[1] In general, girls liked programs dealing with words, without competition and aggressive action, and with a degree of fantasy. Boys also liked fantasy, but preferred more aggressive, competitive action, and preferred pictures and numbers to words. These biases in programs tend to discourage computer use by girls and by minority students.

Little is known about the effect of the format of the program on the learning of content. For example, students often view the simulation "Oregon Trail" as a game, rather than as a serious imitation of the events occurring to travellers on the 2000 mile wagon road to the Oregon Territory.[12] How could the format and content be changed so students learn the appropriate facts and attitudes, rather than irrelevant ones? The degree of competition in many games, the format, the pacing, and the symbols used all affect the student's learning, yet most research has focused on the overall impact of the software (gain in learning) rather than on the impact of the different components. The wide range of results from studies of effectiveness of computers may come from the lack of a coherent use of research about learning in designing educational software.

SOURCES OF REVIEWS

Teachers and schools are now looking for evaluations of software to help them spend their money wisely. Most teachers simply select programs from software catalogs, since reviews are not readily available. In the United States, there are five private ventures publishing reviews of educational software [2] and many public ones.[3] All of these publications together have reviewed less than 1000 software products, out of an estimated market of 10000. Many of these reviews are not accessible to teachers as they select software. The states of New York and North Carolina require software to be submitted for review at the state level. Favorably reviewed software is listed and can be purchased with school funds. California has produced a "preview list" of software favorably reviewed by school software evaluation projects.[3]

Some states are considering including software with textbook evaluation. It is not clear how software evaluation can best be handled, but the crucial issue is making appropriate reviews available to teachers.

TYPES OF INSTRUCTIONAL SOFTWARE

The availablity of software directly affects the uses made of computers. The main uses are drill and practice (47%), learning enrichment (19%), and computer literacy (including programming) (29%).[4] In California, 83% of the schools with computers use them for computer-assisted instruction.[5] Some use is made of simulations, and of those applications often seen in business-- word processing, data management, computation and finances. The availablity of appropriate software is a major issue, even for teaching programming. Much software of types other than drill is designed for the home or business environment, and is inappropriate at school. What is required for software to make computers useful for students in a school environment?

DRILL & PRACTICE

As a quick glance through software catalogs will confirm, most of the educational software available is drill and practice-- computer assisted instruction. Many educators are critical of the "electronic ditto machine" nature of much software. Publishers are critized for rushing their print mater-ials onto the computer without considering the differences in the media, nor taking advantage of the unique capabilities of the computer. For example, the Milliken Math Sequences presents problems with all digits in white. When a student answers correctly, brightly colored, animated figures appear. The educational impact might have been far greater if the color had been used for different digits to indicate place value, or to otherwise support the content, rather than just as part of the reward.

Assumptions about the use of drill and practice also cause overuse. Many teachers provide the same drill at the computer for all students. One of the touted advantages of the computer is the ability to individualize instruction by providing separate, appropriate instruction for each student. While the computer can be used to provide different lessons for each student, the teacher must schedule and keep records on all this--a formidable task. There are some drill programs where the computer can also provide management, but few teachers make use of this feature. (The two main reasons for this seem to be lack of funds to buy multiple copies of software and the time it takes to set up and maintain such a system.)

Many programs use a game format to provide interest. In some of these programs, the students play the game by answering the questions (The Game Show, for example).[12] In other programs, when students reach a set achievement level, they are rewarded with a few minutes to play a game (Stalker).[12] While there has been research to show that the ability to work another problem is strongly motivating (i.e., appropriate drill is its own reward), to my knowledge there has been no research on learning outcomes with such gamey programs.

Another problem with drill and practice software is an underlying bias, as discussed earlier.

SIMULATIONS

Many educators feel that simulations are one of the most promising uses of computers in education. Simulations like Volcano, Factory, Rocky's Boots, and Snooper Troopers have been highly acclaimed in reviews.[12] There is no question that these programs are engaging to students, and that learning takes place.

However, the average classroom cannot provide the amount of time to individual students that many simulations require--from 20 minutes to several hours. There is not enough access time to the computer, and there are too many other subjects to be covered. In addition, many teachers have minimal training in teaching problem solving skills. Many curricula provide little time for, or emphasis on, problem solving skills. Informal surveys of teachers indicate much interest in simulations, but little use of them. These simulations may find significant use in the home; many are being advertised to the home market.

WORD PROCESSING

The use of word processing with students clearly illustrates the problem of lack of appropriate software. Many teachers have begun to use word processing with elementary students, with exceptional results.[6] Until recently, the available word processors were written for secretarial use in an office environment. Many of them had features that made them difficult for students to learn and use, such as multiple key strokes, extensive memorizing of codes, and lack of help or instructions on the screen. Bank Street Writer, released during the fall of 1982, was the first word processor designed specifically for use by students. It is menu driven, always has a prompt/explanation line on the screen, and has other features designed to make it easy for students to learn it and use it.[12]

An ancillary to word processing may cause the next big debate in education: spelling check programs. These programs are used in conjunction with word processing programs to find misspelled words, and mark them. The student may then add the word to the program's dictionary, correct it, or do nothing. There are similar programs which will count word and phrase frequency, and indicate possible grammatical problems. Programs like these provide students with powerful help. Will these programs make spelling classes obsolete? What skills will we need to teach? What effect will this have on the curriculum? It is likely that these problems will be faced again and again as other powerful uses of computers are brought into the schools.

OTHER USES OF COMPUTERS

The Montgomery County MD (7) computer curriculum includes several lessons using data bases (for example, to sort and generate data about population changes for states of the United States). It is hard to see what are appropriate uses of data bases for students, even though it seems that students should be introduced to this powerful use of computers.

The calculating power of the computer can provide information to students and help them understand numerical information. As in data base management, this use of computers has not yet filtered down to elementary level. However, the calculating power of the computer could be used to enormous advantage by helping elementary students achieve a better understanding of numerical relationships. While a calculator can be used for calculating, the computer's ability to provide an instructional dialog using the student's language is a significant benefit at the elementary level. The computer, unlike the calculator, can explain which number to enter, and can comment on results.

PROGRAMMING PROGRAMS/LANGUAGES

Many elementary teachers are teaching programming to their students as computers become available in their schools. These teachers are interested in the development and use of languages appropriate for this age of student. While BASIC is widely available, its mathematical orientation, its lack of structure, and its lack of immediacy make it less than ideal. Logo and PILOT are alternatives. We need to ask, "What are students learning from this language?" We must also be aware of biases within these languages which may make them less attractive to certain groups of students. There is little research to substantiate some of the claims made for Logo.[8,9] Some preliminary information from the Cupertino Union School District (Cupertino, CA) indicates that girls are indeed more likely to enroll in Logo classes than in BASIC classes. On the other hand, to provide the discovery atmosphere desired for Logo requires much effort on the part of the teacher. Learning Logo and learning to provide this atmosphere requires training which doesn't yet exist.

Some teachers effectively introduce programming with "pseudo-languages." These programs mimic some of the attributes of a programming language, providing for storage of instructions with immediate and deferred execution and possibly some control commands. PAK JANA and FACEMAKER are two examples.[12] Because the student sees results immediately, young students who don't have the patience, typing ability, or interest to generate programs in BASIC can have fun and have the experience of programming the computer. Most of these programs use simple commands which require few keystrokes, also making them more accessible to students.

Some of the most important benefits of programming may not be the knowledge-domain results, such as logical thinking, which are usually claimed. The most consistent comment from teachers about student's reaction to programming seems to focus on affective domain results--dramatic changes in student's self-esteem and attitudes towards school. Some of this change may relate to Papert's claim in MINDSTORMS that programming puts students in control of the computer, giving them a feeling of power.[8] The potential for attitude changes seems to be greatest among those students who are least successful at school--special education, learning disabled, and "under achievers."

FUTURE ISSUES IN EDUCATIONAL SOFTWARE

The major issue in educational software is becoming the integration of computers into the curriculum. The use of drill and practice software represents the adoption of computers to meet current curriculum goals. However, the capabilities of computers make possible new activities (programming), and new ways of teaching (simulations, word processing). Will schools change their curricula to reflect these potential uses of the computer, or will they continue to use computers to prop up outdated objectives? What we are looking at is the ability of an institution--public schooling--to cope with change. That ten years of abundant calculators have caused no changes in content or organization of the curriculum is cause for concern.

What use will be made of the increasingly creative, innovative educational software that is available? Computers already are accessible to many students at home and this trend is expected to continue.[5] What will happen with home "schooling" using computers? Already, curriculum packages covering extensive content in math and reading are commercially available, allowing a parent to provide years of instruction in these areas at a home computer. In addition, many of the more innovative programs involve simulations or adventure-game style discovery activities, requiring substantial access to computers. These activities are unlikely in schools where the average student spends less than 3 minutes per day at the computer [4]. Access time is much less of a problem for those students who have computers at home, and there is already widespread concern about the creation of a new division into "haves" and "have-nots"--those who have computers at home and those who don't. The California Assessment Program survey found that there was indeed a strong correlation between socio-economic status (parents' job types) and computer access [5].

The last concern for the future is the issue of copying. LeRoy Finkel paints a picture of a bleak future where most computer use is for programming, and there is no instructional software available; small companies have gone out of business and large ones decided not to enter the market due to widespread illegal copying. [10] Many schools are purchasing disk sharing (networking) systems, only to find that most copylocked software cannot be used. Few vendors have any plan at all for providing software to operate on networks. Many teachers openly flaunt copyright laws, often using the excuse of poverty. There are some possible solutions to this nightmare. Obviously, the educational establishment must stop illegal copying. The software publishing companies in turn must face the existence of network systems and the need for multiple use licensing for schools. Already, backup and replacement policies have become reasonable and appropriate [11], so there is hope.

CONCLUSION

While there seem to be many obstacles in the way of appropriate and effective use of computers in the schools, there are signs that teachers, parents, and students are effectively pressuring schools to adopt computers and to use them wisely. The major problems are just beginning. Software will be abundant only if some solution is found to the problem of illegal copying. Powerful uses of computers, such as word processing, will depend upon having many computers in schools and upon curriculum changes of a wide-spread and far-sighted nature. How these problems are met and solved or not solved will determine the structure of schooling and the importance of a formal school system in our country in the future. It will also affect the position of our country in the community of nations as our youth grow up with or without significant exposure to computers.

REFERENCES

[1] WHAT MAKES THINGS FUN TO LEARN: A STUDY OF INTRINSICALLY MOTIVATING COMPUTER GAMES, Thomas Malone, Xerox Palo Alto Research Corp., Palo Alto, 1980

[2] EPIE, Educational Products Information Exchange; Dresden School Microware Reviews, Box 246, Dresden ME 04342; Courseware Report Card, 150 W. Carob St., Compton, CA 90220; Journal of Courseware Review, Apple Computer, 20863 Stevens Creek Blvd., Cupertino CA 95014; Software Review Digest, School & Home Courseware Journal, 1341 Bulldog Ln. Suite C, Fresno, CA 93710

[3] MicroSift, NWREL, 300 S.W. 6th Ave., Portland, OR 97204; Arizona State University Microcomputer Research Clinic, Gary Bitter, Arizona State University, Tempe AZ; California Library Media Consortium, Ann Lathrop, SMCOE, 333 Main St., Redwood City, CA 94063; Comp-You-Ter Project (IVC), Pat Johnson, Watertown, SD; DISC Project, Carol Kelnow, IICD-Oakland Schools, MI; Florida Center for Instructional Computing; MACUL, WCISD, 33500 Van Born Rd., Wayne MI; Microcomputers in Education, Bill Heck, Robinsdale Area Schools, Robinsdale MN; Micro-Ideas, Fred Bockmann; MECC, 2520 Broadway, St. Paul, MN 55133; North Carolina St. Dpt. of Public Instr., Div. of Evaluation Services, Raleigh, NC; Putnam/Northern Westchester BOCES, NY; Texas TABS, Ft. Bend ISD, TX; TIES, MN

[4] U.S. Department of Education survey, SURVEY OF MICROCOMPUTER USES IN SCHOOLS, October 1982. Figures given for K-6 schools. Instructor Magazine survey, October 1981. K-8 teachers reported 60% drill & practice, 30% problem solving, 45% computer literacy, 40% computer progr.

[5] California Assessment Program, 1981-82 ANNUAL REPORT, "Chapter VIII: Computers in California Elementary Schools," Cal. State Department of Education, 1982. About 20% of students had access to a microcomputer at home, about 20% had access at school, mostly on a once-a-week basis; about 6% had "almost daily" access. surveyed all Cal. 6th graders.

[6] "Word Processing: Can It Make Even Good Writers Better?", Collette Daiute, Electronic Learning, Mar./Apr. 1982, Vl #4, p.29 ff. "Word Processing--Will It Make All Kids Love to Write?," Glenn Fisher, Instructor, Feb. 1983, Vol. XCII #6, p. 87 ff.

[7] MY STUDENTS USE COMPUTERS, Beverley Hunter, Reston Publishing Co., Reston, VA, 1983. Published form of a curriculum developed by HumRRO for Montgomery County Public Schools.

[8] MINDSTORMS, Seymour Papert, Basic Books

[9] BYTE, August 1982. Entire issue devoted to Logo.

[10] Luncheon address at "Forward to the 3 Cs Conference," Arizona State University, March 18,1983. LeRoy Finkel is author of numerous books on computers, and is Computer Curriculum Coordinator at the San Mateo County Office of Education, CA.

[11] A backup disk with the original is $10, $5, or free. Replacement copies are usually less than $25 when the damaged disk is returned.

[12] OREGON TRAIL, SOFTSWAP, SMCOE, 333 Main Street, Redwood City CA 94063,or MECC[3]. THE GAME SHOW, Computer-Advanced Ideas, 1442A Walnut St. #341, Berkeley CA, Apple . STALKER, from Cal. School for the Deaf, SOFTSWAP, Apple . VOLCANOES, Earthware, P.O. Box 30039, Eugene OR 97403, Apple. FACTORY, Sunburst, 39 Washington Ave., Pleasantville NY 14850, Atari. ROCKY'S BOOTS, Learning Co., 4370 Alpine Rd., Portola Valley CA 94025, various. SNOOPER TROOPERS, Spinnaker Software, 215 First St. CAmbridge MA 02142, Apple . BANK STREET WRITER, Scholastic, 904 Sylvan Ave., Englewood Cliffs NJ 07632, Apple. PAK JANA, SOFTSWAP, PET. FACEMAKER, Spinnaker, Apple.

SESSION 9

Session 9 - Discussion Groups

The conference was divided into five groups to discuss the following questions:

1. **HOW SHALL WE USE COMPUTERS IN THE ELEMENTARY CLASSROOM?**

    Is the computer to be used as

    - just another pedagogical device?
    - a drill and practice machine?
    - a creative stimulant to extend the capabilities of the mind?
    - a problem solving medium, for instance through simulation?
    - an expert system for resource based learning?

    AND WHAT ARE OUR AIMS?

    Is our aim to achieve computer literacy, for example through the development of thinking models?

    OR

    Do we wish to enhance the creativity of our pupils?

2. **WHAT STRATEGIES SHOULD WE ADOPT TO PREPARE SOFTWARE AND TEACHING MATERIALS?**

    - Do we use teachers?
    - Do we use publishers?
    - Do we use manufacturers?
    - What about the children?
    - Does government have a role?
    - Who guarantees the quality?

3. **HOW CAN RESEARCH ASSESS THE EFFECTIVENESS OF OUR DEVELOPMENTS?**

    Can research help us with the design of our software and teaching methods?

The groups reported to a main session in which further discussion took place.

GROUP 1

Chairman: H. BAUERSFELD
Rapporteur: D. MARTIN

There was definite interest in examining the issues of research and evaluation and a strong feeling that there was a lack of and need for both at the elementary level. However, the majority felt that aims for the use of the computer at that level should be tackled first. It was suggested that there should be a more relaxed definition of research to include the development stage, the users' experience and the evaluation process into an integrated, self-improving system.

The computer as a pedagogical tool was described as one among many possible devices, with the burden falling upon the teacher to choose the best device to meet a given objective. Computers are different from other devices, however, in that they are non-exclusive, general purpose tools which require great discretion in use because there is the danger of allowing them to assume too much responsiblity to the detriment of education. They are both the medium and the message and must be introduced in such a way as to give children a realistic view of how they are used in society at large.

After some discussion the group attempted to put forward a theoretical framework for evaluating positive and negative aspects of computer use in elementary education. The aim of using computers in elementary education is to enhance elementary education. The aim of elementary education is to help every child reach his/her full human potential and to achieve social, emotional, and mental maturity. When computers are introduced into schools, we should be concerned about three levels of use - the technical level (how and when to use them), the understanding level (why they bring about the results they do) and the reflective level (the personal and societal values involved in using them).

GROUP 2

Chairman: R. LAUTERBACH
Rapporteur: J. STEWART

The group could see a use for the microcomputer in all areas suggested. It was thought, however, that the list may be incomplete. Were children not building computers or using them as toys at home? Should these aspects also be considered by teachers?

It was thought that "aiming at computer literacy" was not as useful a term as "illustrating the relationship between computer and society" when discussing aims. The "this or that" approach was also criticized and the group preferred to remove the word "or" completely and concentrate on listing aims. Several new ones were suggested including enhancing learning and the learning environment and enhancing teaching. Once a list was made however it automatically raised the issue of "aim priorities". Some group members thought however that the latter would discourage teachers from selecting the aspects on which to concentrate. Finally, it was suggested that teachers should not try to achieve all the aims at any one time - the concentration on single aims being preferable.

Instead of considering how individuals should be involved in software production strategies, the group moved to general suggestions. The preference for teams with a common aim was strong. Also it was thought that for these teams software production should be a realistic task i.e. money, time, good programmers and administrators, access to schools and teachers etc. should be readily available. The involvement of young programmers was discussed which raised issues about motivating program writers to document their software well. As a generally difficult, tedious task it was thought that incentives should be found for development teams to see their materials through to a usable state. The successful method of the British Open University in employing seconded teachers for a limited period to produce software was quoted as one example of what might be done.

On the government's role in software production it was thought that individual initiatives should be encouraged but not individual evaluation.

It was felt by some that the quality of programs might be shown in teachers' responses to them i.e. if they were used in school. The rating system adopted by computer magazines for games was discussed and also a "Which?" magazine (a British Publication of a consumer group which evaluates in a ruthless but unbiased way the effectiveness of many aspects of life from washing machines to holidays) on computer programs was suggested. Why should education be different from any other aspect of society?

Finally, it was felt that there was no way forward in teaching with microcomputers without research. Also, that whilst the effects of micros on teaching and learning were one research aspect there was also a need to explore those roles and uses which at present we do not know about - some of which perhaps we cannot even imagine.

GROUP 3

Chairman: R. JONES
Rapporteur: F. KLOTZ

As a starting point, the discussion group agreed that it is not too soon to introduce children in elementary schools to examples of computer uses. But the computer should be used as a tool rather than an end in itself. It must fit in with the existing aims and objectives in the elementary curriculum. Physically, it should be a part of the normal working environment, not set aside in a special laboratory. Teachers should not have the impression that using the computer is essential to good teaching.

The group felt we were still at an exploratory stage in the classroom use of the computer. It is therefore inappropriate to attempt to specify desirable or undesirable methods of use. Each teacher has an individual style in the classroom and might wish to use computers in an individual way. Much of the appeal of the computer for elementary education comes from its ability to accommodate so many different approaches and it is not desirable to limit these. Perhaps when more experience is gained, particular examples of good practice might be identified and publicized.

The group believed that if good quality software and teaching materials are to be disseminated effectively, established publishers must be involved in the process. However, it was also felt that most publishers have a poor understanding of the possibilities the computer introduces and the needs of the schools. Information on these points should be made available to the publishers. Teachers must be involved in the design of educational software, but must first be made aware of what computers can do. Teachers need support from professional programmers.

Recommendations:

1. IFIP should establish a permanent clearing house for the dissemination of information about national projects concerned with computers in elementary education. Access to this information should be provided for elementary teachers.

2. IFIP should also set up a clearing house to disseminate information about current research on uses of computers in elementary education.

3. The conference proceedings should be available in a less expensive form so that elementary and secondary school libraries could afford to buy copies.

4. IFIP should create a permanent panel concerned with the use of computers in elementary education.

5. IFIP should support research directed towards exploring the potential of computers for alleviating the problems of elementary education in the third world.

GROUP 4

Chairman: M. VORBECK
Rapporteur: B. SAMWAYS

The group decided first to consider what were the aims. All agreed that we should first look at education in general and the aims of elementary schooling in particular. Only then could one decide if the computer could be useful and whether or not it will create more effective teaching. The result was that "knowledge of the use of computers was necessary to prepare pupils for a scientific and technological society."

There was much discussion over the way computers might be used in the elementary school classroom; drill and practice and resource based learning were considered less important than use as a creative stimulant and problem solving medium. Most of the group wished to add "play" as a use; though with caution, as with television, this could result in a child losing the natural capability of "playing with nothing" (for example a piece of wood or a stone). Good teachers and good training were felt to be uppermost in achieving successful use of the computer in the elementary school classroom.

It was agreed that programs such as LOGO should be used by teachers and not written by them. Quality software is important, though teachers in the end must be the judges. Maybe they could be helped by regional centres which could evaluate and assess the software available and could also act as coordinators between teachers and programmers. In many countries, commercial people are keen to produce software but the resulting programs are not so good.

Research can of course help with teaching methods but the research should be done from the outset. It would also be better if carried out in depth in a few schools. But again this requires national or regional coordination. Several members felt that such evaluation should be done by complete outsiders and that the influence of teachers, pupils and parents should also be investigated. Research needs to be both short and long term and it may be that the research itself could also initiate development.

GROUP 5

Chairman: M. M. DeVAULT
Rapporteur: J. PETTY

The discussion opened with a query about whether question 1 should read "Shall we use computers in the elementary school classroom?" Concern was expressed about using computers with the young child (4 - 7 years) as it might be used so frequently that social interaction or development was hindered.

With older children, the use of the computer as a teaching or training tool was seen to be useful as long as it was the best medium in that context. "Drill and practice" programs were felt to be the least useful mode of use, whereas simulation or information retrieval programs, for example, offered support for child-to-child discussions, questioning and decision-making.

With regard to the aims of using computers in elementary education, the group wished to include some consideration of the social implications as described by the Scandinavian contingent. The first aim was changed to read "is our aim of for example, to develop thinking models through computer literacy AND at the same time to enhance the creativity of our pupils?" It was considered that our curriculum might have to change in certain areas due to the effect of the technology, such as in mathematics. We were concerned that the on-going hidden costs of software development and teacher training (both pre- and in-service) should not be forgotten in our discussion.

The group considered the second question quickly and a few points were made, though not argued through. The small countries where little money is available are being forced into buying software from publishing houses, much of which has not been evaluated for its educational strengths. The second worry was that materials brought from other countries would also import the culture of that country. This was not considered to be good.

Plenary Discussion

Chairman: T. VAN WEERT
Rapporteurs: W. G. CATHCART AND R. LAUTERBACH

The plenary discussion followed the some sequence as the questions suggested for the group discussions as outlined above.

Question 1.

BAUERSFELD asked Group 3 what they considered the function of a general clearing house to be. JONES said that it would allow for some international cooperation in documenting and disseminating courseware.

LOVIS commented on the discussions in IFIP to date with regard to all the recommendations as stated by Group 3.

1 and 2. IFIP does not have sufficient manpower to implement these recommendations.

3. North-Holland has a long standing, iron-clad contract to publish the proceedings. There has been discussion in IFIP about less expensive ways to do this. This is of increasing concern as more attention is paid to the elementary scene.

4. IFIP has discussed the formation of an elementary working group. The possibility of its formation was likely to be increased by a recommendation from this conference.

5. IFIP's involvement with the use of computers in third world countries would have to be done in cooperation with UNESCO.

BOSLER commented on point 5, saying that we should not tell others what to do until we have our own house in order. M. DeVAULT added that, while nationally some of us may be forced to take action, it is useful to share questions internationally.

VAN DeWOLDE asked what age range an elementary IFIP working group would include. LOVIS responded that it would probably include children up to 12 years of age.

In response to a question from MARTIN to Group 5, PETTY said the group discussed the question of whether computers should be used at all in elementary education. The group felt that computer use with very young children might detract from their social development. (Little danger of this in the near future due to lack of hardware. Editors.) With older children computers should be used only if they are the best means to achieve a desired objective. The group concluded that the impact of computers on social life needs to be included.

VORBECK pointed out that in 18 of the 23 countries in the European Council, a fundamental rethinking of the aims of primary education is taking place. After this has been done an analysis of how the computer can assist in achieving these aims needs to be made. WATKINS argued that the use of the computer will, in itself, make a fundamental change. However, this is not the major reason for introducing it. LEVRAT said that governments all engaged in long range planning but all we can give are short term recommendations.

Question 2.

BAUERSFELD asked Group 4 how quality of software is defined and how can quality be guaranteed by centres. VORBECK responded that countries could determine which programs are used most frequently and have teachers' comment on the programs when they used them.

BERDONNEAU argued that the number of teachers using a program is not necessarily an indication of quality. She gave the example of a widely used French textbook which most agree is of very poor quality. SCHMIDT said that curriculum centres in Denmark are moving into courseware evaluation and the qualitative labelling of programs. He believes that this evaluation is the responsibility of the teachers. PLANCKE-SCHUYTEN supported the idea of teachers evaluating programs but that that is not enough to guarantee quality. SCHMIDT suggested that children should be observed while using programs as a part of the evaluation procedure.

LEVRAT said that quality has to be assured because programs cost money. He felt that centres were in the best position to provide this assurance. BERDONNEAU said that quality depends on who judges the product. To some, quality is implied when the program runs; to others a worthwhile educational objective must be achieved.

BAUERSFELD said he is suspicious of centres for the control of quality of educational materials. He gave the example of German centres for the distribution of educational films which use to describe and judge the films educationally. Now they only describe the films and give a suitable level for use. More confidence in teachers' judgements is necessary.

WATKINS said teachers need to have all the programs or be able to go where they have access to all the programs. This access defines a centre. WEAVER added that software collections should be included in subject libraries where you find qualified personnel to judge the content.

WALDOW said that some teachers have good software but are unable to share it because of copyright.

Question 3.

HANSEN observed that the discussion groups did not raise many points with regard to research. This may be an indication that the groups felt that pure research would not be very helpful at the moment. More development needs to occur followed by research.

BAUERSFELD asked Group 4 if they had considered the role of the researcher as a full participant in the development of a software project. VORBECK responded that the group had not discussed their specific research needs but every project should at least have input from a researcher.

(There seemed to be a general agreement that the first priority must be the education of the children, both to live in society and to develop their potential in the best possible way. The second priority was not so much mentioned, that of making the best possible use of the most precious and expensive contributors to children's learning, namely the teachers - and also the parents, siblings and school companions. Computers, however great a boon, must come third to these two, although their arrival is changing society. Editors.)

SESSION 10

COMPUTERS IN ELEMENTARY EDUCATION
A SOLVABLE PROBLEM WITH PROBLEMATIC SOLUTIONS

Roland G. Lauterbach

IPN Institute for Science Education, Kiel
Federal Republic of Germany

While questions about computers in elementary education are
mainly concerned with how to introduce hardware and software
into schools this article is concerned with what to teach. Five
principles are used from object centered learning in German
elementary schools to come to terms with computer interaction.
The result is characterized as dependent on the background of
children who have increasingly less opportunities to learn by
overcoming the resistance of reality.

THE PARTICIPATING OBSERVER (Introduction)

After having read Seymour Papert's "Mindstorms" (1980) I have to consider myself
a participating observer among computer specialists. Computer interaction takes
people into math-land where they talk mathematics. My field is primary science
in the Federal Republic of Germany. I come from thing-land where we observe
things, handle things, and ask questions in a language things understand. Permit
me to comment and talk like "Kongor M-III LVKX 4" (as his friends from his home
planet call him) did with the French psychologist Gue R. Lefrançois on human
learning (1972, 1976). Kongor tried to understand human learning specialists
up to the point where his own principles limited his acceptance of their theory
and practice. You will find me in a similar situation.

A SOLVABLE PROBLEM

As far as I see it, you are dealing with a double-bonded question: Can elementary
school children learn to handle a computer and how can computers be introduced
into elementary education? From literature and from my own experience I consider
this problem solvable.

In 1969 I was asked to participate in a project to introduce Science and New Math
into German elementary education. While mathematics was well established as
arithmetic, science had no home in elementary education. It started in grade 5
as biology, in grade 7 as physics, and in grade 8 as chemistry. In the elementary
grades there was some nature study as part of community or vernacular studies
(Heimatkunde). Regardless of the different starting conditions, New Math and
Science had to cope with similar problems: Were children able to learn what they
should? And how could these topics be introduced into schools?

American psychologists, scientists, mathematicians and educators had proved that
children were able to learn Science and New Math (and had demonstrated that it
was possible to teach them). New curricula for elementary science and mathematics
had been developed and tried out in many schools with hundreds of teachers and
thousands of students (e.g. SCIS, S-APA, COPES, ESS, PIS). Elaborate evaluation
studies accompanied these efforts guaranteeing the soundness of results and
promising good products. They were then offered on the world's educational market
for adoption and adaptation.

As in many other countries, psychologists, subject specialists and teachers as well as educational planners in the Federal Republic of Germany responded to the American advances. They began to adapt the material and to introduce the hypotheses, theories and values: Gagné's learning hierarchy with its iterative teaching strategy (1965), Bruner's warrant for teaching anything to children at any age level (1961), Bloom's 80% deadline for stabilizing a child's personality at age eight (1964), the AAAS notion of the child as a scientist. The European contribution was soon identified. The founding fathers were the French Bourbaki-Group, the Swiss Geneva School of Piaget, the Hungarian Dienes. Early studies by Jean Piaget were rediscovered and replicated (Duckworth 1964). In England, Sweden and the Netherlands follow-up studies increased and culturally modified products sprang up (e.g. Science 5/13, AVOL, Elkind/Flavell (1969)).

The project I participated in also started with the adaptation of an American Curriculum: "Science - A Process Approach" by the American Association of the Advancement of Science (AAAS). We could convince ourselves that children were able to learn new mathematics and the type of science this curriculum conceptualized. For children it was easier to learn this new content than for most adults, including their elementary school teachers (Arbeitsgruppe für Unterrichtsforschung 1971).

That experience substantiated what others had reported before: elementary school children have a remarkable potential to learn almost anything when the subject is given a suitable form. There should be little doubt that they are also able to learn a computer language to handle a computer and to interact with it. Sceptics should read Papert's report. So this part of the Problem I consider solvable.

The other part of the problem seems more difficult. How to introduce the innovation into schools? While the mouldability of children's minds is probably greater than that of adults, their resistance to educative measures may be smaller. They do not have stable sets of cognitive structures, attitudes, values and habits. Teachers, educational administrators and parents do. There are ideological traditions in subjects, concept of student, role of teacher and values of educational fundamentals. Moreover, a school system also has material manifestations in its buildings, equipment, media and written documents. There exist regulative expressions in time tables, schedules and administrative rules. Innovation theory and practice has dealt with these problems and made suggestions how to cope with them more or less effectively (Havelock 1970, Hameyer 1978). Again, the experience with New Math and Science laid the grounds for the knowledge of implementation and innovation strategies in education.

To summarise, for a strategy to implement computer education in the Federal Republic of Germany, the following steps are recommended:

1) Prepare a fairly convincing line of argument pointing to the need of technological know-how in a highly industrialized society like the Federal Republic of Germany.

2) Propose a research program to examine the plausibility, desirability, and effects of computers in primary education, maintaining that this program will set no precedent for the school system.

3) Persuade a computer company to participate in this program, "altruistically".

4) Persuade the ministries of the states to permit schools and teachers to participate in the research project.

5) Involve teachers and head teachers.

6) Arrange some learning opportunities for teachers in the schools.

7) Organize an evaluation to identify the increase in knowledge.

8) Collect opinions of pupils, teachers, parents and administrators at the end of the project.
9) Publish your results.

From my own experience in curriculum development in primary and secondary education as well as from teacher training and from many research reports in science education, I contend it can be proved that the outline developmental strategy of projects which intend to introduce new methods, new topics, or new media into school lead to significant results for the trial period. Only after the results are published and the good of the research deed is proclaimed by the authors and their collaborators do the hawks of criticism attack their prey. And sure enough theory was lacking, the design was too narrow, the evaluation was faulty, the splendour of the results was due to the halo of the research situation, and the undesired side effects had been ignored. If one is neither on the side of the researchers, the developers, or the participants nor on the side of the critics, one usually will find on both sides truth as well as contradiction: This is an excellent guide to improvement.

You are probably familiar with the solutions proposed to this part of the problem as you were with that on children's plasticity. So the solubility of the problem should no longer be the topic, but the validity of the proposed solutions. This is my proviso. I shall confine myself to ask: <u>What</u> should children learn in elementary school?

PRINCIPLES OF THINGLAND

At the beginning I introduced myself as a participating observer who may perceive our problems and solutions differently than most of you because of different principles regulating thoughts and actions. I also briefly referred to the special nature of our tradition.

In German elementary school we have a subject called "Sachunterricht" or "Heimatkunde". Even though not directly translatable it means "study of things" or "community studies" or "vernacular studies". This subject is considered central to German elementary education and its leitmotif is, "Talk of, about, around things, which constitute the natural, social, geographical, historical, intellectual, and emotional environment of the child!" It is considered to be fundamental for all of teaching and learning in the elementary grades. The history of this subject goes back to 1816 and the leitmotif relates back even further to Comenius in the 16th century. The German elementary school in its present structure goes back to the early twenties of this century. Educational and didactic theory for this school level was developed during that time. It was quite abruptly stopped during the thirties due to political and cultural mania. About 10 years after the end of World War II a gradual revival of educational thinking could be discerned. But even at the end of the sixties it had not regained enough momentum to put forward strong arguments against the tidal wave of American curriculum development for elementary education rolling across Europe and the rest of the world. The flood settled and permitted the seeds which had rested for about fifty years to spring up.

I am going to state five principles which may be considered basic for this subject. They can be considered constitutional for thingland. And as the comparison of two different cultures illuminates both, we may shed light on the question, of what a child should learn in elementary school. Educators, subject specialists and philosophers do not use identical terminology to discuss this question. When looking through German syllabi and educational literature one will notice shifts of emphasis during the last 100 years based on changing educational purpose and conceptualisation. This is why any terms chosen to label the principles cannot be taken literally. They require historical analysis and are best described in dialectic terms to show the constructive tension in them and the need to avoid a simple either-or-conceptualization. Unfortunately, the English translation increases the difficulty.

The principles are:

1) From child-centredness ("Kindgemässheit") to subjective generality

   Teaching starts and ends with the child. Each thing has a subjective reality for the child. Even those things a child meets for the first time may induce associations, fear or delight, attention, motivation to act. This educational principle would require to begin with this subjective reality ("vom Kinde aus"). The child is then confronted with the intersubjective validity of a thing, its names, usages, relationships, characteristics, semantics in different contexts, etc. Education leads the child to recognize, learn about and accept as his own what is generally accepted as valid. While assimilating and accommodating, the subjective reality changes to a more general level of subjectivity.

2) From nearness ("Lebensnähe") to vernacular universality

   The individual child lives in a community with other people, with animals and with objects. They are close to him; they are unique. This geographical, social, ideological, aesthetic, emotional, and personal environment constitutes his home. It includes the experiences of the distant made possible by modern transport and communication. Other people have other homes. Being at home is different in different cultures. Education begins at home and conceptualizes the things at home in its vernacular structure. It then confronts the child with "foreign" cultures and things. Getting to know them, to accept them in their uniqueness, and to deal with them on their terms will expand as well as deepen the child's perception of home.

3) From vividness ("Anschaulichkeit") to conceptual concreteness

   Perceiving things is a sensual as well as a cognitive act. Observing with all the senses it the basis for cognitive, affective, and motor development. Education starts with multi-sensory perception of things, it conceptualizes the experience in concrete operations and abstracts from them symbolic operators. The conscious use of the senses and the available concepts increase the quality and quantity of perception and conceptualization as well as that of concrete actions.

4) From wholeness ("Ganzheitlichkeit") to analytic integration

   A thing is an entity. It is perceived in its wholeness. As entities things have their own value. They seem simple. Education starts with this simple thing and explores its existence. Yet, a thing can be described by a complex of properties, it can be taken as an example for a class of things, it can be seen as a system of interrelated parts, or it can be looked at as part of another system. These analytic views are developed functionally to integrate things into higher order systems, i.e. into new entities. Thereby, things turn into determinants of the new entities as those in turn redefine the original things.

5) From active learning ("Selbsttätigkeit") to self-reliance

   When child and thing meet, two entities interact. The interaction changes both, child and thing, however small the change may be. The child experiences how the thing determines his actions, the thing undergoes change depending on the child's inventiveness. Education starts with offers of interaction. It promotes the child's change as learning and

growth. Growing awareness of the limitations things set as well as the
chances they offer for action increase the child's competence and confidence to participate in shaping things and self. An advice Jean Jacques
Rousseau is said to have given a young mother may illustrate the point:
If your child cries for an apple, don't bring the apple to the child,
but take the child to the apple. This will teach him from the beginning
that nature is not man's servant.

These principles are derived from the most commonly expressed requirements for
"Sachunterricht" and "Heimatkunde" (e.g. Spranger 1923/1964), Schietzel (1948),
Kopp (1972), Salzmann (1982) and from educational theories dialectically mediat-
ing between the learning subject (child) and the object of learning (thing)
(e.g. Weniger (1952), Klafki (1965), Walgenbach (1979)) trying to overcome rigid
"either-or" positions, shallow "in-betweens", and the fatalistic notion of a
pendulum swinging back and forth between subject and object didactics. This is
why they are best described as regulating ideas (Hübner 1979, 197) indicating
the direction educational efforts should take from a definite historical
situation.

To illustrate these principles in the context of computers and elementary
education I shall draw upon the experiences of children as described by Seymour
Papert in his convincing project on "children, computers and powerful ideas"
which he has been working at with his colleagues at MIT. In particular I would
like to recall the hypothetical conversation between two children who are
working and playing with the computer (Papert 1980, 77-93). They command a
"Turtle" as an "object-to-think-with".

In this conversation the children discover the potential of procedures for moving
the turtle in ever more complex ways to create a pictorial environment. Procedures for enlargment, repetition, translation and rotation become
tools for the expression of their imagination. Papert's intentions in using
Turtle geometry with children are quoted as follows:

> "Two fundamental ideas run through this book. The first is that it is
> possible to design computers so that learning to communicate with them
> can be a natural process, more like learning French by living in France
> than like trying to learn it through the unnatural process of American
> foreign-language instruction in class-rooms.
>
> Second, learning to communicate with a computer may change the way
> other learning takes place. The computer can be a mathematics-speaking
> and an alphabetic-speaking entity. We are learning how to make computers
> with which children love to communicate." (1980, 6)

And pertaining to "Turtle geometry":

> "Turtle geometry, too, has a fundamental entity similar to Euclid's
> point. But this entity, which I call a "Turtle", can be related to
> things people know because unlike Euclid's point, it is not stripped
> so totally of all properties, and instead of being static it is
> dynamic. Besides position the Turtle has one other important property:
> It has "heading". A Euclidean point is at some place - it has a position,
> and that is all you can say about it. A Turtle is at some place - it,
> too, has a position - but it also faces some direction - its heading.
> In this, the Turtle is like a person - I am here and I am facing north
> - or an animal or a boat." (1980, 55).

One may allege that discussing Papert's intentions, experiences and visions within the framework of the presented principles is not justified. He is concerned with teaching a language. I am not going to refute this assumption. But, as far as possible, I shall try to remain on Papert's terms.

1) Child-centredness

How much do we know about the subjective reality computers have for children? As far as I have been able to find out this question points towards educational no man's land.

The production and sales of personal computers is increasing rapidly. Eventually, they will be part of every home like TV-sets, home worker tools, or electronic toys of today. This vision is used to construct the rationale for computer interaction in schools. Another line or argument pleads for computer literacy to avoid mathophobia. Unfortunately, it does not consider that the remedy may lie in avoiding the phobia causing therapy in the first place, or if a therapy is needed.

According to this first principle, only the first argument would be acceptable here. As computers become a reality for children, they will cause an educational issue. For that Papert's approach may well be of indispensable value. He wants children to learn the rules of dealing with the computer in order to foster their independence from the computer by turning it into an instrument to extend human thinking whenever there are good reasons for it.

"I have described myself as an educational utopian - not because I have projected a future of education in which children are surrounded by high technology, but because I believe that certain uses of very powerful computation technology and computational ideas can provide children with new possibilities for learning, thinking, and growing emotionally as well as cognitively." (17f)

In agreement with this first principle he designed Turtle geometry. It had "to be something children _could_ make sense of, to be something that would resonate with their sense of what _is_ important." (63) It had to be firmly related to the children's sense and knowledge about their own bodies and be coherent with children's sense of themselves as people with intentions, goals, desires, likes, and dislikes.

2) Nearness

The vision of a personal computer in every home reduces computer interaction to an issue of triteness. Yet, it need not be of less explosiveness than that of watching TV. Television contributes to the degeneration of personal nearness, living experiences, and creative home-making, wherever its use is uncontrolled. Alienation from home is not uncommon. We do not know if computers in the home will have similar effects. So what is the nearness computers may have?

Papert speaks of computer cultures, of computer language, of thinking like a computer, and of computer environments (19 ff). His vision of the computer age seems total. But he is aware of the problem:

"People often fear that using computer models for people will lead to mechanical or linear thinking: They worry about people losing respect for their intuition, sense of values, powers of judgement ... The advice 'think like a computer' could be taken to mean _always_ think about everything like a computer. This would be restrictive and _narrowing_. But the advice could be taken in a very different sense, not precluding anything, but making a powerful addition to the person's stock of mental tools." (155)

3) Vividness

This principle, it seems, cannot be convincingly satisfied. In computer interaction it is not the computer as a concrete object which is conceptualized but its language through which examples of reality are symbolized. Indeed, the multi-sensory perception of things is not represented in computer images.

"Children working on an electronic sketchpad are learning a language for talking about shapes and fluxes of shapes, about velocities and rates of change, about processes and procedures. They are learning to speak mathematics, and acquiring a new image of themselves as mathematicians." (13)

But even though Papert aims at "thinking" he, at first, introduces a movable robot turtle. The children are asked to identify with the turtle in moving back and forth, right and left, speeding up and slowing down. This permits the children to conceptualize their own movements and improves the physical awareness of themselves. Only after that, the turtle is symbolized on the screen. And by identifying with it geometric forms are produced or geometric representations of real objects. The computer is not used to reconstruct the concrete thing on the basis of concepts.

But is that really visionary enough? A concrete object could be taken as a prototype from which the mathematical functions are abstracted to have the computer "plan" production. From computer-controlled machines we know that Turtle geometry need not end with 2- or 3-dimensional moving pictures.

4) Wholeness

This principle, probably, does not regulate mathematical learning. The turtle is neither a composition of sub-units nor does it constitute new entities as their maintained part. The reason is obvious: for one, the constructions in turtle geometry are not material systems, for another, the symbolic turtle is a tool in the generation of the symbolic systems. Tools leave their marks on products but they are not part of the products. And yet, there is an aspect in Papert's approach which needs attention under this principle. The construction of an entity (flower) by trial and error experiences which are transformed into analytical steps is the prototype procedure in constructing artificial systems. The similarity to construction procedures in technology are striking. The difference is that for today's technology the physical, chemical, or biological basic units as well as the natural laws regulating their interaction have to be discovered first, before they are synthesized.

There, probably, would not be any didactical sense in having the children discover the man made rules. That is why creation is left to the composition. As Papert formulates himself: "Children are builders (Piaget), therefore, give them materials to build with." (7)

5) Active learning

This principle appears to be satisfied best by Papert's scene. Step by step the children experience how their intention (to draw a flower) has to comply to the computer's structure. In accepting these determinants they learn to construct their own creation. And when they would like a garden, the appropriate command forces the computer to make one.

"The dialogue structure of communication humanizes the computer to the child's partner. Yet it remains servant to the child. Do children recognize the difference between servant and tool? The edginess of reality, its resistance against commands to be at will is not available. Action is limited by the frame of communication."

All in all, Papert's hypothetical scene does not appear alien to the five principles of thingland even though they were neither his topic not did he construct them in recognition of these principles. Does this mean that computer interaction qualifies as a topic for elementary education?

WHAT SHOULD BE TAUGHT IN ELEMENTARY EDUCATION?

On first sight, one may suggest that both types of learning are needed for elementary school children: experience with things (having Rousseaus's advice in mind) as well as experience with the computer as a tool. That would seem a comfortable solution. Unfortunately, educational reality is of a different kind. Children's opportunities to learn from objects, organisms and people directly is diminishing.

When Eve was coached into picking the apple in the Garden of Eden by the serpent and offered it to Adam there were only two choices: refuse blindly or take a risk. We are in a somewhat different situation. With the advent of each new technology we are reminded of the blessings and curses of the preceding ones: automobile, nuclear energy, chemical technology, instrumental medicine, television, gene technology, computers. The association of the myth of mankind's expulsion from paradise and the persistent effort to regain it by means of technological development is used here to orient attention toward the speculation that a bit of the apple of knowledge may be all that it takes to find out whether we could gain paradise or lose it for good in elementary education.

1) Child-Centredness

Today apples come in containers with a hygienic plastic-film. They are called Golden Delicious, Granny Smith or Red ... Each of a kind is guaranteed to look and taste more or less like the other. They are available all year round. They are available at the super market. And if they are out just ask for more from the storage room or wait until tomorrow. The reality of apples is that of any merchandise: attractive, buyable, disposable. If educators tell the whole story of their production including mono-cultures, fertilization, pesticides and insecticides, cadmium content, surplus destruction, price control, South Africa and the American Fruit Company, will the children understand? And if their don't, would not a morality argument require additional educational efforts?

Or:

How many children have been with flowers in gardens, on fields, in forests? Have they smelled, serenely looked at them, picked a bunch? Or are flowers colourful shapes in books or moving pictures? Are they, too, store products only? How convincing can an educational rationale be that helps to reduce for most children chances or experiencing flowers in their natural settings - for the sake of language, mathematics, or science? It is a question of priority and one of responsibility for education to help the child come to himself.

2) Nearness

There is little difference between children living in different cities of industrialized societies: food at MacDonald or Kentucky Fried Chicken, TV-series with American stars, cars and Shell Oil, Aspirin and Alka-Seltzer, learning New math and science, Pepsodent and Lux soap, and even music and language adapt to one another.

This trend toward cultural uniformity would be no topic, if it were not for the loss of traditional individuality. The personal computers from APPLE or Texas Instruments with the same language just focus this issue. If the children's experiences outside of school tend toward uniformity obliterating traditions, should education re-enforce this development or does it become necessary to promote the regeneration of culturally deprived areas? Again, it is a question of priority and one of responsibility for education to help the child find a home.

3) Vividness

Here reference is made to the questions under the heading of the first principle: If the children's world is becoming more and more one of pictures, the need increases to supply the target conceptualization with a concrete basis. To command an instrument to draw semi-circles in a certain order, naming the results, flowers and their random distribution and size, a garden, degrades the children's potentialities to perversion, if they are not given the opportunity to be with flowers in their natural settings.

4) Wholeness

When the children's reality comes in packages, foods as well as toys, clothes as well as 45-minute learning units, where are their possibilities to experience relationships of meaningful unity? Are apples part of the fruit market or of trees? Or are they just and only for sale and for consumption? What is the sense of the mathematics lesson or that of science? To experience today or to learn for tomorrow? Can an educational rationale be ignored that argues for meaningful entities at every level of understanding? Here, an old educational problem comes up: should a tool or a language be taught regardless of its subject and object? This is not a question of priority but one of educational theory: there always is a subject and an object.

5) Active learning

Child and object meet as separate entities. Even if the child is given the chance to actively deal with the object, it will have difficulty finding an object of individuality or uniqueness. The objects which children meet are more or less identical mass products. As such, they have no identity, they are dressed in preplanned properties to promote their sale. In so far, there is little individuality offered to children. Either their world seems totally able to be made and controlled by man or it appears impervious to his actions. Standards and regulations dominate. And yet, there is a chance for children to discover objects with a history challenging them for interactions. The educator should not hesitate to require the children to take on the challenge. This is no longer a question of priority, but one of responsibility.

At the beginning I referred to Kongor M-III LVKX 4 the visitor from another planet. He not only had some difficulty getting emotionality and rationality integrated when dealing with human learning. He also had some difficulty understanding why people take risks - even if they know there are no winners.

I argued for the historical situation of today's elementary school children. As soon as personal computers begin to enter most homes the question of priority may be answered differently. Is the identification with computer thinking part of the liberation from it or the socialization into its acceptance as faultless delineator of man's better future? Does it lead to a type of self-consciousness that impedes or even stops the appreciation of being human in our thinking, as Joseph Weizenbaum (1976) fears or will it lead to the self-consciousness in Hegel's understanding of where we recognize and love ourselves as the (self-) conscious creator of our own future, as Seymour Papert suggests?

LITERATURE

Arbeitsgruppe für Unterrichtsforschung: Weg in die Naturwissenschaft, Stuttgart 1971.

Bloom, B.: Stability and Change in Human Characteristics. New York 1964.

Bruner, J.: The Process of Education. Cambridge 1961.

Duckworth, E.: Piaget Rediscovered. In: JRST, Vol. 2, Isne 2, 1964, pp. 172-175.

Elkind, D., Flavell, J.H. (eds.): Studies in Cognitive Development. New York/Toronto/London 1969

Gagné, R. M.: Conditions of Human Learning. New York 1965.

Hameyer, U.: Innovationsprozesse. Analysemodell und Fallstudien zum sozialen Konflikt in der Curriculumrevision. Weinheim 1978.

Havelock, R. G.: A Guide to Innovation in Education. Ann Arbor 1970.

Hübner, K.: Kritik der wissenschaftlichen Vernunft. Freiburg 1979.

Klafki, W.: Studien zur Bildungstheorie und Didaktik. Weinheim 1965.

Kopp, F.: Von der Heimatkunde zum Sachunterricht. Donauwörth 1972.

Lefrancois, G. R.: The Psychological Theories and Human Learning: Kongors Report. Belmont 1972.

National Society for the Study of Education: Teaching Science in the Elementary School. In: Victor, E., Lerner, M. S.: Readings in Science Education for the Elementary School. New York 1967.

Papert, S.: Mindstorms. New York 1980.

Salzmann, C.: Die pädagogische Aufgabe des Sachunterrichts. In: Die Grundschule. (1982) 2, 46-50)

Schietzel, C.: Das volkstümliche Denken und der sachkundliche Unterricht in der Volksschule. Hamburg 1948.

Spranger, E.: Der Bildungswert der Heimatkunde. Stuttgart 1964.

Walgenbach, W.: Ansätze zu einer Didaktik ästhetisch-wissenschaftlicher Praxis. Weinheim 1979.

Weizenbaum, J.: Computer Power and Human Reason. San Francisco 1976.

Weniger, E.: Didaktik als Bildungslehre. Weinheim 1952.

THE DISPARITY OF COMPUTER EXPERIENCE
- A CASE FOR ORIENTING THE SYLLABUS
FOR ELEMENTARY EDUCATION?

Heinrich Bauersfeld

IDM der Universität Bielefeld, FRG

Recent studies of memory and knowledge in Cognitive Science as well as case studies on children's learning in pre-school and in early school ages support the assumption that learning starts and proceeds through disparate domains of subjective experiences (the "society of mind" metaphor). Due to their rigid characteristics the integration of such computer-related subjective domains with other domains of experience is of particular difficulty. Cases and possible consequences are discussed in this paper.

Difficulties in educational reform are man-made difficulties - mostly. Reformers suffer from the stability of what has been learned yesterday as well as from the uncertainty of their predictions for future action, and they live in the present tense of a given historical and societal situation, like their objects do. Now computers join that unpredictable game of stability and change. In particular the man-made invasion of computers into elementary education is raising a complex field of interdisciplinary problem dimensions, and is producing specific theoretical challenges aside and above of all of the pragmatical approaches and answers which exist already. Computers have come over us like TV, or nuclear fission, or E.T., and many related recommendations reflect naive fascination rather than serious and responsible analyses of conditions and processes.

Since my interest is with the teaching and learning of mathematics, I am not a computer specialist, my theoretical key questions are:

What does it mean for a child to "learn" with a computer?

Clearly, there are important differences with everyday experiences, e.g.:

- the totality of the closed system - it is you and the machine and nothing else
- the severe reduction in the complexity of language
- the limitations of action and reaction
- the split of operation and product - the kinestesia (complex of related movements) of the keyboard versus the screen features etc.

And if these computer systems are so strikingly powerful and so different from all of our usual procedures and routines how then will an individual integrate experiences with these systems into his/her everyday (i.e. non-computer) knowledge and activities? Is it a case just of "applying" the experiences from within of these highly specialized, closed microworlds of prestructured meanings?

I shall stop questioning here and will group my sceptical remarks and answers around three aspects:

1) The issue of "learning" - using recent research outcomes an alternative view of human learning will be outlined
2) Papert's approach as the present most sophisticated example will be discussed in comparison with other reforms of mathematics instruction
3) The nature of a "computer culture" and the metaphor of "application" are called in question along with a few guidelines for special research work.

THE ISSUE OF "LEARNING"

One of the many anecdotes of David Hilbert sees the great mathematician a few minutes before the opening of a party in his house, caught by his wife: "You can't meet our guests in that fashion, go upstairs, please, and change your tie at last!" After a while, his wife wondering about his absence goes upstairs and finds him in his pyjamas in his bed and fallen asleep deeply.

The reconstruction leads to the interpretation, that Hilbert finding himself in his room, his bed nearby, and opening his tie just reactivated the daily procedure of going to sleep - successfully as we know in terms of the procedure but not of the party. Here one step in the chain of situation-specific actions has activated the whole subjective reality of going to bed, supported by the specific environment.

Sometimes we use the totality of such domains of subjective experiences the other way round: When an intention (or an idea) has dropped out of our mind suddenly, we go back quickly into the very same situation, where we created it.

Recent theories of memory and of Cognitive Science describe the fundamental nature of such domains and their specificity to situations using concepts like

- "scripts" (R. Schank and R. Abelson 1977, R. Schank 1982), the prototype of which is "eating in a restaurant" (R. Schank 1981, p. 115, and Anderson 1980, p. 149), but also the above "going to bed"
- "production systems" (A. Newell and H. Simon 1972, Simon 1979), which form a model of mind as a non-hierarchical system of conditions and actions
- "frames" (R.B. Davis 1979, 1980, 1982), based on an early concept of Minsky (1975), characterized as "assimilation schemata for the organisation of recognitions" and in the analysis identifiable across errors (R.B. Davis 1980, p. 193), and
- "microworlds" (R.B. Lawler 1979, 1981), using Papert's name for computer arrangements for the inner (subjective) representation of domains of experiences.

Though the development of these models followed different research interests in different fields - I skip the discussion of the historical roots here - the models coincide in relevant aspects: the organisation of experiences (or of memory) in certain domains, the separateness of these domains against each other, and the totality of the transmitted orientation for recognition and action. Differences among the models appear with the descriptions of the stability of such domains, of their size and of their inner structure, of their parallel or exclusive functioning, and of the nature of control in the system.

"Each subsociety of the mind must still have its own internal epistemology and phenomenology, with most details private, not only from those central processes, but from one another."

"Each part of the mind sees only a little of what happens in some others, ... most knowledge stays more or less where it was formed, and does its work there." (H. Minsky 1980, p. 130).

All these models are cognitive models. I therefore prefer the notion of "domains of subjective experiences" which in contrast covers the totality of human recognition and action (Bauersfeld 1983).

Most interesting for the discussion of computers in elementary education are the "Intimate Study" of Robert W. Lawler (his doctoral thesis under Papert's supervision 1977-79) and more recent case studies of his. For about 6 months before school entrance Lawler worked with his oldest daughter Miriam in the LOGO-laboratory at M.I.T., using different programs of the "turtle geometry", and also guiding fundamental arithmetical activities, like written addition and subtraction, without a computer.

Lawler found Miriam's knowledge split up into strictly separated "microworlds" such as

- the "money-world", in which all relevant experiences concerning coins, pocket money, change etc. are represented, and wherein she quickly can respond to the question: "How much is 75 cents plus 26 cents?" saying: "three quarters, four ... and a penny, a dollar one!"
- the "count-world", wherein early number experiences, including calculations following the finger-counting strategy, are represented, and wherein Miriam solves the task "75 plus 26" like "seventy, ninety, ninety-six, ninety-seven, ninety-eight, ninety-nine, one hundred, one-oh-one (counting the last five numbers on her fingers)"
- the "decadal world", which arose with TURTLE Geometry, related to the commands of rotation "right 60", "left 20" etc. and their combinations in the SHOOT game. Here, Miriam quickly came to know that "90 plus 90 equals 180", due to the specific result of taking the opposite direction.

In a "money"-situation Miriam would calculate all problems exclusively along with her strategies of dealing with the (US-American) coinage. Never would she do so in a "count"-situation. Also the mental addition and subtraction of large numbers is available (or accessible) to her only in TURTLE game situations, that is within the "decadal world", but not in others. So at the same time, when she "knew" 90 plus 90 equals 180 for the TURTLE, she solved the problem "9 plus 9" with "count"-strategies as "8 plus 8 plus 2". Therefore the recognition of a problem within a given situation is done through the activation of the adequate microworld, and there is no connection among these early microworlds, though the words (number names) are phonetically the same and also are the number symbols (on key-board or paper). Thus the microworlds - or more completely; the domains of subjective experience (DSE) - are not only specific to situations, but are specific in terms of language, of meanings, of available options for actions etc.

If human mental activities are organized this way, principally, and there is more support from other research activities also (Bauersfeld 1982, 1983), then we can identify at least two types of "learning":

* enriching and differentiating an existing DSE and
* developing a new DSE.

The first case is a permanent and regular issue, because whenever a DSE gets activated, the situation will leave it in a somewhat elaborated or reformed or stabilized fashion. What is called learning usually might be seen as related to the second case. New DSE's can integrate the perspectives of two or more older DSE's. But, since "memory never subtracts" (Minsky), the older DSE's survive and can become activated still without change in a given situation (the classical gase of "regression"). Also there is no "comparison" possible between different DSE's, no "transfer", no "generalisation" or "abstraction", without the supportive functionning of a third (new) DSE, which provides for the necessary perspectives - language, actions, meaning etc. The total view of organisation in the individual is the "society in mind", which consists of competing DSE's of various types and degrees of development.

Experiences with a computer, so we can learn from Lawler's protocols and interpretation, produce DSE's of an extreme peculiarity - no matter how much tricks software producers may have employed for making things smooth. The characteristics of computer environments as described at the beginning are so different from everyday experiences and from usual school situations, that inevitably at a first stage strictly segmented knowledge will come out of the activities. At a later stage special and extended effort is needed, if an integration with other everyday DSE's is to become successful. There is nothing like "application" in the sense of an easy employment of ready-made available skills; the "bringing together" requires new DSE's, which make the connecting procedures feasible.

PAPERT'S APPROACH

The "Mindstorm" issue is chosen here, as it appears to be the most sophisticated approach for the earlier ages, and because of the exuberant promises and predictions which Papert has published (1980). Other ideas and software, like drill and practice programs, computer games etc. are either in a less perfect status or were released with much weaker theoretical foundations (if at all they offer a "philosophy").

Papert uses the notion of "microworlds" in the sense of planned educational arrangements, wherein the computer functions as a "partner of the student":

"The TURTLE world was a microworld, a 'place', a 'province of mathland', where certain kinds of mathematical thinking could hatch and grow with particular ease. The microworld was an incubator." (1980, p. 125)

Papert's computer microworlds are objective means and no inner (subjective) realities. Thus it is the concept of informatics and not of psychology (as it is with Lawler). Papert designs "classes of TURTLE worlds" using three design criteria (1980, p. 126/128):

1) "let the learner acquire the concept of laws ... by working with a very simple and accessible instance"

2) "the possibility of activities, games, art, and so on, that make activity in the microworlds matter"

3) "all needed concepts can be defined within the experience of that world."

The third criterion, by the way, expresses the "closedness" which I have claimed for computer experiences in a direct manner.

In terms of setting up educational reforms through new directions for learning the three criteria may remind the reader to the "Mod Math" affair and to the special approach, which Zoltan Dienes has produced. He tried to organize students' concept development via the students' engagement and activities in structured games, which he designed as morphisms of mathematical structures:

"We need to create mathematical learning-situations, partly as if we were practising an art-form, and partly as if we were devising an original research situation." (Dienes 1960, p. 15)

For a general critique the comparative view on these two approaches is promising. In the following paragraphs I shall limit myself to the discussion of three relevant aspects: the prestructured nature of the exploration in the didactical arrangements, the particular transfer problems they bring about, and the type of communication in the related learning situations.

1) Both, Papert and Dienes, offer <u>prestructured arrangements for student's learning</u>.
Both also share the difficulties from opening access to a limited subset of
mathematical activities only: those which fit into the system.

With Papert's TURTLE geometry the mathematical conditions as well as modes and
format of representation are build into the computer program (1980, p. 122). That
the learners "can shape the reality in which they will work" and that they "can
become the active, constructing architects of their own learning" (p. 126/128)
is one of the exuberant promises, which comes true within very narrow, disparate,
and closed domains of activities only.

Dienes has used the mathematical structures to be learned for building up the rules
of his "Structural Games". Thus in both approaches the learner can make explorations only along prescribed paths and only through using given presentations.
Related to the "what" of this exploration, the learner is the captive of the
system's inbuilt logic, without becoming aware of it.

2) Therefore both didactical approaches bring about their <u>special transfer problems</u>.
Dienes failed to integrate his fascination with structural games and his partly
brilliant items into a more or less organized curriculum. Papert's LOGO enthusiasm
likewise cannot obscure the fact that a reasonable relation between his marvellous
examples and any kind of curricular framework and of general orientation has to
be established. The idea, which Papert forms for this purpose at the end of his
book (1980, p. 216):

> "the most likely bearer of potentially relevant cultural change in the
> near future is the increasingly pervasive computer presence."

is not a sufficient answer - apart from the question of what "cultural" might
mean in this context. How do we develop relations to everyday experiences? How do
we steer clear of just adding another curiosity to the dissonant concert of
school subjects and of subject matter goals?

3) The <u>analysis of communication</u> as constituted with the two approaches will
deepen the troubles with Papert's ideas in a principal manner. The structural
games of Dienes do their function through the social interaction among the
participating students. Papert organizes a man-machine-relationship. The computer
is addressable only through a normed language with stringent, unequivocal
denotations of words and symbols. Compared with the possibilities of reflexive
understanding and of multidimensional actions of a human partner, the computer's
repertoire is of extremely reduced dimensions, both semantically and sensorically.
Naming the computer as an "interactive being" (Papert 1980, p. 126) is using the
same amputated concept os Cognitive Science does when speaking of "interaction
of persons, societies, and machines" (Norman 1981, p. 282). The increasing ease
of computer addressing is achieved through organized learning processes during
the initial encounter, and these processes mask the fact that they are made for
adapting the "user" to the limitations and conditions of the system. In particular
computer languages do not allow figurative speach, which through metaphors and
mainly through metonymics can support the tentative transgressing of DSE rims
(Bauersfeld and Zawadowski 1981). All this contributes to an heightening of the
disparity and seclusion of computer-related DSE's.

Finally one should not overlook the special conditions of Lawler's study with
Miriam and LOGO. Miriam's experimenting with the TURTLE cannot be taken as typical
for an institutionalized man-machine relationship, because of the father's
permanent presence and his transmitting aids. This encounter was much nearer to
usual human interactions. Adding to our problem is the fact that in spite of the
positive conditions, Miriam's computer experiences have appeared in such isolated
microworlds. In order to avoid the recurrence of the "Mod Math" pattern of reform
- much fascination, weak theory, disappointment in general - informatics requires
a better guided processing, the developing of more alternatives, and last, but not
least, more informed reflection.

"COMPUTER CULTURE" VERSUS REFLECTED INSTRUMENTATION

It is interesting that it was exactly the conspicuous seclusion of the TURTLE-related "decadal world", which made Miriam's everyday experiences appear as distant and alien issues, and which therefore led Lawler to the general concept of microworlds. Hence learning with a computer has changed our understanding not only of learning in general, but also of "transfer", "abstraction" etc. But this was achieved by sensitive, interdisciplinary research work.

On the other hand, if we allow the human adaptation to computers to develop, latently and uncontrolled in parallel with the soft take-over of the machines and their omnipresence, then clearly we can expect changes in human communication. If computer environments win a reasonable influence on human thinking, then the unequivocal denotations will drive away the variety of connotations in natural language. Since this variety provides for a main source of creative ideas, human creativity will change in effect, if not become poorer. Perhaps this is necessary in an "technological world" or within a computer "culture", but I doubt it.

But there are many problems which are of more immediate concern and perhaps are easier to solve or at least easier to bring nearer to a solution:

1) <u>The side-effect problem</u>. As it is with methods in school teaching: every new system for learning brings about its own new deficits and difficulties in learning.

> Typical are Miriam's addition problems in her "decadal world": "In playing SHOOT, precision was not required." Initially Miriam added rotations like "50+20" by "dropping the zero's", then adding 5+2=7, and using one of the dropped zeros to make the result 70, a procedure, which leaves "an extra zero".

> Later she added rotations like "55+26=76", because she dropped the ones, then added 5+2=7, and filled in the 6 for 76, just "dropping the five" as she did with the extra zero. (Lawler 1981).

Therefore the development of computer programs for educational purposes should be accompanied by carefully designed case studies, not only for the direct "debugging" procedures, but also, and this in particular, for the identification and control of the many possible side-effects, which do not arise on the track of the program's aims, but just nearby. For SHOOT "dropping the zero's" was such a nearby problem.

2) <u>The language problem</u>. When children work with a computer there are at least four different types of languages in function

- the language in which the child addresses the computer
- "   "   "   "   the children communicate about their work
- "   "   "   "   the computer expert has programmed the computer
- "   "   "   "   the scientists communicate their observations of these different processes.

My problem is with the last type. We discussed the change of the notion of "learning" already. No doubt there are many more concepts used in the new context, which were not coined definitely for it. The metaphorical nature of this use and the tentative function for the description of the new context are helpful to get started at all. (In my language: you construct new DSE's here!). But these concepts need careful clarification, not just by definition, but in the course of the abductive process (Bauersfeld 1983) of generating new knowledge and hypotheses about the work with the computer. Sureley "environment", "embodiment", "action", "motivation" etc. are such deficient concepts. They all mark theoretical deficits in the end.

3) <u>The content problem</u>. The question of "What to do with the computer?" is answered in the first instance by looking out for available good examples from other fields which can be treated inside the border lines of the available computer system, and which inspire the program writers. Thus the answer turns out to become a mix of old content, system constraints and programmer's competence. Clearly, this triad will not work for long, neither alone nor effectively. There is some complementary effort necessary. So, where are the little home-made projects, the grass-root level inventors and their new problems and ideas? Where is the sensitive network to encourage and guide such productions, and for coordinating the distributions of promising issues? Who will develop an adequate theoretical frame work? I think there is not much hope for good solutions except through organizing the problem solving as a multidimensional process in itself.

4) <u>The distance problem</u>. If the integration of computer experiences with other experiences takes special effort, which one then? It the work with the computer is made as smooth as possible for the child and if the child does this work without much reflection of what he does, then we are back to the analogy with usual classroom learning. This way will lead to the generation of another sad school subject. Therefore, raising the reflection about the procedures seems to be one possible way for to overcome the segmentation and disparity of the computer experiences. The difficulty is that nobody can raise reflection directly, because it takes a super ordinate DSE as basis. And an adequate DSE for such meta-level discussions has to be developed within the process. So, we need a certain organization of the working process, which in itself requires reflection for the progress. That is to say the computer should be taken as a serving instrument, as a technical problem solver as well as a model producer, rather than as a non-transparent, unbeatable intelligence machine, which is treated like a miracle. Thus reflection has to be developed within the process, but at a distance from the machine rather than through adaptation to the machine's constraints.

REFERENCES

Anderson, J.R., Cognitive Psychology and Its Implications (Freeman, San Francisco, 1980)

Bauersfeld, H., Hidden dimensions in the so-called reality of a mathematics classroom, Educational Studies in Mathematics 11 (1980) 23-41

Bauersfeld, H., Analysen zur Kommunikation im Mathematikunterricht, in: Bauersfeld, H., Heymann, H.-W. et.al.(eds.), Analysen zum Unterrichtshandeln (Aulis Verl. Deubner, Köln, 1982) p.1-40

Bauersfeld, H., Subjektive Erfahrungsbereiche als Grundlage einer Interaktionstheorie des Mathematiklernens und -lehrens, in: Bauersfeld, H., Bussmann, H. et al. (eds.), Lernen und Lehren von Mathematik (Aulis Verl. Deubner, Köln, 1983) p.1-56

Bauersfeld, H. and Zawadowski, W., Metaphors and Metonymies in the Teaching of Mathematics, Occasional Paper no.11, IDM Universität Bielefeld, 1981

Davis, R.B. and McKnight, C., Modelling the Processes of Mathematical Thinking, Jrnl. of Children's Mathematical Behavior 2 (1979), no.2, 91-113

Davis, R.B. and McKnight, C., The Influence of Semantic Content on Algorithmic Behavior, Jrnl. of Mathematical Behavior 3 (1980), no.1, 39-79.

Davis, R.B., Young, S. and McLoughlin, P., The Role of Understanding in the Learning of Mathematics, Curric. Laboratory, Univ. of Illinois, Urbana, 1982

Dienes, Z.P., Building up Mathematics (Hutchinson, London, 1964, 2nd)

Lawler, R.W., One's Child's Learning, unpubl. Doct.Dissert., M.I.T. 1979

Lawler, R.W., The Progressive Construction of Mind, Cognitive Science 5 (1981) 1-30

Lawler, R.W., Extending a Powerful Idea, Jrnl. of Mathematical Behavior 3 (1982), no.2, 81-98

Lawler, R.W., The Articulation of Complementary Roles, A.I.MEMO 594, A.I.Lab., M.I.T. (May 1981)

Minsky, M., A Framework for Representing Knowledge, in: Winston, P. (ed.), The Psychology of Computer Vision (McGraw-Hill, New York, 1975), p.211-277

Minsky, M., K-lines: A Theory of Memory, Cognitive Science 4 (1980) 117-133

Newell. A. and Simon, H.A., Human Problem Solving (Prentice-Hall, E.C., 1972)

Papert, S., Mindstorms (Harvester Press, Brighton 1980)

Norman, D.A., Perspectives on Cognitive Science (Ablex, Norwood, N.J., 1981)

Schank, R.C., Language and Memory, in: Norman, D.A. (ed.), 1981, 105-146

Schank, R.C., Reading and Understanding (Erlbaum, Hillsdale, 1982)

Schank, R.C. and Abelson, R.P., Scripts, Plans, Goals and Understanding: An inquiry into human knowledge structures (Wiley, New York, 1977)

Simon, H.A., Models of Thought (Yale Univ. Press, New Haven, Conn., 1979)

Session 10 - Discussion

Rapporteurs: P. BOLLERSLEV, R. PETTY

LAUTERBACH expanded on his paper and drew a parallel between the situation as it was in the 60's with introducing science into the elementary school. It had the following **aims**:

To develop

- science process skills
- science concepts
- problem solving ability
- experimenting
- appreciation of science
- creativity
- scientific literacy
- communication skills

with the concept of the child as "little scientist" and the concept of the teacher as "arranger, facilitator".

The results of this science experiment were:

Short term	Long term	Side effects
children: achieved	achieved	* (below)
teachers: worked hard	worked: somewhere else harder less	reluctance to work in school
scientific community: learned from it appreciated it	did other things	reluctance to work in school
administrators: encouraged	withdrew money, personnel	filled up syllabus, called the reform a flop
publishers: supported	were disappointed	produced materials for themselves to sell
schools: were interested	were using books on science	two cultures: contra/pro science lower secondary science

* The side effects for children were observed as follows:

- less time for non-science activities because the topic was of interest to the children
- objects, animals, plants no longer a matter for play
- objects, animals, plants lost or never gained identity
- objects, animals, plants were isolated from their natural surroundings
- meal worms received names and there was mourning when they died

- precise terminology acquired
- increase in disciplined and concentrated learning
- convergency in thinking
- communication between children increased during experiments
- building up a new language and way of interpretation not useful in normal everyday life
- destruction of plants and objects to find out how they worked
- experimental reports reduced to the formula required by the project
- group work increased

LAUTERBACH then questioned if a "Computers into Elementary Education Programme" could do better?

His contention was that computer education will not adequately satisfy the following requirements for learning experiences:

1. child-centredness
2. nearness
3. vividness
4. wholeness
5. interactiveness

Keeping in mind that the individual's personality, intellectual development and motoric differentiation are formed basically in the early years of life, the questions remaining unanswered are:

How will the use of computers affect:

- the child's perception of nature and people?
  (controllable, incalculable, imperfect, makeable)
- the child's imaginative capability?
  (literature, art, dreams)
- the child's body experience?
  (handicrafts, sensuality, instrument play)
- the child's interaction with things, animals, plants and people?
  (empathy, conflict, tolerance, love)
- the child's language, communication with people?
  (appx. 800 words suffice, cartoon communication, gesture)

In his opening remarks BAUERSFELD also drew a parallel between the development of computers in education and the introduction of 'new' maths. He expanded on his paper in the following way.
"The issue of DSE's has appeared at several places in the Conference:

1. Firstly, Ron JONES taked about the "hidden curriculum" and, in particular, he explicitly described computers as "segmented experience for children". His answer is near to my consequence: "talking about connections".

2. It also has to do with Margaret DeVAULT's distinction of "the child as a responder or as an initator when working with a computer". Clearly, the responder-type will create narrower DSE's.

3. Most striking was Colin WATKINS's short remark: "If we put a teacher in front of a computer to write a program he stops being a teacher!"

So a teacher's behaviour is also guided by DSE's, and experiences with the computer obviously are so unique that teachers even forget about their professional role.

I cannot give a better example!

"Why are DSE's important for informatics? It is a psychological concept, not a mathematical one. The discussion gave the impression that there is a polarization in this group. I cannot say whether it is typical for Informatics or for IFIP, I just state it:

- The one pole is represented by Colin WATKINS who made clear that "there are only three problems: 1) Software, 2) Hardware, 3) Teachers". Children are no problem. This is the **computer-centered subgroup.**

- The other pole, the **child-centered subgroup,** is characteristicly presented by women, Margaret DeVAULT, Toni KUBATH (and their husbands).

But I think both groups might profit from the DSE-concept, because both **love** and **neglect** work better on an informed basis.

"Finally, as a man from the floor without official functions and independent from IFIP, I feel obliged to say plainly what I mean. My key impression is that particularly with very young fields of science, fresh disciplines on the scene, as is informatics, suffer from severely underdeveloped **interdisciplinary relations.** This means that in dealing with question on their borderlines or even beyond, young disciplines start far behind the status of information in older disciplines. In other words they have tremendous deficits in their foundation and their theory. I myself come from another young discipline. As with the reflection of children, conferences like this one should be realized as a process which has to develop the reflection of its own discipline as well. This will mean:

- extention of cross-discipline cooperation, learning from mistakes
- sensitive case-study research
- developing the process-structure of the discipline's activities".

Discussion

LEVRAT asked if we were in danger of writing programs that would induce children to be controlled by computers. BAUERSFELD answered that the computer can be seen as an object, a tool, or an aid, but the computer can become a pseudoteacher. The distinctions between these should be kept clear and it should be used as a tool for learning so that children do not become dominated by the computer.

LAUTERBACH agreed with LEVRAT. This is not a deliberate action but as a result of the computers's function being seen as a word processor. Thus people adapt to it. He said that schools themselves act in a similar manner in the way that they parcel up knowledge in separate units of 45/50 minutes of time, which acts as a control mechanism.

JONES thanked LAUTERBACH for bringing us down to earth. He said we are optimistic but not always realistic. The U.K. had passed through these early stages of optimism and now faced the more realistic problems. We must play with computers and learn to relax with them, then teachers will again be teachers and children will be children.

LOVIS then quoted LEVRAT: "There is no possibility of the computer not being used." It is not a question of whether but of how. Be pragmatic, we will use them. LAUTERBACH thought that this was possibly just a British/American point of view and that the German one was more sceptical. We know that school is not independent of society but we have a change for a new approach. BAUERSFELD asked that we do not nationalise the problems. There is a pressure from outside. We needed to be aware that education should be child-centered. Is informatics a field related to school issues? If it is you should have a better background in it and not just ask "How?".

SCHMIDT said that of course we would have to cope. He said that most of his colleagues outside the Maths/Science areas of the curriculum have regarded the problem as having nothing to do with them. We must develop a healthier attitude to the relevance of computers to other subject areas. MARTIN thanked the conference for the many questions she could take back to the States. In America there was a panic as to how fast they could get things going.

LAUTERBACH described the possbility of a widening gap between different types of schools, that of:

- those with more and more technology,
- those with less and less technology.

This would create a contradiction in life styles. He questioned the need for 'schools' at all in this context.

LOVIS amended his earlier statement and asked why the conference had been mounted (an aside from BAUERSFELD: "To write the book!"). For himself he thought it was to look at the pragmatic issues **and** the wider ones. M. DeVAULT said that in her region elementary schools have three computers each and will receive no more until the question why we need them is answered. It may well be different in other states. They may even decide there is **no** need for computers with very young children.

Toni BONELLO-KUBATH asked BAUERSFELD how does transfer occur in the child's mind, if we take computers out of the picture? He replied that the Lawler study gives a good answer to that, as described in his paper. PETTY said that good teachers are always good teachers. They intuitively know how and what to teach and which medium to use. KLOTZ pointed out that computers make learning fun for children. That's an advantage and a reason for being optimistic.

In summary LAUTERBACH said that he had come to the conference to be an observer but had found himself drawn into looking for solutions to problems in areas he had not wanted to investigate.

SESSION 11

CLOSING ADDRESS

Bernard Levrat

I am about to close the parentheses in our lives which I opened on Monday. We have been away from our usual worries, meeting with people with interesting but often unexpected ideas and being challenged on some of the things which we have always defended as the absolute truth, at least in the face of the outside world. We won't go back to our job exactly the same as we came and I hope the world will also be changed as a result of our concerted efforts.

The first thing to go by the board was the concept of "computer literacy". There is no way to define it properly in English and it cannot be translated. It was decided not to replace it with a single concept but to recognize the necessity of both becoming familiar with the use of computers and illustrating the relationship between computers and society.

Few elementary schools possess even one computer and fewer still have more than one. We are far from the situation in which many machines are permanently available in the library or, alternately, in which a machine sits expectantly in every classroom.

To most participants, including me, it came as a great surprise to learn of the British Government's initiative in offering a half-price computer to each of 27 000 primary schools and in starting at least to train 54 000 teachers to use these machines.

JONES gave a convincing demonstration of the efficiency of the U.K. national scheme. Then WATKINS described the work of the Birmingham Centre and WEAVER that of the London project. Finally, PETTY and STEWART demonstrated some of the software produced for the ITMA project. The whole picture was very impressive although nobody is quite sure of where this is leading. The amount of governmental help is important, yet there is some scepticism as to its long term relevance.

The finality of introducing computers in schools was excellently addressed by LAUTERBACH and BAUERSFELD. Although they take very different approaches, they converge on the idea that much caution must be exercised for fear that the instrument should get in the way of the learning process.

Coming back to the subject of didactics, it was clear that teachers who will be in contact with computers do need to receive special attention. MARTIN proposed a model based on her own experience where the teachers moved from a purely personnal interest to the ability to advise others. There are some doubts on the time needed to complete that evolution. V. DeVAULT offered an integrated scheme where children, teachers and graduate students interact during the Wisconsin Summer Computer Fest. A lot of experimentation is going on there, producing insights on curriculum development, on the relationship between learners and machines and on language choices.

LOGO occupied a prominent place in a number of presentations. Its promise for turning the school computer into a valuable teaching tool was emphasized by LOTHE while BERDONNEAU showed us how to use sprites with first graders to conduct very interesting research. But action languages are not the only things that can be taught to children. AKIRA gave some statistics on teaching ASSEMBLER, BASIC and LISP in Japan, which were quite surprising in the sense that young children did not seem to have trouble in managing the LISP syntax. Finally, the paper by FISHER gave a general idea of the software available at the elementary school level, along with the difficulties of evaluating and using it efficiently.

It is not at all certain that children have to learn a programming language to gain experience with computers. They can use ready made packages for drill and practice, word processing or computer based learning activities. YOSHIMURA showed some material developed in a private school in Japan. He also indicated that, in his technologically advanced country, very few elementary schools had been given computers.

Many interesting presentations tried to give a glimpse of what children could learn when they are given access to computers. SCHMIDT and TOVGAARD indicated their way of giving the machine control over some pieces of machinery, Karl AHLSTROM explained how to go from physics lessons to computers and society while FONJALLAZ tried to offer a general scheme to introduce children and parents to programming and to relate computers and society. The attempt of CATHCART to teach problem solving with the help of structured programming seemed to run into some difficulties when he was forced to use BASIC.

DeVAULT proposed a very simple model of the child going from receiver to initiator. I am sure that will, in many cases explain the behaviour or children - and teachers - in front of a machine. With a variety of languages and probably as many models, Frank and Toni BONELLO-KUBATH presented a bag of very interesting ideas, experimentation and reflexions. In view of a rapidly changing technology, I found their attitude very positive in the sense that we need individuals to try new ideas. Let us hope that we can think of ways of sharing and disseminating the positive results and to pass the word so that the same mistakes are not repeated over and over.

In a more refreshing vein, SCHMIDT and TOVGAARD took us to a tour to Greenland, where their efforts to bring computers to a non-technical population were inconclusive. That was a reminder of the many problems related to technology transfer and to third world countries. Although this Conference was not able to address the problem in any way, every participant was aware that elementary education plays a fundamental role in the widening gap between developed and developing countries. The one-sided introduction of computers can only accelerate the process.

In fact, we don't really have a choice about introducing computers in elementary schools. The pressure is there from parents, politicians and manufacturers who would gladly do our jobs if we hesitate too long. We must keep in mind all the questions that were raised during this fruitful week and warn the proponents of a simple-minded solution of the dangers for the children and for the stability of the school system. Nevertheless we must accept our part to play in encouraging projects for a thoughtful introduction of computers in elementary schools. In doing so, we will avoid teachers feeling more and more remote from the technological society in which we live and we will increase the chance that children from different social backgrounds have equal opportunities in life.

Session 11 - Final Discussion

Rapporteurs: E.D. TAGG, J.D. TINSLEY

BAUERSFELD drew attention to the special circumstances in Japan. The time taken to understand the pictorial characters prevented time being available for other activities such as computer education. On the other hand the great variety enriches children's perception.

SCHMIDT pointed out difficulties in the Greenland language. There were 20 words for snow but none for computer. The translation for 'Press Return' made children laugh since it also meant 'Please go and eat'.

Recommendations

LOVIS asked whether there were any proposals that IFIP should involve itself further. JONES made such a proposal. BOSLER warned of the necessity of collecting only 'computer freaks'. TAGG pointed out the two-way flow of information. The computer experts needed to be informed of the progress and problems of computer education at all levels.

LOVIS read out some specific proposals which had been sent to him.

1) It was proposed that a list of questions be prepared by the participants for their mutual help and consideration.

2) A proposal was made that the first half of the conference should consist of papers with the questions raised - and others - discussed in the second half as well as demonstrations.

BONELLO-KUBATH wanted more opportunity to discuss the questions asked on the Conference Programme. The questions for Thursday's discussions were handed out too late for proper thought before discussion. WALDOW said that small groups were much better for discussion.

3) It was proposed that the conference should be held annually. LOVIS pointed out financial and organisational difficulties. MARTIN underlined the time needed for research, and for results to be fed back. PETTY wanted to make sure that those involved should not be a closed group. A straw vote suggested that every other year was the most widely accepted proposal.

4) Specific proposals from one discussion group were
   (a) IFIP should establishing an International Clearing House for information about projects, software etc.
   (b) Research results needed to be more widely known. IFIP might be able to collect information about research papers and make it available.
   (c) A Working Group on Computers in Elementary Education should be established.
   (d) The proceedings of the Conference should be made available more cheaply so that they might be read by primary teachers.
   (e) IFIP should support research in the Third World.

LOVIS pointed out that the establishment of the suggested working group had already been agreed by TC3. He would be the first chairman to steer it through the initial stages. IFIP already was concerned - with UNESCO - in projects in the Third World. These proposals received general support and would be transmitted to TC 3.

CHAIRMAN of 3.1 LOVIS announced the end of his six years as chairman of WG 3.1. P. BOLLERSLEV would be the new chairman in 1984. One of his first occasions would be at the WG 3.1. conference on Teacher Training (Elementary and Secondary) to be held at Birmingham July 16-20, 1984.

Finally LOVIS as chairman expressed the thanks of the conference to
1) The Director and staff of the Gustav-Heinemann-Stiftung for excellent care, catering and accommodation.
2) Dr. Ulrich Bosler and his Organizing Committee for all the arrangements they had made including the choice of venue.
3) The IPN staff who had given such great help with the equipment for demonstrations, in particular Hans-Jürgen Waldow, Klaus-Henning Hansen and Günter Jacobsen; also Mr. Jacobsen for driving to and from Kiel and to Günter Haupt for his carrying out all of the required printing even by working outside normal office hours.

A Statement on behalf of ATEE by Peter Gorny

On behalf of the president of the Association for Teacher Education in Europe I want to make the following short remark:

ATEE is very much interested in the efforts which resulted in the invitation to this IFIP-Conference and it is supporting them. The association understands itself also as a link between the educational and computer experts and the political bodies deciding on educational matters.

The ATEE-Working group on Information Technologies will meet next time at the annual ATEE-Conference in Aalborg (DK) in September 1983 and hopefully will make some progress in designing recommendations for a curriculum for "Literacy in Information Technology for all teachers" (pre- and inservice). As soon as possible we will present the result of our work to IFIP for critical discussion and improvement.

The ATEE will be glad to include the insight gained at the conference into the recommendations.

WORKING GROUP 3.1
WORKING CONFERENCE INFORMATICS IN ELEMENTARY EDUCATION

AHLSTRÖM Karl-Gösta p. 39
Gravörsgatan 12
528 66 Linköping
Sweden

AKIRA Aiba p. 137
Department of Mathematics
Faculty of Science and Technology
Keio University
Hiyoshi 3-14-1, Kohoku-ku
Yokohama-shi, Kanagawa-ken 223
Japan

BALDURSDÓTTIR Halla-Björg
Holmgardi 45
108 Reykjavik
Iceland

BAUERSFELD Heinrich p. 199
Fahrenheitweg 23 B
4800 Bielefeld 1
FRG

BECERRIL GASCO José Luis
IBM Madrid Scientific Center (1411)
Paseo de la Castellana 4
Madrid-1
Spain

BERDONNEAU Cathérine p. 157
Université Paris 7, I.R.E.M.
Tour 55-56 3ème étage
2, place Jussieu
75251 Paris Cedex 05
France

BOLLERSLEV Peter
Røjlevangen 40
2630 Taastrup
Denmark

BONELLO-KUBATH Toni p. 19
152, Madison Avenue
Toronto, Ontario M5R 2S5
Canada

BOSLER Ulrich p. 7
Institut für die Pädagogik
der Naturwissenschaften
Olshausenstr. 40-60
2300 Kiel 1
FRG

CATHCART George p. 115
Faculty of Education
543 Education South
University of Alberta
Edmonton, Alberta T6G 2G5
Canada

DeVAULT Marge p. 73
4242 Wanda Place
Madison, Wisconsin 53706
U.S.A.

DeVAULT Vere p. 53
Department of Curriculum and Instruction
University of Wisconsin-Madison
Teacher Education Building
225 North Mills Street
Madison, Wisconsin 53706
U.S.A.

FONJALLAZ Julien p. 145
Centre de Recherches Psych.Pédagogiques
Direction Générale du Cycle d'Orientation
Av. John Mohl 15A
Genève
Switzerland

GORNY Peter
Universität Oldenburg
Ammerländer Heerstr. 67-99
2900 Oldenburg
FRG

HANSEN Klaus-Henning
Institut für die Pädagogik
der Naturwissenschaften
Olshausenstr. 40-60
2300 Kiel 1
FRG

JENSEN Peter
Amundsenvej 8
2800 Lyngby
Denmark

JONES Ron   p. 27
Education Department
County Offices
Lincoln LN1 1YQ
United Kinydom

JØRGENSEN Karl Johan
Slettensvej 107
5270 Odense N
Denmark

KERNER Immo
Pädagogische Hochschule Dresden
Sektion Mathematik
Wigardstr. 17
8060 Dresden
GDR

KLOTZ Frederick
Dept. of Mathematics
St. Patrick's College
Drumcondra
Dublin, 8
Eire

KUBATH Frank   p. 19
152, Madison Avenue
Toronto, Ontario M5R 2S5
Canada

KURODA Ryo   p. 99
2-28-10 Aobacho, Higashimuraya
Tokyo
Japan

LAUTERBACH Roland   p. 189
Institut für die Pädagogik
der Naturwissenschaften
Olshausenstr. 40-60
2300 Kiel 1
FRG

LEVRAT Bernard   pp. 9,213
Centre Universitaire d'Informatique
Université
24, rue Général Dufour
1211 Genève 4
Switzerland

LÜTHE Herbert   p. 45
Jägerstr. 18
7053 Rommelshausen
FRG

LOVIS Frank
Faculty of Mathematics
The Open University
Walton Hall
Milton Keynes MK7 6AA
United Kingdom

MARTIN Dianne   p. 61
Computer Science and
Electrical Engineering
Academic Center
George Washington University
Washington, D.C. 20052
U.S.A.

NAKANISHI Masakazu   p. 137
Department of Mathematics
Faculty of Science and Technology
Keio University
Hiyoshi 3-14-1, Kohoku-ku
Yokohama-shi, Kanagawa-ken 223
Japan

PETTY Jane   p. 161
The Shell Centre for
Mathematical Education
Nottingham University
Nottingham NG7 2RD
United Kingdom

PLANCKE-SCHUYTEN Gilberte
University of Ghent
Jemappesstr. 8
9000 Ghent
Belgium

PLETT Peter   p. 3
Bundesministerium für
Bildung und Wissenschaft, II B 1
Heinemannstr. 2
5300 Bonn-Bad Godesberg
FRG

List of Participants

SAMWAYS Brian
Birmingham Educational Computing Centre
The Bordesley Centre
Camp Hill
Stratford Road
Birmingham B11 1AR
United Kingdom

SCHMIDT Erling pp. 93,105
Revlingbakken 40
9000 Aalborg
Denmark

SCHMITZER Ursula
Draschestr. 75/6
1232 Wien
Austria

SCHULZ-ZANDER Renate
Institut für die Pädagogik
der Naturwissenschaften
Olshausenstr. 40-60
2300 Kiel 1
FRG

STEWART Jan p. 161
ITMA Project
College of St. Mark & St. John
Derriford
Plymouth
United Kingdom

TAGG Donovan
1, Newmarket Avenue
Lancaster LA1 4NG
United Kingdom

TAUBER Michael
Wissenschaftliches Zentrum
IBM Heidelberg
Tiergartenstr.
6900 Heidelberg
FRG

TINSLEY David
Education Officer
Further Education Division
Education Offices
Margaret Street
Birmingham B3 3BU
United Kingdom

TOVGAARD Niels pp. 93,105
Flittig Lisevej 18
5120 Odense SV
Denmark

VAN DE WOLDE Jan
Onderafdeling der
Toegepaste Onderwijskunde
Postbus 217
7500 AE Enschede
Netherlands

VAN WEERT Tom
Stichting Lerarenopleiding
Ubbo Emmius
Postbus 2056
9704 CB Groningen
Netherlands

VORBECK Michael
Council of Europe
Secrétariat Général
BP 341 R6
67006 Strasbourg
France

WALDOW Hans-Jürgen
Institut für die Pädagogik
der Naturwissenschaften
Olshausenstr. 40-60
2300 Kiel 1
FRG

WATKINS Colin p. 79
Birmingham Educational Computing Centre
The Bordesley Centre
Camp Hill
Stratford Road
Birmingham B11 1AR
United Kingdom

WEAVER Brian p. 125
Inner London Education Authority
Room 291, County Hall
London SE 1PB
United Kingdom

WIBE Jan
Nyheimsveien 22 A
7058 Jakobsli
Norway

YOSHIMURA Satoru p. 99
1-17-12 Ookayama - Meguro-ku
Tokyo 152
Japan